P9-EMC-775

The Plains States: the natural scene

The topography of the seven Plains States is typified by landscapes of seemingly uniform flatness, though there are areas of hills and valleys. The fertile Central Lowland rises gently to around 1,500 feet at its western limits before giving way to the semiarid Great Plains, which are about a mile high where they end at the edge of the Rockies.

The state flowers of the Plains States, shown clockwise from top left: Kansas' sunflower grows as high as eight feet; Missouri's hawthorn blooms in clusters of tiny flowers that resemble apple blossoms; Nebraska's goldenrod gets its name from yellow flowers that crown its long branches; Minnesota's showy lady's-slipper is a striking orchid that has a crimson-flecked pouch set off by pure white petals; North Dakota's wild prairie rose has large pink or crimson blossoms; the South Dakota pasqueflower bears a single light blue or purple blossom; and Iowa's ubiquitous wild rose presents pink flowers that grow singly or in small clusters.

The climate of the Plains States produces some of the widest and most violent seasonal variations in the nation. Summer is a time of soaring temperatures—climbing as high as 110 degrees—sudden thunderstorms and damaging hailstorms. Wintertime brings blizzards and prolonged cold spells with temperatures often as low as -20 degrees.

Scale of map: one inch to 94 miles

The Plains
States

TIME
LIFE
BOOKS ®

LIFE WORLD LIBRARY
LIFE NATURE LIBRARY
TIME READING PROGRAM
THE LIFE HISTORY OF THE UNITED STATES
LIFE SCIENCE LIBRARY
INTERNATIONAL BOOK SOCIETY
GREAT AGES OF MAN
TIME-LIFE LIBRARY OF ART
TIME-LIFE LIBRARY OF AMERICA
FOODS OF THE WORLD

TIME-LIFE Library of America

Blairsville High School Library

The Plains States

**Iowa Kansas Minnesota
Missouri Nebraska
North Dakota South Dakota**

By Evan Jones
and the Editors of
TIME-LIFE BOOKS

TIME-LIFE BOOKS, New York

14404 ESEA '77

The Author: Evan Jones was born in Le Sueur, Minnesota in 1915. He began his writing career as a journalist and during World War II served in Europe as an editor of the army newspaper, *The Stars and Stripes*. After a five-year postwar sojourn in Paris, where he worked as a writer and editor, Mr. Jones returned to the U.S. in 1950. Since then his articles have appeared in such magazines as *Collier's*, SPORTS ILLUSTRATED and *Gourmet* and he has had several books published, among them *The Minnesota: Forgotten River, Trappers and Mountain Men* and *Citadel in the Wilderness*. Mr. Jones and his wife now live in New York City.

The Consulting Editor: Oscar Handlin, Charles Warren Professor of American History at Harvard University and director of the university's Charles Warren Center for Studies in American History, is one of America's foremost social historians. His work on U.S. immigrants, *The Uprooted,* won the Pulitzer Prize in 1952.

Plains States Consultant: Professor Allan G. Bogue, now at the University of Wisconsin, taught history at the University of Iowa for 12 years. His specialty is the American West.

The Cover: Combines work into the night completing the wheat harvest on a farm in southwestern Kansas, the state in which about 20 per cent of the nation's winter wheat is grown.

TIME-LIFE BOOKS

Editor
Maitland A. Edey
Executive Editor
Jerry Korn
Text Director   **Art Director**
Martin Mann   Sheldon Cotler
Chief of Research
Beatrice T. Dobie
Picture Editor
Robert G. Mason
Assistant Text Directors:
Harold C. Field, Ogden Tanner
Assistant Art Director:
Arnold C. Holeywell
Assistant Chief of Research:
Martha Turner

Publisher
Rhett Austell
Associate Publisher: Walter C. Rohrer
General Manager: Joseph C. Hazen Jr.
Planning Director: John P. Sousa III
Circulation Director: Joan D. Manley
Marketing Director: Carter Smith
Business Manager: John D. McSweeney
Publishing Board: Nicholas Benton,
Louis Bronzo, James Wendell Forbes

TIME-LIFE Library of America

Series Editor: Oliver E. Allen
Editorial Staff for *The Plains States:*
Assistant Editor: Peter M. Chaitin
Picture Editor: Robert W. Bone
Designer: John Newcomb
Assistant Designer: Jean Lindsay
Staff Writers: Tony Chiu, Lee Greene,
Marianna Kastner, Frank Kendig, Victor Waldrop
Chief Researcher: Clara E. Nicolai
Text Research: Marian Taylor, Evelyn Hauptman,
Doris Coffin, Clare Mead
Picture Research: Victoria Winterer, Marcia Gillespie,
Toby Solovioff, Margo Dryden, Myra Mangan
Art Assistant: Mervyn Clay

Editorial Production
Color Director: Robert L. Young
Assistant: James J. Cox
Copy Staff: Marian Gordon Goldman,
Patricia Miller, Susan Galloway, Florence Keith
Picture Department: Dolores A. Littles,
Marquita Jones
Traffic: Arthur A. Goldberger
Studio: Jean Held

The text chapters of this book were written by Evan Jones, the picture essays by the editorial staff. Valuable aid was provided by Jean Strong of Cedar Rapids, Iowa, and by the following individuals and departments of Time Inc.: LIFE staff photographers Alfred Eisenstaedt and Michael Rougier; Editorial Production, Robert W. Boyd, Jr.; Editorial Reference, Peter Draz; Picture Collection, Doris O'Neil; Photographic Laboratory, George Karas; TIME-LIFE News Service, Richard M. Clurman; Correspondents Robert Sanford (St. Louis) and Jack Cannon (Rapid City, S. Dak.).

The Plains States © 1968 Time Inc.
All rights reserved. Published simultaneously in Canada.
Library of Congress catalogue card number 68-18049.
School and library distribution by Silver Burdett Company.

Contents

Introduction

The Plains States are the heart of our nation, and that heart beats slow and sure year after year while the cities on the coastlines, crowded, competitively industrial, cosmopolite and more seemingly vulnerable to foreign influences as well as attacks in time of war, manifest our nation's violent anxieties and antagonisms. Nowhere can we find a closer correlation of landscape and character than in the Plains States. The people there are, for the most part, as plain and level and unadorned as the scenery. New fashions, new inventions seldom emanate from this region, and its native artists usually go to some other part of the country to find appreciation and encouragement. In recent years at least, one has seldom heard of riots, strikes or demonstrations in Kansas, Missouri, Nebraska, Iowa, Minnesota and the Dakotas.

Human violence, when it does occur, is all the more frightening because one does not expect it in such a quiet, innocent land. The bloody murdering of a wheat farmer's family in a peaceful Kansas community horrifies us more because of the unlikeliness of the setting than because of the deed itself, which might not seem so grotesque in a populous, strife-torn, industrialized city.

Violence on the plains exists more in nature than in man. A person lives in this mid-country with an inherent consciousness of the sky. One is always aware of the sky in these states, because one sees so much more of it than in the mountainous regions where the horizons are blocked and the heavens are trimmed down like a painting, to fit a smaller frame. And human life on the prairie is more dependent upon and influenced by the sky and its constant maneuverings than in other regions. Men here look at the sky each morning as soon as they get out of bed, to see what kind of a day is indicated. Life and prosperity depend upon that sky, which can destroy a season's crops in a few hours, by hail or blizzards or tornadoes or a relentlessly burning sun that can desiccate the land like an Old Testament curse.

During my growing years in Kansas, I witnessed every extreme of weather and learned that it is as unpredictable in all the Plains States as the pictures that show up on a slot machine. I attended the University of Kansas, at Lawrence, in the early 1930s, when dust storms were periodically enveloping the land. The dust darkened the sun and filled the atmosphere, seeping into houses and stores. There was no way of escaping it. It discolored all the air and made the necessary act of breathing a hazard and a discomfort.

The spring when I graduated from the university, there was a deluge. Between mid-April and early June there were but three days when there was no rain at all. Graduating seniors had to march in the rain to the vast Hoch Auditorium, where we sat in moist attendance in our damp caps and gowns, smelling of wet wool. All the rivers and streams overflowed their banks and the entire eastern half of the state was flooded. Train and bus service was either stopped or rerouted. When the rains finally ceased, the sun came out in full force, creating a steamy heat that lasted the summer. The following spring and summer there was a tragic drought. The rivers and streams withered dry, livestock died on the plains with parched throats, and the record-breaking heat (for two weeks temperatures reached 118 degrees in my own section of Kansas) kept people closed up inside their homes, hanging wet sheets over electric fans to create a semblance of air and refreshment. The entire earth looked as if blasted in a furnace. The Plains States were a partition of hell.

In April of 1938, when I was teaching high school in a small mining town close to my home, I experienced my first tornado. It struck unexpectedly at noon after a still and sunny morning when students and faculty had walked to school with no anticipation whatever of the freakish violence that the elements were preparing for them. About one third of the town, as I remember, was leveled.

But of course there is beautiful weather on the plains. Nowhere in the world is the morning sky such an innocent blue. And nowhere is the sunset more awesome; a burning globe covers the land with a phosphorescent glow before it sinks into the far horizon. When spring comes early, the month of April can be joyous with bright green grass, budding leaves and yellow daffodils. And sometimes the sun is gentle to the summer months, providing days of pleasant warmth and nights that are cool and sweet with the smell of honeysuckle. In October there is a quickening of life when the trees turn orange and yellow and red, and the harvest brings apples, melons and pumpkins to the markets. The new school year is begun by now, and the daytime world is left to the elders, while the young attend classes and cheer at football games. And there is always good hope for a mild winter.

Once a New York friend, a genuine sophisticate who has lived for varying periods of time in most of the world's great cities, told me of a visit to Kansas much as one would describe a chance sojourn among the Fiji Islanders. "I found the people to be genuinely sweet," he told me. And I believe they are. Perhaps this *sweetness* of character becomes instilled in a group of people who are more dependent upon the elements than are those in other parts of the country. This sweetness, I believe, is of a spiritual nature. Men in the prairie states have long had to deal with forces they cannot always control. They often have to surrender to these forces and deal with them as best they can. This surrender to forces greater than one's self cannot but create a humility in human character that is a part of all religious faith. Prairie people, most of them descendants of Puritan New Englanders or of God-fearing Scandinavians or Central Europeans, know and live with the knowledge that man is not all-powerful. That may explain why people in the Plains States are (I believe) more solemnly religious than those in other parts of the nation. There are the fanatically religious, too, but they are a small minority. The general tendency in this level land is to be conservative in all things, and to be suspicious of all extremists.

But these peaceful states have had their share of dissenters. Rebellion is not foreign to them. John Brown and Carry Nation and Billy the Kid all lived in Kansas. So did the Communist leader Earl Browder. And the notorious James brothers came from Missouri. Every town and city in the Plains States has its share of misfits, people hostile to the environment, who feel themselves in a broad land that is full of narrow minds. They seek their destiny in other parts of the country. Some are criminal; some are creative. Los Angeles, San Francisco, New York, Chicago, Miami, Houston, all owe much of their color and culture to these sometimes gifted misfits from the plains.

When I lived for a while in western Massachusetts friends liked to tell me about a woman from Minnesota who had come to the Berkshires for a vacation that she did not appear to be enjoying. She took no pleasure at all in the lush, romantic landscape. When asked what she thought of the scenery, she replied, "There isn't any. The mountains get in the way." I appreciated the story and realized that I felt the same way. No mountains can be as beautiful to me as the far horizon, level as a floor, 20 or 30 miles in the distance. The sight fills me with a wonderful feeling of personal freedom, and also with a sense of infinity. Man finds his solitude here and in the still atmosphere cannot help but wonder about the nature of all being.

Not all the land in the Plains States is level. Much of it is gently rolling, and there are a few mountains. But those areas are exceptions in this level land. Level, but not flat. When we speak of anything as *flat* we imply that it holds no content of interest. But we use the word *level* as synonymous with honesty and truth.

Instinctively, I call the land *level*. People who do not appreciate this region call it *flat*. And perhaps one has to be born and raised in the Plains States to see and feel their serene and understated beauty. People from the East are slow to respond to it, if at all. And they deplore its lack of Eastern culture. When I was a boy in Kansas, my family had neighbors who had just moved to our town from Colorado. The mother of this new family never became happy in what she called "this flat country." She became seriously neurotic there, unable ever to feel "at home" or to make friends. She never ceased to long for the mountains that were native to her. Eventually, her husband gave up his job and took her back to Colorado, where they made their home again and have lived happily ever after.

Maybe we find beauty only in what we know. Mountains have never intrigued me. They have none of the mystery of the prairie, where one can always feel close to some eternal truth concerning man and his place in the universe.

—WILLIAM INGE
Playwright

The broad, gently undulating countryside of central Iowa recalls the lines written by Nebraska author Willa Cather in the introduction to *O Pioneers!*, a novel set on the plains:

Evening and the flat land,
Rich and sombre and always silent;
The miles of fresh-plowed soil,
Heavy and black, full of strength and harshness.

1

Limitless Vistas of Land and Sky

There is a dryness in the air, a lingering loneliness in the atmosphere; there is a hint of danger—almost of doom—in the wailing wind that blows unrestrained across the all but empty landscape; there are nuances in the natural light that alert all the senses to the pervasive and somehow threatening spaciousness. Here a solitary stand of trees and there a lone building silhouette themselves against the distant horizon, where the sky seems to lean down to create the illusion of a flat world reaching a precipice from which it drops off into a void. It is a large world in the daylight; in the pitch black of a starless night even a strong man might yield for an instant to a feeling of panic. For the surrounding land is vast and open, as if scaled for long-striding giants rather than for humankind. Here,

on the Great Plains of America, man is aware of his smallness and loneliness, and he stands exposed to nature—a violent and capricious nature that denies the comforting shelter of the forest with its safe and familiar sound of a bird's song. Small wonder then that through much of the 19th Century Americans called the western reaches of the plains the "Great American Desert" and believed that only a savage could survive within its realm.

Man is indeed relatively alone in the Plains States. Almost the same number of people (15 million, give or take a few) live in the 10 counties of New York City's metropolitan area as in the seven trans-Mississippi Plains States—Minnesota, Iowa, Missouri, Kansas, Nebraska and the two Dakotas. Yet Greater New York's millions are squeezed

The Plains States' varied terrain

The Plains States' physiographic provinces, shown in different colors on the map at right, reveal that the seven states fall into five major areas. The map labels name the sections of each area. The western area forms part of the extensive Great Plains Province ▨▨▨▨▨▨ a broad highland. The northern part of this province, the Missouri Plateau, is highly eroded terrain. In the glaciated section, deposits left by glaciers have smoothed the surface. The unglaciated section, however, is rougher and includes the weirdly carved Badlands. Jutting above the plateau in the west is an isolated mountain range, the Black Hills. South of the plateau is the flat, little-eroded High Plains section. Erosion in the Plains Border section, however, has created low ridges and shallow valleys.

The largest province is the Central Lowlands Province ▨▨▨▨▨ an immense and generally flat basin. In the north the Western Lake section is marked with small lakes. Just below it are the Dissected Till Plains, eroded into small valleys and low ridges. In the east are edges of the topographically varied Wisconsin Driftless section—missed by glaciers—and the relatively flat Till Plains. In the southernmost section are the Osage Plains, a land of low relief.

Three other major physiographic provinces extend into the eastern Plains States. The Superior Upland ▨▨▨▨▨▨ is a highland worn by glaciation and erosion. In the southeast is a corner of the Ozark Plateaus ▨▨▨▨▨ which include the Springfield-Salem Plateaus, a terraced land of increasing altitude. Bordering this area on the east is the Mississippi Alluvial Plain. It is part of the Coastal Plain ▨▨▨▨▨▨ that slopes gently to the south and east.

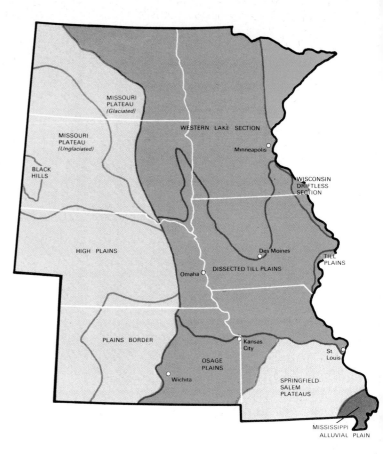

cheek by jowl into 2,843 square miles of Atlantic littoral while today's plainsmen have 200 times the space—roughly half a million square miles—in which to stretch out.

There is so much space stretching empty from horizon to horizon that the dominant impression most people carry away from these states is of an oceanic expanse of flat terrain. This theme of the endless, sealike plain recurs again and again in the literature of the region. More than 90 years ago one observer wrote: "Like an ocean in its vast extent, in its monotony, and in its danger [the plains country] is like the ocean in its romance, in its opportunities for heroism and in the fascination it exerts on all those who come fairly within its influence." The description remains apt, for anyone who casts his gaze across the broad, open corn fields of Iowa or the wheat fields of Nebraska, Kansas and North Dakota must be struck by the similarity of the land to an encircling sea. A man set down in a Kansas wheat field might find no natural landmarks to guide him and, like a mariner, might be forced to set his course by the sun or stars.

The special quality of light on the plains contributes to this sense of oceanic vastness. Light turns Kansas wheat fields to gold, brightens the dusty green leaves of Iowa and Missouri corn, and causes poplar trees along the Platte River to flash with dazzling brilliance; reflected off stretching expanses of snow, it can almost blind. Near the western limits of the region the plains light probes deep into eroded canyons to reveal a vivid spectrum of color, each color characteristic of a separate layer of rock or earth. Throughout the seven states the light and space continually create optical illusions, making distant objects appear miles closer than they actually are.

From a vantage point in the great limestone cliffs called the Slim Buttes that jut from the expanses of northwestern South Dakota, for example, a man can turn in almost any direction and clearly perceive landmarks tens of miles away. The big, humpy outlines of the Cave Hills, 25 miles distant to the northwest, leap into view; 50 miles to the west the chalky, green-topped crest of the Long Pine Hills of Montana pokes upward on the horizon. To the southwest the Crow Buttes and the two peaks called Castle Rock and Square Top—50 miles off—rise to meet the eye. And beyond these peaks, and a sea of sticky gumbo soil, a low row of dimly seen knolls—the wooded Black Hills of South Dakota—seem to undulate, their form and color blurred by 100 miles of flat, oceanic space.

The natural origins of this vast apron of land are not fully understood, but geologists have unearthed a number of clues to the area's beginnings. They trace its history to the formation of the Rocky Mountains, which came into being more than 60 million years ago, heaved up from the bowels of the earth by volcanic forces. Those rivers and streams that flowed east from this newly created Continental Divide distributed great quantities of gravels, sands, clays and silts over the flat land as the meandering courses drifted from side to side. The result was a wide expanse of wasteland, many hundreds of feet thick and sloping toward the southerly flowing river that is the Mississippi.

The glaciers that followed in future eons brought rich topsoil and left it in layers upon the wastes, making the northern plains one of the most fertile agricultural areas in the world. But for almost all of its history the region's chief crop has been grass. The wide grasslands nourished a richly varied animal population that included deer, wolves, beavers and antelope. Most important of all was the buffalo, the primary source of nourishment for the first human inhabitants, the Indians who wandered into the plains thousands of years ago.

The wide and trackless sea of grass created over the geologic ages is, like a real ocean, neither unbroken nor unbounded. The plains have a "coastline" that frames the region with a marvelous variety of landforms. On its northeastern rim—Minnesota's Arrowhead country and lake district—the terrain is heavily forested with towering Norway pines. Far to the south, from out of Arkansas, the Ozark Hills bulge up into Missouri, bringing with them bubbling streams, rushing cataracts and deep stands of deciduous trees—woodlands so colorful in autumn that they rival the glory of a New England October. In the distant west, beyond the borders of the region, the Rockies rise up to terminate abruptly the plains' great sweep.

It is about 1,100 miles from Hermondale, in Missouri's Boot Heel, to the U.S.-Canadian border town of Penasse, on Minnesota's Lake of the Woods, and it is about 750 miles west from the Mississippi at Clinton, Iowa, to Bushnell, on the Nebraska-Wyoming border. Within these limits are expansive landscapes, many of them almost pancake flat, like the broad basin of the Red River Valley near the Canadian border in North Dakota and the oil-well-studded prairies on the Kansas-Oklahoma line. But elsewhere the land takes on a more varied character. In the northwest, for example, it is punctuated by high, towerlike buttes, formed by wind erosion, and east of the Wyoming boundary line, near Scottsbluff, Nebraska, there is a natural column covering 40 acres at its base and crowned by the 475-foot-high Chimney Rock. This landmark, visible for 40 miles, was a welcome guidepost for the earliest pioneers whose wagons crossed the plains on the journey to the forested lands of the Oregon country. To the north of Chimney Rock are 3,600 square miles of utter desolation—the eerie Badlands of South Dakota, formed by thousands of years of water erosion. In 1850 an intrepid traveler described the Badlands as "a chaos of tormented buttes and deep ravines that yawn like the maw of some monstrous serpent, disclosing a row of fangs."

Rivers help define and shape the region, too. Along the eastern edge of the Plains States the Mississippi River flows slowly southward to separate lower Minnesota from Wisconsin and mark the eastern boundaries of Iowa and Missouri. On the Missouri shore of the river are steep bluffs, enclosing deep caverns where stalactites and stalagmites build from the ceilings and floors into long, pointed skewers that look like gaily colored icicles. Just north of St. Louis, the Missouri River—"Big Muddy"—joins the Mississippi. Although the Mississippi sets the eastern limits of the Plains States region, it is the Missouri, cutting through the heart of the area, that has played the more vital role in the development of the plains civilization. Forming far to the west in Montana, the Missouri enters the Plains States in North Dakota, flowing southeast through that state and down through South Dakota. Farther on to the south and east it marks the border between Iowa and Nebraska. Finally it slices Missouri in two with a swift plunge to the east before it is swallowed by the Mississippi. Because the Missouri courses through the center of the Plains States it was long the primary travelway for the pioneers who settled along its banks. They moved upriver, northward and westward, from the early settlements in Missouri and established their farms and river towns along "Big Muddy's" banks, first in Iowa, then Nebraska and finally in the Dakotas. Only when each new territory's riverside land had been claimed did the pioneers push inland to settle the vast interior reaches of the plains.

Clearly, then, the Plains States are not entirely of a piece. To describe them merely as arid grasslands is to ignore their mighty rivers, Minnesota's pine-bordered lakes, the sculptured canyons, and the pastoral green rises of the region's eastern and western edges, where dairy cows and beef cattle graze away the day. But the mountains, hills, lakes and forests that add drama to the Plains States are not truly characteristic of the region. Most of these formations are along the region's borders, where the plains have disappeared and the topography is similar to that of neighboring areas. Or they exist as occasional oddities that suddenly rise from the prairie to emphasize the prevailing flatness around them, like volcanic islands poking up from the sea. It is the treeless, limitless, level expanses that typify the Plains States. Their spaciousness and their unlimited vistas give the area its unique character.

The openness of the landscape has also helped shape the inhabitants. The early plainsman found space in the long reach to the horizon and in the bigness of the sky; he found it in the barely discernible roll of the prairie that tumbled away from the Mississippi Valley and extended straight out from the Missouri and the Platte; he found it again in the bleakness of the Sand Hills in Nebraska. In the plains he was free of the closeness of the forest, of wooded land that blocked the view of the sky and masked the miles that separated a man from the end of his day's journey. He sensed a new freedom in the vastness of the land, and perhaps that was the reason he developed an attitude that was essentially optimistic and self-sufficient. O. E. Rölvaag, the Scandinavian-American novelist, expressed the early pioneer's unbounded joy in the land through the thoughts of Per Hansa, hero of *Giants in the Earth.* "Once more Per Hansa's heart filled with a deep sense of peace and contentment. . . . Was he really to own it? Was it really to become his possession, this big stretch of fine land that spread here before him? . . . His heart began to expand with a mighty exaltation. An emotion he had never felt before filled him and made him walk erect. 'Good God!' he panted. 'This kingdom is going to be *mine!*' "

But Per Hansa's wife, Beret, saw the plains in a different and ominous light: "Beret sat down and let her gaze wander aimlessly around. In a certain sense, she had to admit to herself, it was lovely up here. The broad expanse stretching away endlessly in every direction, seemed almost like the ocean— especially now, when darkness was falling. It reminded her strongly of the sea, and yet it was very different. This formless prairie had no heart that beat, no waves that sang. . . . The infinitude surrounding her on every hand might not have been so oppressive . . . if it had not been for the deep silence, which lay heavier here than in a church. . . . Here no warbling of birds rose on the air, no buzzing of insects sounded. . . . Could no living thing exist out here, in the empty, desolate, endless wastes of green and blue? . . . How *could* ex-

istence go on, she thought desperately? If life is to thrive and endure, it must at least have something to hide behind!"

Per Hansa's dreams and Beret's nameless dread together sum up man's attitudes toward the plains. On the one hand much of the soil seemed rich beyond compare, and for many years the land was there for the taking. Here a man of humble birth, with little wealth, could carve out a decent livelihood for himself and his family.

On the other hand the odds against the settler were terrible. He was a hostage of the elements— the worst weather nature has to offer. In summer the thermometer may rise to 100 degrees or higher, to all but suffocate the farmer in his fields. And nowhere in the nation, according to climatologists, is there greater reason to be awed by the wind. "Does the wind blow this way all the time?" a greenhorn visitor once asked. "No, mister," a plainsman replied. "It'll maybe blow this way for a week or ten days, and then it'll take a change and blow like hell for a while."

Insolent gusts scud along the ground and eerily whistle through the grass, corralling tumbleweeds in fence corners, flapping loose anything not nailed down. Hot winds—impenetrable waves of torrid air, varying from 100 feet to half a mile in width— prevail throughout July and August, maintaining velocities of 10 to 12 miles an hour almost ceaselessly. Sometimes the winds whip up into monsters of destruction as seasonal tornadoes with velocities of up to 65 miles per hour. Like a black finger of doom a spiral funnel of swirling dust and debris advances, shifting and weaving across the plains. Touching down here and there along its unpredictable course, it topples fences, rips houses loose from their foundations, and destroys any man or beast unlucky enough to feel the full fury of its breath.

Even in average warm weather the winds and their burden of dust parch the throat, crack the lips and burn the eyes. Small wonder that many plainsmen find the summer a season that tries their patience. But winter is hardly less troublesome. Temperatures can remain below zero for days on end. The people of the region are assaulted by howling blizzards in which winds of 50 miles per hour may be accompanied by snowfalls of 22 inches in 12 hours, with drifts sometimes piling up to depths of 15 feet. It may be no accident, as historian D. W. Brogan has written, that much modern central-heating equipment was perfected in the plains, "where the winter cold can kill ten times as often as it can on the milder Atlantic."

The plains pioneer, of course, had no modern conveniences and only rudimentary shelter, and often his only protection against the winds was a bandanna tied around his face. If he was lucky enough to survive the expected terrors in nature's arsenal, he was still fair game for the unexpected that might lay him low and dash all his dreams. Wheat planted under a warm April sun might very well succumb beneath the icy blasts of a May freeze; drought might stunt his crop or torrential rains inundate it. Windstorms blowing in from the west might bury his land under a thick coverlet of dust or, conversely, lift his topsoil from the earth, carrying it thousands of miles away to God knows where. For the early plainsman there was a final and particularly cruel blow. In September, as the wheat or corn stood gleaming in the sun, waiting for the harvest, a dark cloud might sweep in from the north; a cloud that moved inexorably forward, blacking out the daylight. No mere harbinger of an approaching thunderstorm or early blizzard was this, for the cloud lived. In fact, it was not a cloud at all, but an infestation of millions of grasshoppers that swooped down upon the crops to strip them bare. To the plains settler, typically devout and often superstitious, it must have seemed like a visitation from an avenging God, punishing man—as in the days of Pharaoh—for his sins. Often the grasshoppers came several years in a row, and the pioneer who could withstand both their raids and nature's numerous other afflictions was indeed among the fittest—and a prime candidate for survival in a seemingly merciless world.

There were compensations for such agonies. There had to be. "When spring comes again," a pioneer wrote, "when soft green covers the vast expanses . . . when bounteous crops . . . luxuriantly spring forth . . . when the wild prairie grasses provide sustenance for the grazing herds; then everything else is forgotten." But the plainsman did not really forget for long the peril that surrounded him. There was too much to remind him of the awful reality of his condition. Perhaps a child, frozen by the winter's cold, lay buried in a corner of one field; perhaps a wife driven insane by loneliness and fear sat muttering incoherently inside the farmer's sod house. And slowly the plainsman put aside his early, naïve dreams of quick fortune and replaced them with hopes more solidly based in experience. Recurring tragedy had taught him that passive acceptance of the rigorous plains environment was suicide; mastery of that environment was essential, and such mastery did not come easily. It is of course no news that the region is now one of

Bane of the plains region, grasshoppers gnaw away at a cornstalk *(left)* that soon will be as bare as the clover plant *(right)* upon which a swarm of the insects rest after eating their fill. Periodic infestations of grasshoppers were once a huge problem to plains farmers, but today insecticides help control these insects.

the world's major agricultural producers; what is forgotten is that it took decades of trial and error to learn to farm on the flat, open land.

A few of the pioneers who went west expecting to plow the soil were lucky enough, or perceptive enough, to give up that idea and turn their new environment quickly to profit by making use of what was already there—grass in abundance. Near the small North Dakota community of New Salem, for instance, a bronze plaque is affixed to a granite boulder beside U.S. Highway 10. The inscription reads:

> *"Wrong Side Up"*
> *These words were spoken to John Christiansen on this spot in the spring of 1883 by a Sioux Indian. John was plowing under the prairie grass. Pondering this phrase made New Salem a successful dairy center.*

John Christiansen was sufficiently untypical of his fellow settlers to provide one of the few cases in which an Indian's advice was heeded. Accepting the Sioux's warning not to disturb the native grass, Christiansen renounced the plow and introduced dairy cattle to the still-unbroken prairie. Nearby settlers followed Christiansen's example and New

Salem soon became the center of a rich dairy area.

The average plains settler was harder to dissuade from breaking up the sod. He had come to the heart of the American grassland to grow cash crops. But before bumper crops could be forced from the essentially inhospitable prairie, farmers would suffer decades of hardship and privation as they painfully groped toward an understanding of the land and its demands. Few are the plainsmen of today who do not remember, either through personal experience or through stories told by their fathers, the grim days of the 1930s dust storms when thousands of tons of plains topsoil simply blew away and left the farmers penniless.

The tragedy of the Dust Bowl was the most recent chapter in a decades-long lesson that finally taught the plains farmers to perfect the techniques of scientific agriculture. They have learned to nurture the soil, enrich it and protect it from erosion; they have found that they must vary their crops and develop new and hardier strains of wheat and corn. But, even now the struggle for survival and prosperity continues. For although the plainsmen have made Kansas the leading producer of wheat in the nation, turned two million acres of once-barren Nebraska semidesert into rich cropland, made Iowa the state "where the tall corn grows" and made agriculture the chief industry of the Dakotas, the farmers' scientific defenses have not totally protected them from the capricious plains weather, nor has their political power shielded them from falling commodity prices.

The author Hamlin Garland, himself a plainsman, wrote of his fellow farmers at the turn of the century: "Writers and orators have lied so long about the 'idyllic' in farm life, and said so much about the 'independent American farmer,' that he himself has remained blind to the fact that he's one of the hardest-working and poorest-paid men in America." Nor was Garland alone in his embittered point of view. The farmers of the plains were being economically exploited, and they knew it. Throughout the last decades of the 19th Century and the first decades of the 20th, the Plains States were hotbeds of political agitation, as farmers formed political organizations and lobbies to press for reforms that would ease their lot. Among their adversaries were the railroads, with their high charges for shipping produce to market; the banks and moneylenders, with their high interest rates for loans needed to purchase seed and equipment; the speculators who forced up the price of land; the produce wholesalers who bought cheap and sold dear; and the Eastern financiers who espoused

a rigidly valued dollar against rural pressures for inflation, which would ease the farmers' burden of debt. In time, some of the ardently desired reforms were enacted to help protect the plains farmers from more powerful economic interests, but poverty and calamity would continue to stalk them well into the fourth decade of this century.

Even today's typical plains farmer finds himself in an ever-tightening economic squeeze. To compete successfully and take full advantage of government subsidies he must expand his holdings. More acreage means more sophisticated and expensive equipment, which in turn may require the purchase of even more land if the equipment is to be used to its fullest potential. Add to this the fact that commodity prices have not kept pace with the farmers' production costs and it appears not at all surprising that ever-larger numbers of plainsmen are fleeing the soil.

Thus the small farm recedes into history while the large, efficiently operated, highly mechanized farm thrives. Many farmers, leaving the land, seek shelter in the towns and cities. A number of communities that were once mere supply stations for neighboring farms and railway depots for transporting produce to market are now booming small metropolises, engaged in what is often called "agribusiness." Today's average city dweller on the plains is probably much closer to the rural economy than his counterpart in other regions of the nation. Kansas' agribusinesses—dairy production, meat packing, milling, alfalfa dehydrating and turkey processing, as well as the sale of goods and services to the farmer—gross $4.5 billion annually. Omaha, Nebraska, boasts a variety of titles, including "Agricultural Capital of the World," "The Nation's Largest Producer of Quick-Frozen Meat and Fruit Pies" and "The World's Largest Livestock Market and Meat-Processing Center."

Any visitor who is tempted to smile at such slogans need only remind himself that they represent the same spirit of regional pride that helped build every state of the Union. Plains communities consistently have been typical examples of American "get up and go," and their boasts are not always extravagant—or inaccurate. For decades Minneapolis, near the head of the Mississippi, was rightly called the "Mill City" because the power inherent in the Falls of St. Anthony had been combined with wheat from the nearby plains to make the metropolis the largest producer of flour in the nation.

Like Minneapolis, other plains communities that have become major population centers often owe their success to their locations on rivers; this was particularly important in the days of river transport, before railroads snaked out across the prairies to provide the farmer with an alternate means of moving his produce. All but one of the state capitals (Lincoln, which began as a Nebraska salt center) are river towns, and three of them (North Dakota's Bismarck, South Dakota's Pierre and Missouri's Jefferson City) are on the same stream —the Missouri, that fickle artery that cuts the plains in two.

Whether located on a river or not, few plains cities are of any great size. Only St. Louis and Kansas City, Missouri, can boast more than half a million citizens, and only a score of cities have more than 50,000 residents. Such major urban areas as exist are widely separated, unlike those in other regions of the country where cities, towns and suburbs often seem to melt into one another, forming one huge and ugly industrial jumble.

Increasingly, today's plainsman finds himself a city dweller, but his attitudes remain those of the farmer and cattleman. For chances are, though he may work as an insurance salesman or a mill hand, his outlook was formed by memories of the plow and horse. Though he may live in a city, he has retained the patterns of thought and speech that served him well in earlier times. Perhaps a visitor's most immediate impression of the plainsman is that he more nearly approaches the personification of the American dream than most of his compatriots. The twang in his voice, the rawboned, loose-limbed quality of his body and the no-nonsense style of his speech combine to create an aura of self-reliance and hardiness. The very word "plainsman" evokes a Gary Cooper type—honest, hard-working, tough, courageous.

The plainsman of today generally seems as deeply rooted in the wide-open spaces as a Boston Brahmin is in New England. But in fact, though the roots have sunk deep they are seldom more than a century old. Most prairie residents can trace their ancestry back to mid-19th Century Europe whence their grandparents or great-grandparents began the long journey to the American grasslands. Occasionally the immigrants traveled in groups; sometimes an entire community in Bohemia or Sweden or Germany or Norway would pack up and travel as a unit. It was not unusual for these people to think of themselves as the creators of a New Sweden or a New Swabia on the beckoning prairie. They must have been very disappointed to see their young, nurtured in a plains environment, adopt the relatively free-and-easy ways of the American frontier. So rapidly has assimilation tak-

PRECIPITATION

The area west of the 100th meridian and east of the Rockies has an average annual rainfall of 5 to 20 inches. This makes farming difficult without irrigation.

East of the 100th meridian the average annual rainfall is 20 to 25 inches, much of which falls during the growing season, when the crops need it the most.

NATURAL VEGETATION

Little changed since the first explorers crossed the continent, much of the land west of the 100th meridian is covered with short grass. Cattle now graze on the lands where great herds of American buffalo once roamed.

East of the 100th meridian tall grass once grew as high as three feet, and a great variety of flowers added color to the plains. Today, most of this natural vegetation has been replaced by vast expanses of wheat, corn and other crops.

SOILS

The soil west of the 100th meridian is rich in lime and low in acid. When rainfall is sparse, this combination is bad for the growing of wheat and corn, but it is perfectly suited for grazing cattle, which need the calcium that lime introduces into their forage.

Because of their original tall-grass cover, lands east of the 100th meridian were rich in organic matter. During the dry season, the grass died away and the decaying matter (humus) restored nutrients to the soil. Today's farmers nurture the soil to preserve its richness.

An historic dividing line

Moving westward across the nation, early explorers noticed that the tall-grass prairies with their excellent soil and favorable climate ended at approximately the 100th meridian. Across this line lay what these explorers called the "Great American Desert." Today, the 100th meridian is the approximate boundary between the rich eastern lands of the Plains States, used mainly for farming, and the western, more arid stretches, where grazing is a major land use. This seemingly abrupt division is partly governed by rainfall. Warm air masses moving up from the Gulf of Mexico bring considerable moisture to the region east of the 100th meridian. Beyond the 100th meridian, however, rainfall is dependent on air masses moving in from the Pacific Coast. These drop most of their moisture on the Rockies and have little rain left to nourish the western plains.

15

en place that a visitor to the plains today might be hard pressed to find a household in which any language but English is spoken. In fact, the plainsman whose central European or Scandinavian ancestors came to these shores only decades ago is almost indistinguishable from neighbors who trace their American lineage to pre-Revolutionary times.

Facilitating the quick assimilation of the sons and daughters of the plains pioneers was the rapid decline of immigration, a decline caused by improving economic conditions in Europe, World War I and, most of all, by postwar restrictions on immigration. With few arrivals from the Old World coming to the plains, the cultural ties to ancestral homelands were soon loosened. In typical American fashion, the evidence of European background is now noted primarily in such surnames as Hansen, Jensen, Schmidt and Svoboda painted on mailboxes and listed in telephone directories. Sometimes a visitor can find a Czech or Scandinavian celebration in progress in some city or town, but these tend to reflect sentiment rather than any substantive attachment to Europe.

What has happened is that the European heritages have been overshadowed by the more immediate experience of the American prairie. The prairie heritage is a source of great pride to the typical plainsman, although very few elements of the harsh life remain. The grandson of the pioneer remembers the past, enshrines it and romanticizes it. He delights in the ancestral stories of battling blizzards, standing off marauding Indians and defying claim jumpers—tales of trial and triumph. Many families carefully preserve yellowing photographs of a grandparent posing before a sod house or attending a meeting in a log church. Such personal mementos remind today's plainsman of the hardships his forebears endured and the legacy of strength and will power they bequeathed him. But the log churches and sod houses are no more—except as museum pieces. They have been replaced by sturdy frame structures not very different from those found in New England. Farm and ranch buildings are no longer ramshackle, and often the blessings of affluence have even been extended to the barn where the livestock is soothed by the dulcet strains of specially programed, piped-in music.

Today there is a certain uniformity about life in the Plains States that seems to deny the diverse ethnic backgrounds of the inhabitants. Even towns separated by distances of several hundred miles seem quite interchangeable. Although the western half of the region—Nebraska, the Dakotas and western Kansas—was settled in the post-Civil War

decades, fully a generation later than the eastern half—Iowa, Missouri, Minnesota and eastern Kansas—the towns on both sides of the Missouri River bear striking resemblances to one another. The only characteristic that distinguishes many towns east of the Missouri from those farther west is that the former, having been founded earlier, have larger trees that afford more ample shade from the searing summer sun. Nor do the customs and folkways differ greatly from state to state, for all plainsmen share a common bond in the remoteness, loneliness and harshness of their vast land and in the tribulations of their ancestors. Indeed, the average resident clings to the conviction that his folkways are more meaningful—and somehow more typically American—than those of inhabitants of other regions. He holds countless repetitions of rodeos, wild West shows and square dances he claims to have either originated or brought to the peak of perfection.

The plainsman has not neglected such homely events as church suppers and county fairs; nor has he shunned more esthetic activities. From the Plains States have come such distinguished painters as John Steuart Curry, Grant Wood and Thomas Hart Benton; such musicians as jazzman Charlie "Bird" Parker and composer Virgil Thomson. Nor has literature been slighted. Hamlin Garland, Willa Cather, Sinclair Lewis and Mari Sandoz made generations of Americans familiar with the manners and mores of Middle America. Mark Twain's Huck Finn and Tom Sawyer evoke everyman's memory of boyhood, even if his own was lived on the hard pavement of a city street.

Thus the plainsman's life is fertile in many fields. In politics he is notoriously unpredictable— and woe betide the Presidential candidate of either party who takes the region's support for granted, as Thomas E. Dewey discovered much to his chagrin. The man who defeated Dewey, Harry S. Truman of Independence, Missouri, was a true son of the plains, as was his successor, Dwight David Eisenhower, who grew up in Abilene, Kansas. Though the two Presidents differed in political philosophy, they both expressed in their down-to-earth styles of speech and pragmatic approaches to problems those roughhewn, honest qualities that Americans everywhere have learned to associate with a man of the Great Plains. Perhaps in his own eyes, and certainly in the eyes of others who revere his hardy self-reliance, the plainsman still stands larger than life, a man who has not broken faith with the simple rural values, a tamer of the wilderness, a super-American.

Its funnel churning up the landscape, a death-dealing tornado twists across the flat Nebraska horizon in a frenzy of destruction.

The tumult
of plains weather

Taken by themselves, the flat, treeless plains would be a study in boredom. But upon this vast terrain, the weather, in all its vagaries, works miracles of beauty and cataclysms of violence. With few natural barriers to moderate the weather's force, warm and cold air masses clash freely and unpredictably. The wind blows almost ceaselessly, its hot summer breath swirling drought into dust, its cold winter blasts driving snow into deep drifts, its warm spring caresses melting snow into floods. And always there lurks the threat of a tornado *(above),* whose narrow column of wind-tossed debris leaves a swath of destruction. Even in their most reckless moods, however, the elements can transform the otherwise monotonous land into a scene of dramatic beauty.

17

Drought and dust:
perils for the plainsman

Dust clouds, raised by hot winds, blow over a dried-out field. These clouds are symptoms of drought, which is the plains farmer's most persistent enemy.

A trail of dust follows a Kansas farmer across a plowed field. Such fields, devoid of vegetation, are very vulnerable to the wind's erosive force.

Beauty—and danger—from a violent downpour

Seen through a rippling sheet of wind-whipped rain water upon a windshield, a South Dakota townscape takes on the delicate beauty of an Impressionist painting.

Menacing thunderclouds, portents of a downpour, gather over a plains farm. Sudden storms, dropping more water than the ground can absorb, often damage crops and soil.

The silent onslaught
of floodwaters

An ironic welcome awaits unlikely travelers along a flooded highway that was swamped when quickly melting snows caused the Red River of the North to overflow in April 1966.

A lone boat is tied up next to a marooned church as the waters slowly recede near Humboldt, Minnesota. This flood inundated hundreds of square miles of flat farmland.

Hail—a menace
to ripening crops

Hail-bearing clouds boil up over a Kansas wheat field in July. Minutes later, hailstones—formed by rain blown through ice-cold air—were drumming down on the land.

Limp and lifeless, wheat crushed by marble-sized hailstones lies in a field. Hailstorms—with stones that are often as big as golf balls—are a common occurrence in the Plains States.

The blizzard:
winter's howl of rage

Caked with ice, cut off from food and struggling to keep its footing in a deep North Dakota snowdrift, a steer awaits help after a 1966 blizzard. Ranch hands will dig it out of the drift.

Huge snowdrifts, created by furious blizzard winds that have scraped nearby fields almost bare, pile up between North Dakota farm buildings and block a rural highway.

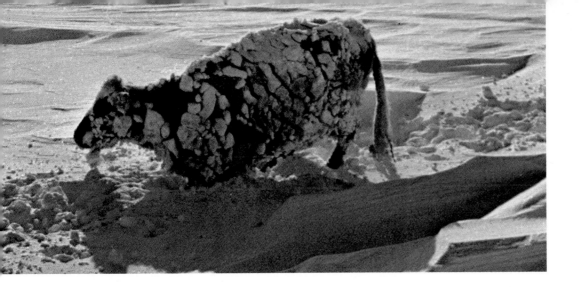

Ice—the most beautiful hazard of all

Icicles weight phone lines after a 1965 storm in South Dakota. Formed when rain freezes on cold objects, ice can wreak great damage; this storm felled 3,500 phone poles.

Seemingly trapped in a maze of glittering ice crystals, a solitary Kansas farm horse stands near his owner's windmill and waits for the dazzling blanket to melt from his pasture.

2

The Red Knights
of the Grasslands

High upon his steed he sits, regal of mien, war bonnet glittering in the sun, eyes scanning the distant horizon, body tensed to respond to the brain's command—this was the legendary figure of the American Indian of the plains, the noble savage who ranged the grasslands and was the first human to bend the prairie to his will. There is some truth in the legend, but it is a truth that shone for less than two centuries—approximately 1700 to 1880—before it entered the realm of history—and myth. When the white man first saw him, the Plains Indian had not yet reached his moment of destiny, his brief summertime of glory before the long winter of sorrow set in.

The first European to enter the plains was a Spanish conquistador from out of Mexico named Francisco Vásquez de Coronado. In 1540, less than half a century after Columbus arrived in the New World, Coronado led a troop of about 250 horsemen, 100 foot soldiers and hundreds of Mexican Indian bearers northward and eastward into the center of what is now the United States. Treasure

Sturgeon's Head, a plains warrior of the Sac and Fox tribe, was one of many Indians who posed in the 1830s for the famous painter George Catlin. The artist has shown the warrior's ceremonial markings: neck stripes and hand prints on his chest.

was the lure that drew the Spaniards deeper and deeper into the unexplored grassland; their imaginations had been whetted by reports of gold, silver and jewels that would make the loot they had seized from the Aztecs seem paltry by comparison. Had not Friar Marcos de Niza reported seeing—from a distance, of course—the fabled Seven Cities of Cíbola? So with high hopes of plunder Coronado set forth on his journey.

Cíbola, in what is now New Mexico, was a disappointment—nothing there but the mud huts of pueblo Indians. But soon the expedition was to capture an Indian dubbed El Turco (the Turk), because of his turbanlike headdress. El Turco spoke of the province of Quivera, far to the northeast, as a glorious land. He is reported to have claimed that in Quivera "there was a river . . . in which there were fishes as big as horses, and large numbers of very big canoes with more than 20 rowers on a side. On the prow [of each] . . . a great golden eagle." Even the common people of Quivera had dining utensils "of wrought plate, and the jugs and bowls were of gold." The Turk also spoke of "the lord of the country [who] took his afternoon nap under a great tree on which were hung many little gold bells, which put him to sleep as they swung in the air." Here was a goal worth a Span-

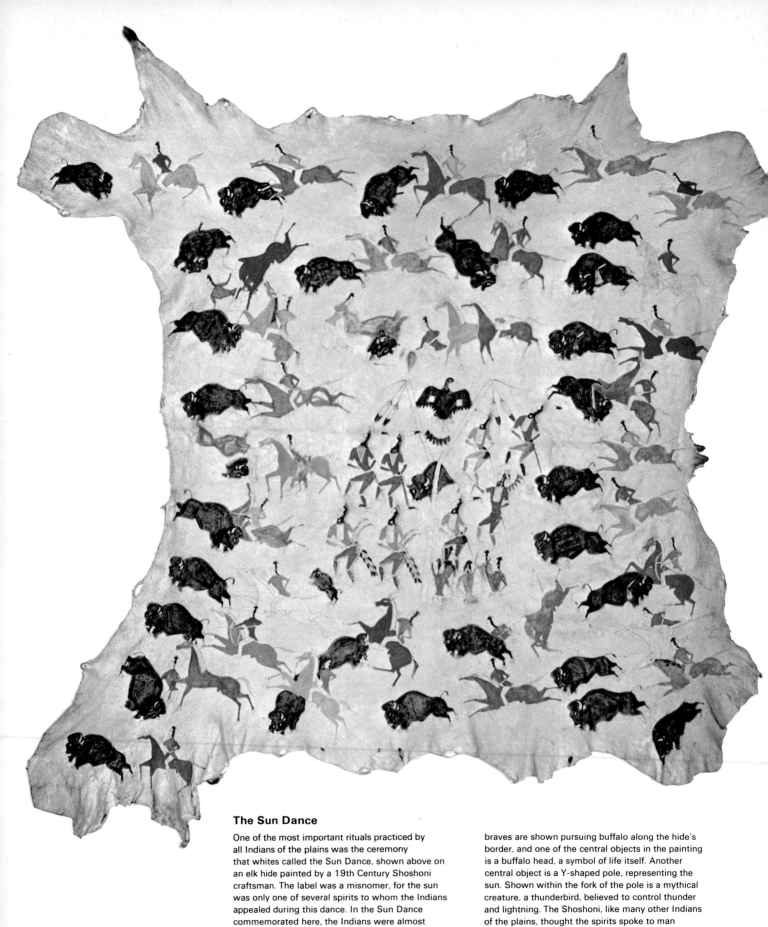

The Sun Dance

One of the most important rituals practiced by all Indians of the plains was the ceremony that whites called the Sun Dance, shown above on an elk hide painted by a 19th Century Shoshoni craftsman. The label was a misnomer, for the sun was only one of several spirits to whom the Indians appealed during this dance. In the Sun Dance commemorated here, the Indians were almost certainly asking for a successful hunt. Mounted braves are shown pursuing buffalo along the hide's border, and one of the central objects in the painting is a buffalo head, a symbol of life itself. Another central object is a Y-shaped pole, representing the sun. Shown within the fork of the pole is a mythical creature, a thunderbird, believed to control thunder and lightning. The Shoshoni, like many other Indians of the plains, thought the spirits spoke to man through deafening and fiery displays in the heavens.

32

iard's time and effort, an El Dorado that would erase the disappointment of Cibola.

By early 1541 Coronado and his men had reached Tiguez, in what is now New Mexico. Then in the spring, led on by El Turco, they traveled eastward into Texas, where the little band of fortune seekers split up. Taking only 30 horsemen, "the most efficient men and the best horses," as one of the conquistador's soldiers later recalled, Coronado turned north toward Quivera. Across the Texas Panhandle, into Oklahoma and finally to Kansas the tiny expedition moved. At last, in July 1541, they reached Quivera. Instead of noble personages, however, they found rude savages; instead of lofty palaces, thatched huts; instead of tinkling bells of gold and tableware of silver, Stone Age implements; instead of silks and satins, skin blankets. As for El Turco, he was garroted for having lied and led the Spaniards astray.

Though the expedition was a failure from the Spaniards' point of view, for the Indians who saw the white men the event must have had almost supernatural import. Here, easing through the tall grass of the plains, were creatures like none ever seen before. The men, clad in armor that glistened in the sun, must have seemed almost godlike to the Indians. Perhaps even more awe-inspiring were the horses they rode—large, strong, fast and somehow fearsome. It would be some time before the Indians realized that the horse need not be feared, but when they finally did—and learned to master these animals—their lives would be dramatically altered.

For more than a century, however, Coronado's foray left almost no mark upon the Indians; even the tall prairie grass that had felt the weight of horses' hoofs immediately sprang up straight to shroud the trail that the Spaniards blazed. The Indians' way of life remained unchanged. Some tribes were nomadic—Coronado's men had likened them to Arabs. The tribesmen traveled on foot, carrying their meager belongings across the prairie on small A-frames dragged by dogs. They stalked the migrating herds of buffalo, approaching the beasts stealthily and sometimes hiding themselves in wolf skins in order to get nearer to the shaggy animals. When a warrior was close enough he might bring one of the huge beasts down with an arrow or a spear. But hunting in this primitive manner offered, at best, a precarious existence and often braves, squaws and young were pinched with hunger.

Some other Indians, particularly those who lived on the eastern edge of the plains—the Kansa, Mandan and Pawnee—were semisedentary and re- mained so. They lived in grass huts or mud houses; they learned to farm the land; and the corn they grew lessened their dependence on the buffalo. It is likely that in the days before the horse, even the tribes known for their nomadic habits—the Teton Dakota, the Crows, the Assiniboin—grew some crops and made some pottery.

This pattern of existence—based partly on hunting, partly on corn-growing, but sharply circumscribed by lack of transport on the prairie's expanses—persisted until the middle of the 18th Century. By that time an immensely significant event had taken place: the tribes of the plains had acquired horses, the descendants of animals that had strayed from the conquistadors and from later Spanish settlers in the Southwest. Once the able-bodied warriors of the basically nomadic tribes took to horse, all thoughts of seed and harvest vanished. These Plains Indians now acquired the aspect of fierce fighters and raiders, men who one day would be prepared to contest the ownership of the plains with the white man.

But at first the tribes had only one another to deal with, and the warrior-hunter culture of the Plains Indian waxed strong and vital. It developed into a unique way of life that in some respects brings to mind the chivalry of medieval Europe. In fact, the Plains Indian has been called the red knight of the prairie.

An authority on the plains tribes, William Brandon, has sketched a vivid picture of the Indian warrior, a portrait of a man who in another time and another place might have made a fit riding companion for Sir Galahad. "Above all," wrote Brandon, "the new world of the horse brought time and temptation to dream. The plains are afloat in mysterious space, and the winds come straight from heaven. Anyone alone in the plains turns into a mystic. The plains had always been a place for dreams, but with horses they were more so. Something happens to a man when he gets on a horse, in a country where he can ride forever; it is quite easy to ascend to an impression of living in a myth. He either feels like a god or closer to God. There seems never to have been a race of plains horsemen that was not either fanatically proud or fanatically religious. The Plains Indians were both."

Like the knights of old, the Plains Indians lived by a warrior's code of honor. Combat was the joy, the vocation and the endless preoccupation of the thousands of tribesmen who were ranging the prairie in the early 19th Century. War, not peace, was considered both a normal and a beneficent state of affairs, but the Indians' concept of warfare was quite different from ours. No thought was given to such ultimate objectives as the permanent securing of a tract of land for one tribe's exclusive use; nor was the physical extinction of a rival tribe a goal of hostilities. Rare, indeed, was a mass confrontation of contending armies. Instead, tribal wars tended to be limited in scope and were characterized by the knife-thrust raid, the ambush, the brief skirmish—all tactics calculated to permit the individual brave to exhibit personal valor. Few if any excuses were needed to set one tribe against another; often the immediate impetus for a raid was simply a desire for more horses. No Indian ever considered that he owned enough.

Central to the warrior's code of honor—a code accepted with only minor variations by most plains tribes—was a concept that came to be known as coups, the French word for "hits" or "blows," which the Indians acquired from French explorers and traders. A brave's valor was measured in the number of coups he was personally able to inflict on an enemy. Riding directly into a troop of hostile warriors, the brave would stick out a pole—called a coup stick—or even his hand, to jab the foeman or disarm him. For many tribes, this was the ultimate in bravery and warriors carefully prized each act of this sort, often painting the skins of their tepees with scenes that recounted their feats. To kill a man from a distance with a bow and arrow, or to scalp a dead enemy—these were considered minor triumphs in most tribes, in no way comparable to the hazardous feat of charging into a hostile host, exposing one's body to lance and knife in hope of "counting coup" upon an adversary.

All of this is not to suggest that tribal warfare was a polite game of tag. On the contrary, it was generally brutal and barbaric. Wounded enemies were slain and scalped, captured braves were horribly tortured, and even women and children were frequently put to death. Often the prairie grass was stained with the blood of hundreds. But to kill and capture were lesser achievements than to prove oneself through feats of daring.

It was the horse that made mobile warfare possible, that enhanced the excitement of battle and that made every Indian boy tremble with impatience for his first taste of combat. As might be expected, horses were worth far more than gold or diamonds in our society. A man's wealth was calculated in the number of horses he owned, and a skillful horse thief, provided he did not steal from his comrades, was an honored member of the tribe. To part with one horse, or several, in exchange for a bride must have made many a brave reflect with some chagrin on the high cost of matrimony, and though a courageous son brought honor to his father, a comely daughter was almost like money in the bank—or in this case, horses in the private herd.

A society that placed such great value on individual action was necessarily loosely organized, without any centralized authority charged with making overall policy. As a general rule no one man could speak for a whole tribe, and any number might bear the title of "chief." Major questions of war and peace were usually decided by consultations among councils of elders, but often warrior bands of younger braves determined a course of action contrary to the wishes of their chiefs. Not even the honored medicine men could make policy for the entire community, although their presumed power to intercede with the spirits won them great respect.

It was the spirits, thought the Indians, who controlled the destiny of man, and it was to the spirits that the Indians appealed for protection and for guidance. In some tribes young braves were expected to spend long periods fasting in isolation to seek out visions; certain objects, such as pipes or bundles of tobacco, were believed to contain kindly spirits that would ward off evil spirits; elaborate rites and dances were practiced to appease the spirits and assure a successful raid, a good hunt or beneficent weather. One of these rituals, the Sun Dance, generally included torture rites through which a brave showed his dedication to the spirits and implored them to grant him great strength and courage.

Of all the many rituals practiced by the various tribes, the Sun Dance was the most important. Most plains tribes performed a version of this ceremony, though the precise rites varied from tribe to tribe. The Sun Dance usually took place once a year, and all the hunting and fighting bands of a tribe gathered together either to witness it or to participate in it. In most tribes, selected braves or volunteers stood exposed before the spirits, and in a frenzy of religious zeal engaged in excruciatingly painful self-torture to please the good spirits and appease the bad. To bear the tortures bravely was also proof of great courage and a portent of success in battle.

In 1832 the American artist George Catlin, while visiting a Mandan village in what is now North Dakota, witnessed one of these torture ceremonies. His journals recorded the event: "In a few minutes about fifty young men . . . appeared in a beautiful group, their graceful limbs entirely denuded, but

Tribes of the plains, 1650

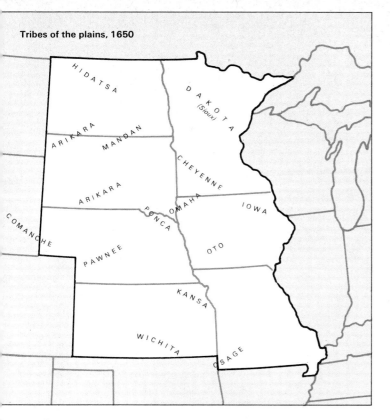

HIDATSA
ARIKARA
MANDAN
DAKOTA (Sioux)
COMANCHE
ARIKARA
CHEYENNE
PONCA
OMAHA
IOWA
PAWNEE
OTO
KANSA
WICHITA
OSAGE

Major migrations after 1650

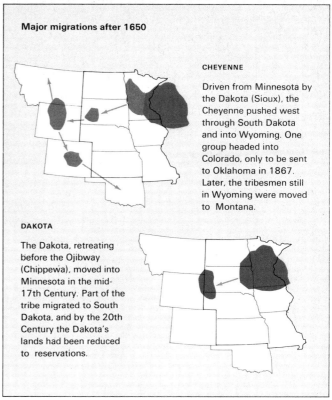

CHEYENNE

Driven from Minnesota by the Dakota (Sioux), the Cheyenne pushed west through South Dakota and into Wyoming. One group headed into Colorado, only to be sent to Oklahoma in 1867. Later, the tribesmen still in Wyoming were moved to Montana.

DAKOTA

The Dakota, retreating before the Ojibway (Chippewa), moved into Minnesota in the mid-17th Century. Part of the tribe migrated to South Dakota, and by the 20th Century the Dakota's lands had been reduced to reservations.

Reservations today

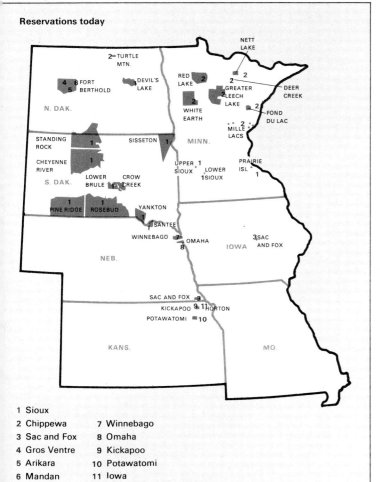

NETT LAKE
2—TURTLE MTN.
RED LAKE 2
4 6 FORT BERTHOLD
DEVIL'S LAKE
2 GREATER LEECH LAKE
DEER CREEK
5
N. DAK.
2 WHITE EARTH
2 FOND DU LAC
2 MILLE LACS
STANDING ROCK 1
SISSETON 1
MINN.
CHEYENNE RIVER 1
UPPER SIOUX 1
LOWER SIOUX 1
PRAIRIE ISL 1
LOWER BRULE
CROW CREEK 1
S. DAK.
1 1
PINE RIDGE ROSEBUD
YANKTON 1
SANTEE
WINNEBAGO 7
OMAHA 8
IOWA
3 SAC AND FOX
NEB.
SAC AND FOX 3
KICKAPOO 9 11 HORTON
POTAWATOMI 10
KANS.
MO.

1 Sioux
2 Chippewa
3 Sac and Fox
4 Gros Ventre
5 Arikara
6 Mandan
7 Winnebago
8 Omaha
9 Kickapoo
10 Potawatomi
11 Iowa

The Indians' lost lands

The shrinking of the territories within the Plains States Indians' domain is traced on the maps above and at left. At about 1650, the earliest date for which reliable information is available, members of some 15 major tribes were scattered in small settlements *(above left)*. By 1750 the Indians had obtained horses, which permitted them to roam freely over the vast reaches of the plains, but by then the pressure of white settlement to the east was being felt in the region. Many tribes, pushed from their eastern lands, made their way westward onto the plains, in turn displacing many of the tribes that stood in their way. The routes followed by two of the displaced tribes, the Cheyenne and the Dakota (now known as the Sioux), are shown at right above.

By the mid-20th Century, the picture of Indian life in the Plains States had changed drastically. The lands controlled by the tribes had been reduced to meager reservations of sometimes only a few hundred acres. In addition, many tribes had disappeared from the region altogether, though in some instances they were replaced by others. Of the major tribes occupying the region in 1650, fewer than half were there some 300 years later. Those remaining include the Sioux, Hidatsa (now known as the Gros Ventre), Arikara, Mandan, Omaha and Iowa. Of the tribes no longer in the Plains States, the Cheyenne, Comanche and Wichita were forced out by other Indians. The Osage ceded their lands—including much of Missouri—to the United States in 1808. They eventually settled in Oklahoma. The Pawnee, Ponca, Oto and Kansa stayed in the region until, in the late 19th Century, the government moved them onto reservations in Oklahoma. Other tribes shown in today's Plains States reservations—the Chippewa, Sac and Fox, Winnebago, Kickapoo and Potawatomi—all moved into the region when white settlement forced them off lands in Michigan, Wisconsin and Illinois. The map at left lists today's plains tribes in order of their population.

without exception covered with clay of different colors from head to foot—some white, some red, some yellow, and others blue and green." Catlin noted that for four days and nights these braves were kept inside the medicine lodge without food or drink, while other tribesmen outside the lodge performed a number of ceremonies. The most important of these rites was the Bull Dance, in which eight principal performers, strangely painted and covered with buffalo skins, imitated the motions of buffalo bulls to the chant of prayers and the rhythmic beat of hands striking water bags. The ritual was a supplication to the Great Spirit, who could reward them by sending large herds of buffalo, but it was also intended to give heart to the braves inside the lodge, giving them the courage that would help them endure the agonies to come.

Catlin then shifted his attention to the rituals about to begin inside the lodge: "Two men, who were to inflict the tortures, had taken their positions near the middle of the lodge; one with a large knife with a sharp point and two edges, which were hacked with another knife in order to produce as much pain as possible, was ready to make the incisions through the flesh, and the other, prepared with a handful of splints of the size of a man's finger, and sharpened at both ends, to be passed through the wounds as soon as the knife was withdrawn. . . . To these two men one of the emaciated candidates at a time crawled up and submitted to the knife, which was passed under and through the integuments and flesh taken up between the thumb and forefinger of the operator, on each arm, above and below the elbow . . . and on each leg above and below the knee . . . and also on each breast and each shoulder."

More tortures followed. The splints were passed through the wounds, and "a cord of raw hide was lowered down through the top of the wigwam, and fastened to the splints on the breasts or shoulders, by which the young man was to be raised up and suspended, by men placed on the top of the lodge for the purpose."

In this way the spirits were appeased and young men exhibited their fortitude. For if they survived such ordeals, what terrors could the battlefield or the buffalo hunt hold for them?

Many of the Indian rituals revolved around the buffalo and the spirits that controlled their migrations and the size of the herds. In the life of an Indian brave the buffalo hunt was almost as significant an event as battle. Here too, the horse made the chase and the kill a never-ending source of high drama. No longer did the Indian have to sneak on foot to approach a herd; no longer need he hang back waiting for one of the shaggy beasts to straggle so that it could be safely attacked with lance or arrow. Now, with the horse, he could more easily stampede the herd this way or that, drive it into a hail of arrows from waiting braves, or route it over a cliff or into a river. The horse also enabled hunting bands to range over hundreds of square miles of prairie while the squaws and young brought up the rear, each family's possessions being dragged along on enlarged A-frames by ponies that were not being used in the chase.

It was a thrilling life, this tracking down of buffalo. A German visitor to the plains, Baron Möllhausen, paraphrased with elegant English the report of an Indian describing a typical hunt: "The buffalo has many enemies, but the most dangerous is still the Indian who has all manner of wily tricks. Buffalo hunting for the Indian is a necessity; but it is also his favorite pastime. Life holds no higher pleasure than to mount one of the handy, patient little ponies . . . and gallop into a herd dealing death and destruction. Everything which might interfere with the movements of man or horse is flung away. Clothing and saddle are cast aside; all the rider retains is a big leather strap . . . which is fastened around the pony's neck and allowed to trail behind. This trailrope acts as a bridle, and as a life-line too, for recapturing the horse should its rider be dismounted. In his left hand the hunter carries his bow and as many arrows as he can hold; in his right a whip with which he belabors his beast without pity. Indian ponies are trained to gallop close alongside the buffalo, providing an easy shot; the instant the bow string twangs the pony instinctively dodges to escape the buffalo's horns, and approaches another victim. Thus the hunt continues until his pony's exhaustion warns the hunter to desist. The wounded buffalo drop out and are dispatched by the wives of the hunter who follow the trail. The choicest morsels are taken home to the wigwam where the meat is cut into thin strips and dried in the sun, while the hide is tanned by a process of great simplicity. Needless to say the rest is left for the wolves, which follow the herd in considerable numbers."

When Möllhausen recorded these observations in 1853, the buffalo still roamed "in great herds; the plains are covered with them as far as the eye can see. There are far too many to count." So long as the buffalo were numerous, the Indians waxed prosperous and rarely knew want. But, in the three decades to follow, the white man hunted down and utterly destroyed the herds. The effect was to deny the Indians sustenance, and the tribesmen were reduced to starvation. It was this destruction of the buffalo, more than any other single factor, that sealed the fate of the Indians of the plains. For the buffalo meant life itself to the red man. Upon its meat he feasted; from its skins he made his tepees, his clothing and his blankets; from its bones he fashioned household and farming implements; and even its dung, called "buffalo chips," served as fuel for his campfire. It is quite possible that no other society in history was so dependent on a single resource as were the Plains Indians on the buffalo.

Into this nomadic, hunting culture came the white men, as explorers, then as hunters and trappers and finally as settlers. At first the number of whites who entered the plains was too small to make much impression on the Indians, and they had little reason to fear the occasional white trapper or explorer who passed their way in the 17th and 18th Centuries. True, the French in the 1600s introduced firearms to their allies the Ojibway, but the only immediate effect of this was to permit this prairie tribe to drive their hereditary enemies, the eastern Dakota, from the woods around the source of the Mississippi onto the open grassland of Minnesota and areas to the west.

But after the French came the Americans, who were to open a new and disastrous era for the red man. In 1803 the United States purchased the Louisiana Territory from the French and thus came into ownership of the vast plains that stretched between the Mississippi and the Rockies. Even before the treaty was ratified by Congress, an expedition authorized by the government set out to explore the new domains. Headed by Meriwether Lewis and William Clark, the expedition traveled up the Missouri, across the plains, and then continued westward to the Rockies and the Pacific Coast. Along the route the captains took careful notes, made maps, collected specimens of the flora and fauna of the area, and observed the various Indian tribes with whom they came in contact—the Oto, Omaha, Arikara, Mandan and Hidatsa, and the Teton Dakota, the most magnificent of the mounted warriors. Other tribes roaming the plains at the turn of the 19th Century were the semisedentary Pawnee and the Crows, the latter admired by all Indians for their talent as horse thieves. To the south, in what is now Kansas, Nebraska, Colorado and Texas, ranged the fierce Cheyenne, Kiowa and Arapaho, among others. From the Lewis and Clark expedition, Americans obtained their first reliable information about the Great Plains and their inhabitants.

While Lewis and Clark were still on the trail, Lieutenant Zebulon Pike went in search of the Mississippi's source and held powwows with the chiefs of the Minnesota Ojibway and the eastern Dakota in an attempt to establish a lasting peace between them. In 1806 he headed west into the plains. He found there the Pawnee, the Osage and the Kansa, who grew corn, watermelon, beans and pumpkins to augment their staple of buffalo meat. During his journey, Pike traced the Osage River west, turned north to the Republican River in today's southern Nebraska, dropped down to the great bend on the Arkansas near Dodge City, Kansas, and traveled up that river to give his name to a Rocky Mountain peak. Pike compared the high plains he crossed to "the sandy deserts of Africa" and branded them "incapable of cultivation." Fourteen years later Major Stephen H. Long followed the Platte River across the Nebraska plains and was equally unimpressed by the terrain. He described the area extending 500 or 600 miles east of the Rockies as being "uninhabitable by a people depending upon agriculture for their subsistence."

Long's term, "the Great American Desert," became firmly fixed in the nation's mind, and the notion that the region was a wasteland kept white settlement to a minimum on the plains west of the Missouri until after the Civil War. For the Indians, this notion was a reprieve of sorts; they could hold their lands for a few decades longer. By the middle of the 19th Century, however, a new and complicating element came into the picture: the indigenous tribes now discovered they would have to share the plains region with tribes that had long lived east of the Mississippi. The white man wanted, and intended to get, the rich farmlands of these Eastern tribes; and since the plains were thought worthless by the federal government, why not, the theory went, resettle the inconveniently located Eastern Indians upon the trackless wastes? Tribes from the Alleghenies and the Ohio watershed—the Delawares, Shawnee, Wyandot, Kickapoo and others—were thereupon forced from their homes onto land in the West—land that was not the government's to give. Quite naturally, the Plains Indians, now required to share their hunting grounds with others, viewed the newcomers with intense hostility and scorned them as farmers unfit to roam the grasslands. Thus the situation that greeted the white men when they eventually began to arrive in force was already troubled.

The first white men to make regular visits to the tribes of the plains were the French traders of the 18th Century, who were later joined by American

On the first leg of its trek westward, a wagon train stops on the main street of Topeka, Kansas, in 1879. Called prairie schooners because their white canvas tops resembled sails, the wagons housed pioneer families that had decided to face the hardships of the plains and the threat of hostile Indians in hope of finding a better life in the West. Each train had its own elected leaders, an experienced guide to lead it across the plains and bylaws that among other things specified proper conduct for all participants.

trappers seeking beaver skins for the burgeoning fur market of the 1820s and 1830s. These mountain men were a special breed, able to live off the land, to read the landscape with the aborigine's whetted senses and to match the red man—and sometimes even excel him—in horsemanship, hunting and fighting. They remain legendary figures in the hagiology of two-fisted American heroes. There was Hugh Glass, who survived a mangling by a grizzly to drag himself halfway across South Dakota in search of aid; there were Kit Carson and Tom Fitzpatrick, both of whom began as Rocky Mountain trappers but later served as guides for government surveys of the plains; there was Jedediah Strong Smith, the first American to lead a party of trappers overland to California, only to be killed by Comanche near the Cimarron River.

The mountain men pioneered the way west and marked the trails that crossed the plains to the Rockies. It was Smith who blazed the Overland Trail and, with David Jackson and William Sublette, demonstrated that it was possible to take wagons and cattle across the mountains. William Becknell of Franklin, Missouri, established the Santa Fe Trail in 1821, thus opening the Southwest for trade and settlement. Carson and Fitzpatrick guided John Charles Frémont—the flamboyant soldier-explorer and political adventurer—across the Rockies and into California.

Romantic and heroic as the mountain men must have seemed to Easterners, they were people forever haunted by the specter of sudden death. Living among Indians who might at any moment turn hostile, threatened by grizzlies, frozen by the winter's bitter cold and scorched by the summer's sun, the mountain men lived in a world of unrelenting fear.

"Folks might call them Indians," wrote the historian Bernard DeVoto of the mountain men in his book *The Year of Decision*, "but they were better Indians. They had usurped the Indians' technology and had so bettered it that they could occupy the Indian's country and subdue the Indian. They had mastered the last, the biggest, and the hardest wilderness. . . . [They] could live comfortably among privations that broke the emigrants' spirit and safe among dangers that killed soldiers like flies in the first frost. They learned not only to survive in the big lonesome, but to live there at the height of function."

Even getting through that indefinable something, "the big lonesome," was to prove too much for many who came later—who came not to stay but merely to cross over the plains on their way to the fertile valleys of the Pacific Coast. Those who did make it likely as not depended on the experience of mountain men to see them through. Fitzpatrick guided the first overland California-bound party of settlers from Missouri to Fort Hall, Idaho, by way of the Platte Valley in 1841, and the intrepid frontiersman Moses "Black" Harris led several covered wagon trains across the Rockies. Getting from the Mississippi to the Far West took the skill of men who knew the terrain and could keep the Indians in check.

These transients were soon to be followed by white men aiming to stay in the plains. They were not held back by the fact that the federal government, in the course of forcibly resettling 60,000 eastern Indians west of the Mississippi, had declared the Dakotas, most of Minnesota and Nebraska, and portions of Iowa and Kansas to be Indian territory barred to settlers.

Though the federal government was undoubtedly sincere at the time in declaring this vast stretch of prairie to be permanently secure for the tribes, the pressures in favor of westward expansion were quickly to make a shambles of this policy. Along the western edges of the plains, miners were soon to make incursions into territory forbidden them by treaty; at the same time, agricultural and railway interests lobbied in Washington to extend the farming frontier ever westward into the heart of the plains. In this way the Indians were to be crushed in a pincers movement of white expansion from both the west and east. In the 1840s and 1850s white settlers began to move across the upper Mississippi and the St. Croix Rivers, and Iowa and Minnesota were admitted to the Union before the Civil War. As early as 1837 the Ojibway and the Santee Dakota had signed away part of their empire and again, in 1851, the Santee renounced their rights to an additional 24 million acres in what is now Minnesota, South Dakota and Iowa. In exchange they were given a 20-mile-wide reservation straddling the Minnesota River and an annual stipend to be paid in cash and supplies. That same year Tom Fitzpatrick, by then an Indian agent working for the U.S. government, met with more than 10,000 Shoshoni, Cheyenne, Dakota, Crows and other tribesmen; he asked for, and received, verbal assurances that the braves would not molest emigrant parties and would permit the government to build roads and forts to protect the wagon trains.

Both the demand and the promise were futile. Fitzpatrick reported two years later that endless traffic by then plying the Oregon Trail had caused

the tribes to be "in abject want of food half the year. . . . The travel upon the road," the agent wrote, "drives [the buffalo] off or else confines them to a narrow path during the period of emigration, and the different tribes are forced to contend with hostile nations. . . . Their women are pinched with want and their children constantly crying with hunger." And, as if this were not enough, the Indians were now being killed like flies by cholera and other diseases brought by the white man. Already the Mandan, whom Catlin had observed only two decades before, had been almost wiped out by smallpox. It could only be a matter of time before the Indians struck out in wrath against the trespassers on their soil.

Incidents were not long in coming. In 1854 a hungry Dakota killed a lame cow along a wagon train trail. Even though some observers believed that the animal had been deliberately abandoned, the owner saw a chance for reimbursement from the government and turned down the tribe's offer of $10. Insisting on $25, he persuaded the Army to let a young, trigger-happy lieutenant, J. L. Grattan, take a task force to a Dakota encampment to bring back the cow's killer. Grattan, a boastful youth who was determined to establish a reputation as an Indian fighter, marched with 30 men to the Dakota camp. He had resolved "to conquer or die" despite his orders to avoid "unnecessary risks." After futile discussion with two chiefs, Grattan, armed with two howitzers, opened fire on the Dakota without warning. Enraged, the Indians leaped to the attack. Grattan retreated hastily, but soon was surrounded by warriors who made short work of him. Within minutes, the lieutenant and his command lay dead in the plains dust.

News of the incident caused a nationwide furor, increased the already intense antipathy toward Indians and established an emotional climate in which the treaty obligations of the government could be ignored with impunity. The new mood also produced a new set of characters. The plains of the West were dangerous. Only now were they beginning to be looked upon with longing by land-hungry pioneers who had previously scorned much of the region as merely a wasteland to be passed through as speedily and safely as possible. But the dangers, Indians and all, had long held considerable appeal for adventurous men. Slowly a new American folk hero—the Indian fighter—came into being.

As early as 1849 a book was published purporting to be based on the life of Kit Carson. Filled with purple prose, the book painted Carson as "a man on horseback . . . erect and lithe as the pine trees." The account went on to describe Carson as "the noble figure of the hunter-horseman, half-Indian, half whiteman . . . with rifle, horse and dog for his sole companions in all that dreary waste . . . to the right [of him] a yelling pack of wolves . . . on his left the thick, black smoke, in curling wreaths, proclaimed the prairie fire, while in the clear gray eye that looked from the picture forth, there seemed to glance a look of proud indifference to all, and the conscious confidence of ennobling self-reliance." In the minds of many Americans such a paragon was obviously the type to wipe out the predatory savages and, given the white man's loathing for the Indians, it was not difficult for many gun-toters, who began appearing on the periphery of the plains in the 1850s and 1860s, to regard themselves as the elite advance guard of civilization.

The gunmen would certainly be needed, for in the 1850s the United States embarked upon policies aimed at destroying the power of the plains tribes. In 1854 the Kansas-Nebraska Act was signed into law. This opened up a considerable stretch of the trans-Missouri plains to settlers, despite the promise previously made that these lands were reserved for the Indians "as long as grass shall grow and the waters run." The hard-pressed red men were expected to evaporate, to seek out new hunting grounds beyond the range of white settlement.

Despite the provocations and humiliations the Indians suffered, they endured their lot with remarkable forbearance until 1862, when at last serious warfare between red men and white broke out. The immediate cause was, perhaps, the result of a misunderstanding and administrative red tape. The Santee Dakota, now restricted to their Minnesota reservation, had suffered a crop failure and were starving. That year the stipend had not been paid, and the Army had received no authorization to open up its warehouses to distribute provisions. At the same time, local traders brutally cut off credit to the Indians; one merchant, Andrew J. Myrick by name, remarked with the lofty indifference that had once brought a French queen to grief: "Let them eat grass." This offhand insult reflected the attitude of many whites of the Minnesota Valley. Soon they would have ample reason to regret their lack of charity.

The Indians, angered beyond endurance by such callousness, struck. On August 17, 1862, the little settlement of Acton was attacked and five of its inhabitants brutally slaughtered. The next day the revolt spread. At Redwood, Jamestown and Redwood Ferry the Indians vented their fury upon helpless settlers, and by midnight 400 whites had been killed. The whites of south-central Minnesota quickly panicked. Within days thousands of fleeing settlers were clogging the roads. About 300 managed to reach the shelter of Fort Ridgely, and many of these, according to an Army officer stationed there, were "wounded and crazed with grief; some had been without food and water."

But even at Fort Ridgely, conditions were critical. Presumably because of the needs of the Union forces engaged against the Confederacy, the installation was short of arms. Major B. H. Randall described the desperate situation of the soldiers and refugees: "When evening came, guards were stationed at all the doors with either axe, shovel, club or anything else that could be used as a weapon. The women worked all night making cartridges out of slugs cut by the men for the small number of guns they had been able to give the sentinels. Twenty old-style Dragoon carbines were found in the magazine and put into condition." The fort also had at its disposal three ancient cannon. When the major Indian assault was launched on the 22nd, these artillery pieces were put into action and it was their booming reports, rather than the damage they inflicted, that frightened the attackers off and saved the installation from being overrun. Aid finally came on August 27 when Colonel Henry Hastings Sibley arrived at the fort with 1,500 troops.

Meanwhile the Indians had run wild. They besieged the town of New Ulm and ultimately burned a part of it to the ground. War parties ranged far and wide throughout south-central Minnesota, looting, burning, raping and killing. One of the earliest white victims of the Santee's wrath was Andrew Myrick. The Indians left him dead with his mouth stuffed with grass.

By the middle of September the Army felt sufficiently strong to go on the offensive. With 1,600 men Sibley marched out of Fort Ridgely to pursue the Indians, and on September 23 his command engaged 700 Santee Dakota at Wood Lake. The odds against the red men were overwhelming: not only did the white soldiers outnumber them by more than two to one, but the Army's artillery decimated the Indians' ranks. This battle at Wood Lake sealed the fate of the Santee Dakota. Clearly, individual bravery was no match for howitzers; ultimate victory would belong to the white man with his fire-breathing cannon.

Not all the Indians were easy to convince. Little

The mass burial of Sioux Indians after the Battle of Wounded Knee on December 29, 1890, marked the end of major Indian resistance to the white man. The battle was the bloody climax to a dispute over a Sioux ritual called the Ghost Dance, which promised the return of lost lands and glory. An attempt by government officials to suppress the ghost dancers resulted in the killing of famed Chief Sitting Bull. Troops were then called in to control the aroused Sioux. One band of Indians was surrounded at Wounded Knee Creek, in South Dakota, by 470 soldiers. When the Sioux fired a single shot, the troops answered with a fusillade, killing 146 men, women and children.

Turtle, a Santee chief, expressed the bewilderment and defiance of the younger braves. After the debacle he told his braves: "I am ashamed to call myself a Dakota. Seven hundred of our best warriors were whipped yesterday by the whites. Now we had better all run away and scatter out over the plains like buffalo and wolves. To be sure, the whites had wagon-guns and better arms than we, and there were many more of them. But that is no reason why we should not have whipped them, for we are brave Dakotas and whites are cowardly women. I cannot account for the disgraceful defeat. It must be the work of traitors in our midst."

Following Little Turtle's advice, many of the Santee Dakota did scatter out over the plains to join forces with Indians farther to the west in the Dakotas and in the Rockies. There, from mountain strongholds, they would continue to harass the white man for more than a decade.

Meanwhile, the U.S. Army had captured more than 1,500 men, and drumhead courts-martial quickly condemned 306 braves to death by hanging. The federal government confirmed only 39 of these sentences, after President Lincoln was advised that most of the real culprits had escaped beyond the Army's reach. It is likely that even among these relatively few, some died for no great-

er crime than the defense of what they considered to be their homeland.

The events that followed the uprising in Minnesota led inexorably to the destruction of the Indian tribes. Once the Civil War was over, the government could turn its full attention to the problems of making the plains safe for settlement—by rounding up the Indians willing to go to reservations and by killing the rest. The self-serving notion that "the only good Indian is a dead Indian" seemed for a time to express the sentiments of most Americans. Typical was General Patrick E. Connor's command to his troops out on an Indian-hunting expedition. "You will not," ordered the general, "receive overtures of peace and submission from the Indians but will kill every male Indian over 12 years of age."

Though most of the major battles between soldiers and Indians after the defeat of the Santee Dakota took place outside the borders of the Plains States—in Colorado, Wyoming, Montana, Oklahoma, Arizona and Texas—these engagements were as important to the development of the region as if they had occurred within its borders. For had the impossible happened—had the Indians won—the entire trans-Missouri prairie would have remained the hunting grounds of the Dakota, Chey-

41

enne, Crows and other plains tribes. Few of the battles were crucial in themselves, and some were even won by the Indians, but certain of them do stand out for a particular quality of horror or a unique significance that is associated with them.

• On November 29, 1864, a troop of cavalrymen under Colonel J. M. Chivington launched a surprise attack on a small band of Cheyenne at Sand Creek, Colorado. The soldiers massacred more than 450 Indians, many of them women and children. The Cheyenne had been camping at Sand Creek at the invitation of the government.

• On August 2, 1867, thirty-three soldiers from Fort Kearny, Wyoming, stood off a large band of Teton Dakota led by a chief named Red Cloud. The soldiers were armed with new breech-loading rifles that permitted rapid fire. An Indian survivor of the skirmish, Fire Thunder, reminisced many years later about the effects of this new weapon. "There were not many Wasichus [whites], but they were lying behind the boxes and they shot faster than they ever shot at us before. We thought it was some new medicine of great power. . . . Afterwards I learned that it was because they had new guns that they loaded from behind. . . . We came on after sunrise. There were many, many of us and we meant to ride right over them and rub them out. But our ponies were afraid of the ring of fire the guns of the Wasichus made, and would not go over. . . . We tried hard, but we could not do it, and there were dead warriors and horses piled all around the boxes and scattered over the plain. Then we left our horses in a gulch and charged on foot, but it was like green grass withering in a fire. So we picked up our wounded and went away. I do not know how many of our people were killed but there were very many. It was bad."

• On June 25, 1876, two hundred and twenty-five men under the command of Lieutenant Colonel George A. Custer were massacred at the Battle of Little Big Horn in Montana. Custer's mission was to scout out the positions of the Indians—the Dakota and Cheyenne—who controlled the foothills of the Rockies. On June 24, Custer sighted signs of an Indian encampment on the Little Big Horn River. Underestimating the strength of his adversary and confident of an easy victory, Custer the next day split his command into three columns before attacking the Indians. But the Indians far outnumbered the whites, and they drove back the first column under Major Marcus Reno without difficulty. Meanwhile Custer had pushed ahead to collide with the main Indian force. In the slaughter that ensued, every soldier in the colonel's column was killed. The third column, under Captain Frederick Benteen, finally joined with Major Reno and helped the major hold off the Indians until reinforcements arrived.

The Battle of Little Big Horn was the worst defeat ever suffered by United States arms at the hands of the Indians, but it would soon be avenged. The Dakota-Cheyenne alliance that had brought about the triumph quickly evaporated, for the Indians lacked the necessary resources to maintain a large army in the field. And the United States was aroused by the news of Little Big Horn as it had never been before. A new and urgent determination to destroy the Indian and avenge the fallen hero swept the lands. Troops under the command of Generals Terry and Howard and Colonels Gibbon and Miles pursued and harried the tribes, keeping them off balance and allowing them no respite. Winter was coming on, and with few buffalo left to hunt, the Indians were faced not only with white troops but with starvation as well. Finally on October 31, 1876, just four months after Little Big Horn, some 3,000 Dakota surrendered after sustaining a defeat along the Tongue River in Montana. For all practical purposes the Indian wars of the plains were over; only mopping-up operations remained. True, Sitting Bull—Custer's proud conqueror—had sworn never to do the white man's bidding, but even he eventually bowed to the inevitable, delivering himself and the ragged remnants of his tribe into the hands of U.S. Army troops on July 19, 1881.

It was Sitting Bull who gave eloquent voice to the Indian's grievance, a grievance that embitters the red man to this day: "What treaty that the whites have kept has the red man broken? Not one. What treaty that the whites ever made with us red men have they kept? Not one. When I was a boy the Sioux owned the world. The sun rose and set in their lands. They sent 10,000 horsemen to battle. Where are the warriors today? Who slew them? Where are our lands? Who owns them?

"What white man can say I ever stole his lands or a penny of his money? Yet they say I am a thief. What white woman, however lonely, was ever when a captive insulted by me? Yet they say I am a bad Indian. What white man has ever seen me drunk? Who has ever come to me hungry and gone unfed? Who has ever seen me beat my wives or abuse my children? What law have I broken? Is it wrong for me to love my own? Is it wicked in me because my skin is red; because I am a Sioux; because I was born where my fathers lived; because I would die for my people and my country?"

Raleigh Leading Fighter and his daughter carry firewood in one of the few horse-drawn wagons left on the Rosebud Reservation. Some Rosebud Sioux eke out a living by selling wood to people who work in the towns.

A glimmer of hope for Rosebud's Sioux

When the plains tribes capitulated to the white man, most of the survivors were herded onto reservations. Their lands gone, the once fierce tribesmen were reduced to docility as wards of the state. The Indians were no longer free to roam and hunt; instead, they were forced to become ranchers and farmers on land that was barely arable. Confronted with the destruction of their traditional way of life, and offered no viable alternative, the impoverished Indians sank into despondence. Today, however, many tribes are reasserting themselves, demanding a full measure of control over their destinies. In South Dakota, one such tribe, the Rosebud Sioux, although faced with problems of education, housing and employment, is making significant gains under its elected tribal leaders. After a century of despair there is hope for better days.

Photographs by Gary Renaud

43

Living in a vast and lonely land

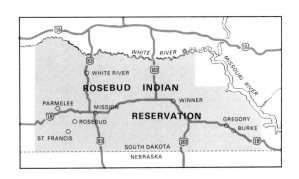

Sprawling across a wind-swept, grassy stretch of southcentral South Dakota, Rosebud Reservation *(map at left)* is a part of the lands set aside in 1868 for displaced tribes of Sioux. Today some 7,000 Indians and 16,000 whites inhabit this desolate land. Most of the Sioux live in small, predominately Indian communities, such as Parmelee *(above and right)*. The grimness of this landscape is reflected in the tribe's bleak way of life. The Indians of Rosebud are American citizens, but they do not have full civil rights. Individually owned plots of land, for example, may not be sold or leased to anyone outside the tribe without the agreement of the U.S. government. Common land, owned by the entire tribe, can often be sold only with the approval of Congress. Some tribesmen support these controls and point out that too much reservation land fell into white hands before the regulations went into effect. Others, however, oppose federal supervision, viewing it as an indignity, a vestige of the time when Indians were thought incapable of handling their own affairs.

A driver offers a lift to an Indian at the Parmelee Catholic church. Many Indians live in the country and depend on passing cars for transportation.

Beside the post office, four residents of Parmelee (population: 140) pause to chat. A few doors away is the general store, that has Parmelee's one phone.

Leaders of a tribe in transition

If there is a sense of hope growing among the Indians of Rosebud, much of the credit must go to the tribe's own leaders, particularly those on the 24-man tribal council. Though the council, elected every two years, has little legislative power, its members speak as the representatives of the Rosebud Sioux, and as such exert moral pressure on government officials. In recent years the council has been conspicuously successful in securing federal funds for housing and job programs. While council members represent the Indians in dealing with governmental agencies—such as the Bureau of Indian Affairs (BIA)—they also help interpret government programs to the tribesmen. Politics among Rosebud Indians, though intense, revolve more around personalities and tactics than goals, for almost all agree on the need for better education and housing and more jobs. The leader of what might be called the radical faction is former council president Robert Burnette *(far right, top)*, whose fiery personality appeals to the poorest group of Indians. More moderate in tone is Cato Valandra *(top right)*, president after 1962, under whose responsible leadership the tribe has made progress.

Tribal council president Cato Valandra (left) wants full self-government for the Rosebud Sioux. A realist, he admits that the Bureau of Indian Affairs will probably continue to exert control for at least another generation.

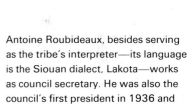

Tribal gadfly Robert Burnette (above), one-time director of the National Congress of American Indians, also presses the fight against discrimination, noting that "Indians exist in a civil rights no man's land."

Antoine Roubideaux, besides serving as the tribe's interpreter—its language is the Siouan dialect, Lakota—works as council secretary. He was also the council's first president in 1936 and helped draft its constitution.

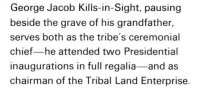

George Jacob Kills-in-Sight, pausing beside the grave of his grandfather, serves both as the tribe's ceremonial chief—he attended two Presidential inaugurations in full regalia—and as chairman of the Tribal Land Enterprise.

Steve Spotted Tail, whose grandfather signed a treaty creating reservations in South Dakota, is off the council but is still respected. Bitterly he decries life in Rosebud as "like being in a corral." His wife appears in the window.

Adam Bordeaux, tribal vice president, is also director of the Arts and Crafts Shop, which was founded in 1960. Among other activities, he works on the program set up to promote tourism on the reservation.

The campaign
for better housing

Tar-paper shacks, chinked log cabins and rusting trailers were for many years the best homes that most Rosebud Sioux could afford. Cheerless and unsanitary, these dwellings served as a reminder to the Indian of his lowly status. But in 1960 the tribal council, with the aid of federal funds, began a program to improve living conditions on the reservation. The few Indians with steady incomes are slowly being moved into low-rent homes and so-called mutual help houses that the tribesmen themselves have helped build. For those without steady income there are "transitional" houses—prefabricated, basic structures with two bedrooms and few modern conveniences. Payments for these houses range from three dollars to $10 per month, and tribal leaders hope that ownership of the new structures will increase the Indians' self-esteem and will encourage them to take pride in maintaining their property. By 1968, 375 transitional houses had been built and occupied on the reservation, and 400 other houses were to be built later in the year.

Joe Good Voice and his wife *(left)* wait patiently in their trailer for the completion of their transitional house *(right),* being erected next door. Like others who are purchasing these houses, the Good Voices will be required to make a $10 down-payment and pay five dollars each month to the Home Improvement Association, which helps Indians adjust to their new homes.

Father Richard Pates, a Catholic priest on the reservation, stands before some transitional houses. It is largely through Father Pates's work as director of the Tribal Housing Authority that the project has succeeded, for he coordinated the efforts of four federal agencies that financed the building program. Each one of the transitional houses can be built for as little as $3,200.

The big push
to create more jobs

The most pressing need of the Rosebud Sioux is for jobs. During the months when there are few tourists to serve and local farmers have little use for labor, Rosebud's unemployment rate soars to nearly 50 per cent —more than 15 times the national average. And while there are a few small factories and workshops *(far right)* on the reservation, these so far employ only a handful. Each year about 700 Indians leave Rosebud, some taking seasonal work in nearby towns, others seeking full-time jobs in distant cities. Most of these return to the reservation. Both the state of South Dakota and the Bureau of Indian Affairs try to help, but neither can give the Indians what they want most—full-time, decently paying jobs on the reservation. Not long ago a white man, Bob Johnson *(on telephone, right)* was hired by the tribal council to direct Rosebud's economic development program. Setting a modest but realistic goal of 700 new jobs within five years, Johnson confers with business and government officials across the country to generate investment in industries that can be operated by the Indians themselves. The tribe has also launched Project Fire Hawk to construct a modern motel, a lodge and a museum.

Bob Johnson, interrupting a talk with George LaPlante *(also shown opposite)* for a call, was with the BIA before becoming the tribe's director of economic development.

Mary Lou Fuller, working in the Diversified Arts Program, holds a print of a western scene that she will mount. Such products are sold to an outside distributor.

Craftsmen assemble plastic-covered countertops at Rosebud Manufacturing, opened in 1966. It employs between 20 and 40 men at wages averaging $1.75 an hour.

Computer components are assembled at Rosebud Electronics with parts shipped in from outside suppliers. The plant employs about 30 and eventually may have jobs for 200.

George LaPlante *(peaked cap),* an Indian working for the tribe under a grant from the U.S. Department of Labor, directs a crew of unskilled Indians working on a dam.

Sandra White Hawk, the youngest daughter of a prosperous Sioux rancher, is the lone Indian at a one-room schoolhouse *(below, left and right)* near her parents' 2,000-acre ranch *(bottom)*. Her schoolmates are all children of whites who live on the reservation. Sandra's parents prefer that she live at home with them rather than board at the dormitory of a distant school, and they note with pride that their seven-year-old daughter is already an avid reader and makes good grades.

The search for
a better education

High-school sophomore Joe Stranger Horse faces a problem that concerns many Indian students—whether to stay in school. Although Joe gets good grades in his classes at the new Todd County Consolidated School and takes an active part in its physical training program *(above)*, he frets that academic studies may be a waste of his time. The boy's parents offer him little guidance, leaving any decision regarding his future entirely up to Joe. Below, he concentrates on homework as his mother and sister sit by.

Lack of good schooling has long hampered attempts by the Sioux to find adequate employment. The Rosebud Sioux took a major step toward overcoming this handicap in 1966 when, with the aid of their Congressman, they persuaded the school authorities of Todd County (a part of the reservation) to build a new public school. Besides offering new facilities, the school has an integrated student body. Inevitably this helps broaden the horizons of Indians like Joe Stranger Horse *(left and below)*. Many problems remain, however. In remote areas, some Indians, like Sandra White Hawk *(opposite)*, still go to inadequate one-room schools. Another difficulty is that many Indian children come from Lakota-speaking families, and their insufficient knowledge of English makes it hard for them to keep up with their studies. And not all Indians encourage their children to get an education, for some do not yet understand that a solid scholastic background is necessary for most good jobs.

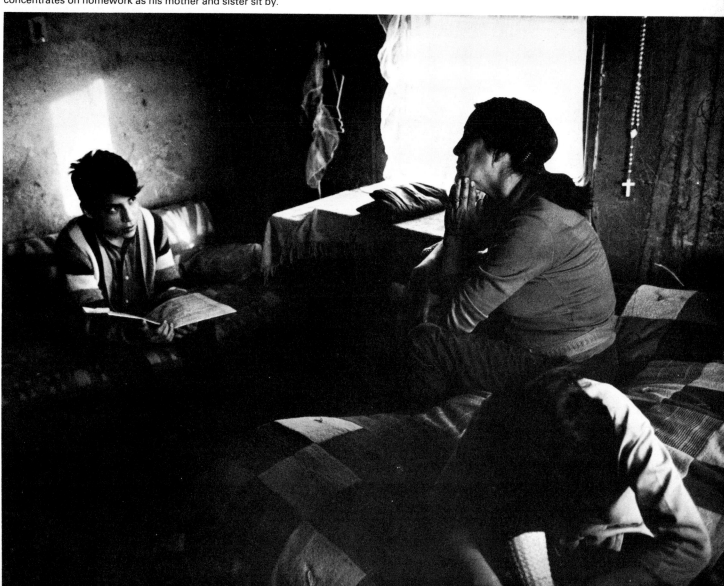

Charles White Hawk, once a professional rodeo rider, is one of Rosebud's more successful Sioux ranchers. He farms 100 of his 2,080 acres and raises cattle on the rest.

Joe Waln, sitting in his basement recreation room, runs a profitable 17,000-acre cattle ranch with his son. Together they own 2,300 acres and lease the rest from the tribe.

John Waugh, a former school teacher, turned to ranching to be his own boss. Despite his success in raising Herefords and race horses, he chooses to live in a modest cabin.

Three who use the land to good advantage

Despite the growing success of tourism and light industry on the reservation, the Rosebud tribe's biggest source of income is still its land. The Tribal Land Enterprise, authorized by the tribal council in 1943 to manage Indian property, today controls some 400,000 acres of South Dakota ranch land, much of which it leases to fellow tribesmen, such as the three successful ranchers shown here. These men pay TLE $240 a year for each quarter section (160 acres). Most of the acreage is used for grazing cattle that are being readied for market. Many ranchers, however, set aside small parcels of land for crops and dairy herds.

Preserving the tribe's hallowed traditions

Although many of today's Rosebud Sioux strive to obtain the white man's goals—security, status, education—few of them wish to cut themselves off from their Indian heritage. As in former days, some Sioux remain indifferent to possessions and the sharing of home and property remains a welcome obligation. Nor has superstition entirely disappeared; medicine men are still consulted, especially by older Sioux. Even some Christian Indians seek out the medicine men when they wish to influence the *yuwipi* (spirits). Elements of tribal ritual are preserved in the peyote cult *(below),* whose members eat the hallucinogenic peyote, a type of cactus that induces visions. Among the most popular of ancient customs, shared by almost all Rosebud Sioux, is the powwow *(right).* Most powwows today are little more than dances in which the guests and hosts dress up in full Indian regalia to celebrate a wedding, a stroke of good luck or a holiday.

As the peyote cult's leader *(above, right)* holds a staff and rattle, the worshipers pray. Peyote, a drug-containing plant, is illegal except for use in tribal religious rites. Communicants believe it brings them close to God.

Convivial tribesmen—including one seemingly bewildered youngster—gather for a powwow held in honor of a newly married couple. Like many of the tribe's celebrations, this one is being held in a Catholic Youth Center.

3

A Time of Growth
and Violence

A family of immigrants, arriving in central Nebraska in 1886, pose
grimly beside the prairie schooner that brought them westward
across the plains. It was about this time that the Plains States were
experiencing their last and greatest influx of settlers.

The summertime tourist in the Plains States is pretty hard pressed to escape a reminder that somewhere not far away a rodeo, Roundup Day, Buffalo Bill Blowout, quarter-horse show or homestead celebration is being staged. In Nebraska, for example, South Sioux City's notion of fun has been an event called Tourist Arrest Days, so rigged that certain passing visitors get tagged as "outlaws," are given reverse fines (free lodging, free gas, free golf, free movie) and are sentenced to eat a "prison meal" of prime steak.

The rough-and-ready aura of the Old West permeates the new. There are, of course, sound commercial reasons for nurturing the illusion that around every corner lurks a desperado primed for the stick-up. And rodeos and Tourist Arrest Days bring in the crowds that buy cowboy boots and ten-gallon hats and spend their money at the local motel. Certainly tourists delight in being shown the spot in the old mining town of Deadwood, South Dakota, where Wild Bill Hickok was shot in the back of the head while playing poker. (The veteran gunfighter held aces over eights, a combination since known as "dead man's hand.") But it is not only the summer tourists who enjoy the nightly re-enactments of the trial of Jack McCall, Hickok's

slayer; even Deadwood residents swell with pride at each retelling of the tale. For, profit aside, the wild West does live on, though often in subtle ways. It is seen in the loping walk of the cowboy, off on a spree after a dull week or two herding cattle in the western portions of the Dakotas or Nebraska; it is manifest in the regional style of speech, slow and deliberate, with a heavy twang that has come to be associated with the spreading range; it pervades the atmosphere of hundreds of small towns that rise from the prairie with all the dingy splendor of a plywood cow-town movie set.

So intent has show business been on raising the history of the High Plains to the status of a legend that many Americans may forget that there was a hard nub of reality at the legend's core. Indeed, the days of cowboys and Indians, of stockmen and homesteaders, of marshals in white and desperadoes in black are almost within living memory. Only in the 20th Century have the Plains States become a region of tranquil, businesslike farms, factories and ranches. We forget that the wildness of the West was not really the invention of show business but was a true American phenomenon, a historical development rooted in political and economic tensions that in some respects have yet to be fully expunged from the now peaceful land.

During the second half of the 19th Century, the raw prairie was developing fast and the last frontier within the contiguous territory of the United States was being subdued. Population, though growing, spread sparsely across the plains, and the institutions of law and order—home and family as well as courts and police—struggled to gain a foothold in an unruly time. The continuing Indian wars, the bloody disputes over slavery, the discovery of precious metals in the hills along the western edge of the plains, the skyrocketing market for buffalo hides, the postwar cattle drives, the clashes between farmers and stockmen for use of the land —all these combined to bring to the plains the type of man willing to gamble all in a quick thrust for fortune, willing to gamble not only his own life but other lives as well.

This era of violence was precipitated by the coming of the railroad. Before the plains could be opened to large-scale settlement, a swift and reliable means of transportation was necessary to link the immense "middle border"—between the Mississippi and the Rockies—with the already well-developed regions to the east and west. Obviously only the railroads could accomplish this task, and by the 1850s Americans were looking forward to a transcontinental line. "Men and brethren!" wrote

New York Tribune editor Horace Greeley, "let us resolve to have a railroad to the Pacific and to have it soon. . . . It will prove to be a bond of union not easily broken, and a new spring to our national industry, prosperity and wealth." Soon there were plans afoot to do just as Greeley suggested. The proposed railroad was to follow a northern route, passing through the Great Plains, a territory still closed to white settlers and reserved for Indians.

The opening of Kansas and Nebraska to white settlement in 1854 had been intended partly to facilitate the building of the railroad; but, far from proving to be a "bond of union," it helped set in motion a chain of events ending in the Civil War, and it ushered in an era of violence that was to plague the plains for many decades. Soon upon the stretching prairie, in both Missouri and Kansas, Southerner and Northerner, slaveholder and free-soiler (opponent of slavery), were to gun one another down with all the abandon that whites had formerly reserved for their Indian neighbors.

The struggle revolved around whether Kansas would enter the Union as a slave or a free state. The legislation that opened Kansas to settlement had charged the residents of the new territory with deciding that for themselves, ultimately through the use of the ballot. But when New England abolitionists began organizing emigrant aid societies to encourage like-minded citizens to settle in the new territory, proslavery Missourians, who lived just across the Kansas border, flooded westward to vote fraudulently, first for a territorial delegate to Congress in November 1854 and then for a territorial legislature in March 1855.

The proslavery tickets won these rigged elections, but the results were not accepted by free-soilers, who formed their own rump regime. In reply, Southerners and their sympathizers—not only from Missouri but from as far away as Alabama—began to form paramilitary bands to destroy the center of abolitionist power in Kansas. On May 21, 1856, a motley group of more than 500 armed proslavery enthusiasts struck at Lawrence, stronghold of Kansas abolitionist sentiment. They sacked the Free State Hotel and smashed the presses of two Lawrence newspapers. In the melee one man was killed. Three days later fanatical old John Brown, Lawrence's self-appointed avenger, and six of his followers raided a settlement on the Pottawatomie Creek and hacked five innocent proslavery men to death. From that point on the level of violence increased as guerrilla bands from both sides took to arms. Terror begot terror, and before the warfare in "Bleeding Kansas" was submerged in the horror of the Civil War, about 200 people were slaughtered and approximately two million dollars' worth of property was destroyed.

This toll was only a foretaste of the suffering that the Civil War was to bring to the plains. In the southern portion of the region, in Missouri and Kansas, the war was fought with the special ferocity that comes when kinsmen and close neighbors fall out. Although all the territories and states of the plains adhered to the Union, Kansas continued to be a battleground for partisan bands on both sides, and in Missouri some of the western counties, with their strong Southern sympathies, were kept out of the Confederacy only at the point of a bayonet. Anti-Union Missourians, who had formerly been content to terrorize abolitionists in Kansas, now extended their operations into their native state, raiding pro-Union towns, ambushing Army columns and generally scourging the countryside, looting and killing. The Union, however, found strong support in St. Louis among thousands of foreign-born workers who rallied to the Yankee cause. At the very beginning of the war they raised four infantry regiments and an artillery battalion, and their steadfast loyalty is generally credited with having saved the state from secession.

Of all the partisan units, certainly the most famous, or infamous, was the one led by William Clarke Quantrill, a young Northerner whose proslavery sympathies eventually led him to make common cause with the South. A man of daring, imagination and ruthlessness, Quantrill directed his men in a series of knife-thrust raids along the Kansas-Missouri boundary. His most notorious depredation was the sack of Lawrence, Kansas, on August 21, 1863. Leading a guerrilla unit of about 450 men—a band that included such future outlaw luminaries as the Younger brothers and Frank James—Quantrill swooped down upon the unsuspecting townspeople at dawn. So startled were the residents that they could offer no effective resistance to the orgy of killing, looting and burning that swept over them like a visitation from hell. Within a few hours at least 150 civilians were murdered and a large portion of the town was reduced to ashes. The wanton and basically senseless nature of this raid has led some historians to characterize it as the worst atrocity of the Civil War.

The Union's response to this act of devastation was swift and terrible. The commander of Federal troops along the Kansas-Missouri border, General Thomas Ewing, issued "Order No. 11," which forcibly removed almost all families from the generally pro-Southern Missouri counties of Jackson, Cass

With piercing eyes and stern expression, John Brown seems the very archetype of the fanatic—a man who could, and did at times, slaughter the defenseless to further the abolitionists' cause. The bloody raids he led along the Kansas-Missouri border in the mid-1850s made him the terror of slaveholders and their sympathizers.

and Bates and parts of Vernon County. By denying Quantrill and his guerrillas the support of the populace, the Union hoped to force them out in the open where they could be destroyed. Under prodding by Federal rifles, the residents of these counties gathered up what belongings they could carry and fled, leaving their houses to be looted by angry Unionist irregulars from Kansas.

Drastic as this measure was, it was only one of the many tragedies to afflict the divided state of Missouri. A total of 1,162 battles or skirmishes were fought on its soil, some between irregulars and others between the contending armies. About 40,000 Missourians swelled the Confederate ranks while nearly three times that number joined the Union Army; when it was all over the citizens of the state mourned 27,000 of their sons.

Even the surrender of Lee's forces at Appomattox, which brought peace to the rest of the land, could not halt the violence on the plains. Members of the guerrilla bands, having tasted the excitement of gunplay, were in no mood to lay down their arms meekly and become model citizens, and their resolve to continue their outlaw ways was strengthened by the knowledge that surrender meant the hangman's noose. Men like Frank James and his brother Jesse (who joined Quantrill after the 1863

A fun-seeking prince, Russia's Grand Duke Alexis *(right)* poses for a photo in 1872 after returning from a buffalo hunt on the plains. His rifle-toting companion is Lieutenant Colonel George A. Custer, the Civil War hero whose foolhardy tactics in 1876 led to the massacre of more than 200 soldiers by Indians at Little Big Horn.

raid on Lawrence) merely shifted their field of endeavor from the political to the financial. Bank robberies and train holdups now became endemic. Third-rate thugs like the Younger brothers and the Dalton boys added new footnotes to the growing legend of the wild West. Bringing more substance to the legend was another element, the cowboy, who was now beginning to drive cattle along the ill-marked trails from Texas to the railheads in Missouri and Kansas.

By 1867 the long stretch of rails had reached out from St. Louis, cut across Missouri and Iowa, and entered the High Plains of Kansas and Nebraska. Coming up from the south to meet the lines were thousands of head of cattle from Texas. Their destination was Abilene, where an alert Illinois livestock dealer named Joseph G. McCoy had established shipping pens beside the Kansas Pacific tracks. This was a crucial development, for it offered the depressed Texas ranching industry a method of shipping its cattle to the beef-hungry East. Though the drive north was arduous, sometimes taking as long as 40 days, and the trail was fraught with danger from marauding Indians and gangs of cattle rustlers, the rewards were handsome, for a Longhorn that might bring a lucky rancher four dollars in Texas was snapped up for

10 times that price at McCoy's shipping pens. On September 5, 1867, the first 20 carloads of beef on the hoof headed east from Abilene. Before the year ended more than 35,000 head had been shipped from that town and a new industry had been inaugurated on the plains.

The cattle boom had a swift economic impact. By 1871 six hundred thousand head were moving through Abilene yearly, and between 1868 and 1871 approximately 75,000 cattle cars carried 1.5 million Longhorns from the Kansas cow town to the slaughterhouses of Kansas City and Chicago. During the early 1870s, however, Abilene began to lose its pre-eminent role as a cattle-marketing center as competing railroads, the Santa Fe particularly, established loading facilities at locations more convenient to the cattle trails. Other Kansas towns, like Wichita, Hays City, Great Bend, Ellsworth and Dodge City, boomed. And on the northern plains, communities like Ogallala, Nebraska, on the Union Pacific line, and Bismarck, North Dakota, on the Northern Pacific, prospered in the service of a nascent local ranching industry.

The grasslands of the north were in many respects even better suited to cattle than was the Texas range, a fact that was quickly appreciated by the Texas ranchers and cowboys driving herds along the Shawnee and Chisholm Trails. Given the sparseness of the population and the easy availability of land, it seemed to make sense to establish ranches in the north, ranches that would be within a few days' drive of the railheads.

Facilitating this growth of the new plains ranching industry was the rapid disappearance of the buffalo. So long as millions of these shaggy beasts roamed the grasslands, stripping the soil of its grass, cattle were effectively barred. But there was a community of interest among whites dedicated to the slaughter of the buffalo. The federal, state and territorial governments wanted to get rid of the buffalo so that the Indians would be denied their chief source of food, clothing and shelter; cattlemen, of course, desired the grasslands for their own herds; railroad men saw the buffalo as a hindrance to settlement; and hunters found these animals excellent sport and a source of quick profit, their hides being used as carriage robes or tanned into leather. Against such odds the buffalo had little chance, and in the 1870s their slaughter reached epic proportions; hundreds of thousands were slain each year, and by 1880 only a few buffalo remained.

The buffalo hunt also spurred a rather odd kind of migration to the plains. The chance to kill these beasts lured hundreds of spirited men westward: hard-drinking, hard-riding men who were handy with guns and horses, who could live outdoors and did not shrink from the sight of blood, who cared little about what they did so long as it offered thrills and money. Joining their ranks, if only temporarily, were Eastern and European dudes who wished to play at being rough-and-ready, and for whom the buffalo hunt offered a welcome relief from the more sedate pleasures of the drawing room. Noblemen and the sons of rich merchants organized safaris, hired specially equipped trains to take them to the buffalo country and then, surrounded by retainers, debouched upon the prairie to search out the migrating herds.

A British baronet, Sir George Gore, was one of the first aristocrats to experience the thrill of the buffalo hunt. His three-year safari, beginning in 1854, carried him, his 40 servants and several friends along a circuitous route through western Kansas, Colorado, Wyoming and the Dakota Territory. Sir George set a standard of roughing it in luxury that later parties were hard put to match. He traveled with three milk cows, 18 oxen and 112 horses. One of the 27 wagons in his train carried no fewer than 75 muzzle-loading rifles, more than a dozen shotguns, a number of pistols and a new breech-loading Sharpe's rifle. After a day's wearying chase Sir George slept in a brass bed set down upon rugs and covered by a green-and-white candy-striped tent evocative of the hunting parties of medieval England. Close at hand was an ample supply of fine French wines and stacks of his favorite books. Sir George spent half a million dollars on his 6,000-mile foray into the plains and took the lives of about 2,000 buffalo and countless other game, including deer, elk, bear and birds.

Two decades later an even more august luminary, Russia's Grand Duke Alexis, arrived on the plains for a spell of shooting. In the company of Civil War heroes General Phil Sheridan and Lieutenant Colonel George A. Custer, escorted by two cavalry companies, serenaded by a regimental band and guided by the already famous William F. "Buffalo Bill" Cody, the party set out on what by then had become a ritual slaughter. To ease the discomforts of life in the open, the hunters could draw upon three wagonloads of champagne and other fine spirits. Perhaps this was the reason why the party accounted for only 56 buffalo during the five-day safari.

The exploits of such newsworthy hunters, combined with the increased market for buffalo bones (for fertilizer), hides and meat, undoubtedly inspired less highly placed but no less adventurous spirits to try their own luck on the plains. The fame of Dodge City arose from its beginnings as an outfitting center for buffalo hunters years before it became a notorious cow town; indeed, its original name, Buffalo City, was rejected by a postmaster simply because Kansas already had a town called Buffalo and another named Buffalo Station.

It may have been inevitable that Dodge City's location in the heart of the buffalo country should have given it a rowdy reputation that has become part of the Old West legend. Money burned in the pockets of Kansas buffalo skinners, while gamblers, whiskey peddlers and willing women descended on the town to reap the rewards of dishonest endeavor. Soon it was known as "Hell on the Plains" and "the wickedest little city in America." By 1878, when cattle drovers had taken over, the Washington *Evening Star* was calling this hell-raiser's hangout "so clearly and egregiously bad that one might conclude that it was marked for special providential punishment." Although Dodge was not really Sodom and Gomorrah reborn, it was certainly a raucous, riotous place, the epitome of the wild and wide-open cow town.

In its days of tinseled glory Dodge was host to most of the gunslingers and lawmen whose lives have since been immortalized (and often bowdlerized) on the nation's television screens. Wyatt Earp and Bat and Jim Masterson, lawmen extraordinary, and the hard-drinking, tubercular dentist Doc Holliday were only a few of the legendary figures to have loped down Front Street, bent an elbow at the Alhambra Saloon and pinched the dancing girls at the Dodge City Opera. In its salad days of the 1870s, Dodge could count a total of 19 saloons. Since the town's resident population was only 1,200, this worked out to one bar per 63 citizens, women and children included. But it was not the residents who spent the money; they made it. It was the hundreds of cowboys, hot and dusty from weeks on the trails, frustrated with the boredom of the long drive and temporarily rich in silver dollars, whom the saloonkeepers, gamblers, shills and prostitutes were anxious to serve.

When a trail drive was over and the cowboys were in town, Dodge roared with a thunder of honky-tonk music and whiskeyed laughter that might have drowned out a cattle stampede. Gunplay, usually staged just for the fun of it, was a nightly occurrence, and from time to time fun turned into tragedy as arguments over gambling debts or rights to a dance-hall girl ended with a bullet through a cowboy's belly. Then, with a minimum of ceremony and a maximum of dispatch, the unlucky wrangler was hauled off to Boot Hill—the original of that name—and deposited beneath freshly turned sod. The respectable citizens of Dodge did not object to these rowdy goings on. Although they wanted some protection from the wranglers' drunken rages and even from their notions of good clean fun, fleecing the cowboys was very profitable. A delicate balance had to be struck, one that would permit a modicum of order for the residents and a spendthrift atmosphere of abandon for the visitors. Local lawmen found a solution they felt sure would satisfy everyone. Along the Santa Fe tracks that ran through the town, the authorities established the so-called "deadline." South of the tracks almost anything short of outright murder was tolerated, but north of the tracks weapons were banned and a reasonable facsimile of peace was enforced. Town officials attempted to increase the ardor of marshals and their deputies by offering them a bonus of two dollars for every arrest. This incentive seems to have had little effect. Though Wyatt Earp, the sometime chief deputy marshal of Dodge, later claimed that arrests often mounted to 300 a month during the summer, the record shows that the number rarely exceeded a few dozen.

Though conditions in Dodge City were considerably less violent than the accounts published in the Eastern press indicated, citizens of Dodge gloried in the inflated reputation their hometown had achieved. One of the popular stories had a drunken cowboy asking a train conductor for a ticket to hell. The conductor replied, "Give me two dollars and fifty cents and get off at Dodge."

Among the busiest purveyors of these wild tales was none other than Wyatt Earp, who talked freely, and with much embellishment of the facts, to anyone who would listen. Typical of his stories was the one that concerned his showdown with a disgruntled gunslinger named Clay Allison. According to Earp, Allison challenged him to a duel in the sun. Earp thereupon allegedly reduced the gunman to the condition of a quivering coward with a few angry snarls. Earp also boasted that he was the chief upholder of law and order in Dodge, hauling malefactors off to the "calaboose" at a prodigious rate. In fact, there is no substantiation for any of the lawman's more heroic claims.

To a casual visitor, however, even the most imaginative fictions about Dodge's brutality might have seemed all too real. One visitor who probably went away convinced was a medical charlatan named Dr. Meredith. He came to Dodge to practice his specialty of phrenology and arranged to give a lecture at the Lady Gay dance hall to demonstrate the principles of reading bumps on the head. The doctor began his speech with the usual disclaimer that he had not really thought to give a lecture but was prevailed upon to do so by numerous town leaders. Suddenly he was interrupted by a member of the audience, one Luke McGlue, who shouted, "You lie!" Ignoring the insult the doctor began again, only to be halted by the same rowdy once more. The chairman of the meeting, none other than Bat Masterson, was just reaching for his pistol to calm McGlue when the lights went out. Gunshots echoed through the darkness, chairs and tables were thrown around the hall, men cursed and women screamed. By the time the lights came back on, the Lady Gay was almost empty and even the doctor could not be found. Many feared he had been killed and hauled away, thus depriving the good people of Dodge of their glimpse into the fantastic wonders of science. But in the end all was well. Meredith was discovered curled up like a baby beneath the lectern; his dignity had suffered, his nerves were shattered, his hat bore a bullet hole, but like most people who came to Dodge, he survived the experience safe and sound.

Numerous towns on the plains envied Dodge its notoriety and sought a full measure of recognition for themselves. Abilene, Wichita and others had their day when badmen staged shoot-'em-ups along their main drags and stalwart citizens banded together to chase the wrongdoers out of town. Abilene's city marshal, Wild Bill Hickok, for example, claimed to have killed more than 100 men (desperadoes all, of course) in face-to-face combat, and his association with the town assured it ample publicity in the *Police Gazette* if not in more polite journals. Hays City, Kansas, got its due in this report of rampant wickedness published in 1869:

"Hays City by lamplight was remarkably lively, but not very moral. The streets blazed with the reflection from saloons, and a glance within showed floors crowded with dancers, the gaily dressed women striving to hide with ribbons and paint the terrible lines which that grim artist, dissipation, loves to draw upon such faces. With a heartless humor he daubs the noses of the sterner sex a cherry red, but paints under the once bright eyes of women a shade as dark as the night in the cave of despair. To the music of violins and the stamping of feet the dance went on, and we saw in the giddy maze old men who must have been pirouetting on the very edge of their graves."

High-spirited cowboy and low-principled thug,

gaudy gambler and painted woman, colorful as they may have been, were all symptoms rather than basic causes of the lawless atmosphere of the plains. One actual cause was the competition among the economic interests—farmers, ranchers, drovers, sheepmen—who would stop at nothing to secure their rights to the land. When conflict arose, each tried to stretch the law to suit his own purposes; failing that, each sought to overwhelm the others through secret societies, vigilante committees and gangs of hired gunmen.

By the 1870s, cowboys driving their herds of Longhorns up from Texas no longer had the High Plains to themselves, and their right of passage across the prairie was being denounced as trespassing by farmers and local ranchers who had claimed ownership of the land. Even the drovers' right to use such well-established trails as the Shawnee and the Chisholm was being disputed, for cattle coming up from Texas often carried fever-bearing ticks that infected local stock. At first the drovers were kept away by informal tactics: a group of heavily armed farmers might meet them along the trail and warn them off on pain of death. Later, state legislatures established so-called fever lines, beyond which the herds could not go. As settlement on the plains moved westward so too did the fever lines, until it seemed quite possible that the entire region would be closed to all drovers except those willing to risk shooting their way through. But slowly the whole controversy about fever lines became academic, for by the mid-1880s the long drives were coming to an end as more and more ranchers settled down on the High Plains.

Often the ranchers did not bother to take legal title to the grazing land they used. The prairie was vast, seemingly there for the taking, and at first there was no one to challenge their grazing rights. Ranching had become big business on the western plains as financial syndicates made up of men as far from the scene as London and Edinburgh invested hundreds of thousands of dollars to stock the area with cattle. In 1883 a prairie editor crowed, "Cotton was once crowned king, but with us grass is king," and at that date few would have contradicted him, for America's hunger for beef seemed insatiable and the grass of the plains was thought to be inexhaustible.

In more remote areas much of the range was still open, but even there ranchers and their faraway financial backers were beginning to protect their investments and bar competition by fencing the land upon which their herds grazed. That the land was mostly in the public domain and not theirs to fence seemed of little import. The howls of farmers cut off from acres they claimed as their own under the Homestead Act were brushed aside, as were the outraged cries of sheepmen and open-range ranchers barred from pastures and water holes. So rampant was the fence-building fever of the 1880s that whole counties of western Kansas were encircled by barbed wire, and in 1883 one Nebraska ranch established an enclosure that ran for 11 miles in one direction and more than 12 miles in the other, while another ranch in that state counted 143,000 acres of fenced range. Finally the federal government stepped in to give moral support, but no more than that, to the hard-pressed farmers. The Secretary of the Interior advised homesteaders to cut down all fences on federal land that they wished to farm, and in 1885 Congress enacted a bill to fine and imprison those who erected fences on the public domain. Some ranchers complied, at least for a time, with the new law, but others ignored it, and as late as 1905 the Public Land Commission reported that wholesale violations of the act were continuing.

Not surprisingly, since little more than advice, good intentions and unenforced regulations were forthcoming from Washington, the farmers—together with disgruntled sheepmen and open-range advocates—often formed secret societies to cut the fences, burn pastures and terrorize ranchers. The cattlemen retaliated swiftly by employing range thugs to drive off nomadic herders and occasionally shoot down farmers who attempted to establish homesteads within a cattle baron's self-proclaimed domain. For a time it seemed as if there would be no end to the terror and counterterror, but then the grim laws of economics combined with the calamitous interference of nature to end the cattle boom on the plains.

By the fall of 1885 the seemingly impossible had happened: the nation had been glutted with beef, and in less than six months prices dropped about 40 per cent to a mere three dollars per hundredweight. The very success of the High Plains ranchers was proving their undoing. That winter was colder than any the ranchers had yet experienced, and their cattle, left to graze in the open, often succumbed to exposure and starvation. The summer of 1886 did nothing to ease the stockman's woe, for it was unusually hot and dry and the cattle could not find enough water to slake their thirst. By fall the ranchers were panicky and an exodus to Canada and Montana began. Normally, one would expect such tragedies to lead to a shortage of beef that would drive prices up. But so overcome with fear were many of the High Plains ranchers that many of them did the worst possible thing: they dumped their remaining herds on the market, and the price of beef took another tumble.

Cattlemen who remained on the High Plains were now hoping for a turn of luck that would help them recoup their losses. Instead, the winter of 1886-1887 proved a disaster beyond their most nightmarish fears. Blizzard followed blizzard and the temperature dipped below the zero mark for days on end. Even the tough Texas Longhorns found it difficult to survive in such a climate, and the less hardy but more meaty breeds, which had recently been developed on the plains, died by the tens of thousands. Despite the sobering experience of the previous winter, ranchers had neglected to provide food and shelter for their herds, and as a consequence many a cattleman discovered in the spring that he had been completely wiped out.

It is impossible to gauge accurately the extent of the financial losses suffered by the plains ranchers and their backers through the two disastrous years, but in the long run the cattle industry of the prairie probably benefited from the tragedy. Weather and the oversupply of beef forced the industry to retrench and reorganize on a sounder basis, which included the providing of winter feed and shelter for the cattle. It also began a long though intermittent process of informal accommodation between farmers and ranchers, for although the remaining cattlemen now began fencing the range with increased vigor, there were fewer of them with whom the farmer had to contend. In fact, cooperation between farmer and rancher slowly began to replace hostility as each came to realize that there was land enough for both crops and cattle. The two groups also found areas of mutual interest: native corn, for example, could be sold to fatten native steers, to the profit of sodbuster and stockman alike.

It was, of course, imperative that the range wars should cease, for by the late 1870s the tide of immigration into the plains had reached flood proportions and showed no signs of receding. Between 1870 and 1880 Nebraska's population soared from 132,000 to 453,000, Kansas almost topped the million mark, and even the Dakotas, long thought to be an utter wasteland, became host to thousands of immigrants. In the same 10 years the number of farms on the High Plains nearly doubled.

Behind the tide of immigration to the plains stood the ever-growing power of the railroads. At the start of the Civil War there had been only about 1,400 miles of track in the Plains States region; 40 years later this had grown to nearly 40,000

miles. More than the federal government, more than the local boosters, more than land speculators, it was the railroads that were responsible for peopling the Great Plains by offering an efficient means of transporting goods to market. More than anyone else it was the railroad entrepreneurs who encouraged immigration and drummed up enthusiasm for farming the plains. To attract immigrants, they launched promotion campaigns that today's advertising executives might envy. Their agents spread out from the previously settled areas east of the Missouri to the distant reaches of Central Europe and Scandinavia, singing the praises of the prairie and comparing it to the Biblical land of milk and honey. By hook or by crook they attracted thousands and still more thousands of immigrants.

The motives of the railway magnates were anything but altruistic. Settlers on the plains meant freight, and freight in turn meant money pouring into rail company coffers. But the private interests of the railroads dovetailed nicely with the public interest of the federal government, which wanted to connect the East and West Coasts with a network of steel. In order to get it, Congress was willing to offer the railroads some powerful inducements: low-interest loans and outright gifts of huge chunks of the public domain.

The Union Pacific, for example, received 20 sections (or 20 square miles) of public land for every mile of track laid. The states and territories through which a rail route ran often upped the ante by turning over still more land to the companies. In Nebraska, for example, the railroads were granted more than eight million acres, fully 16 per cent of the total area of that state.

Land in itself held little interest for the railroads; their executives were neither farmers nor ranchers. But land that might be sold to farmers whose crops would be shipped to market in thousands of freight cars—that was valuable indeed, and the railroads spared no effort to get their holdings into productive hands, at a high price if possible, at a low price if necessary. Generally their terms were generous, for the immediate sale was not as important to them as the freight revenues to follow. Often land was sold for as little as four dollars per acre, loans to cover the purchase price were extended at low interest rates over a number of years, and large discounts were allowed for cash purchases or early payment of the loans.

Sometimes huge chunks of prairie were sold to nationality and religious groups. In the 1870s the Santa Fe Railroad, for example, received $250,000 in gold for 60,000 Kansas acres from a colony of nearly 2,000 German Mennonites. In an act of generosity quite untypical of 19th Century business enterprises, the Santa Fe not only chartered a ship to bring these immigrants, free of charge, from Europe, but also built temporary barracks to house them on their new holdings until the Mennonites could build permanent shelters of their own. These thrifty and hard-working people quickly made a success of their colony. More important, they introduced to the state a strain of wheat, Turkey Red, so well suited to local soil and climate conditions that it revolutionized agriculture in Kansas.

But whether traveling in groups or singly, many immigrants found ample inducement to settle on the plains. One of these was the railroads' practice of offering extremely cheap transportation on specially outfitted passenger cars from the port of entry to the "promised land." While not luxurious, these cars, often equipped with primitive sleeping arrangements and community cookstoves, were generally no worse and sometimes a good deal better than the steerage accommodations that the Europeans had endured on the ocean crossing.

Sometimes the people who came to settle on the prairie helped lay the tracks, but more often they could not be induced to postpone their plowing. Instead, the railroads relied upon transient laborers, men recruited from the recently defeated Confederate Army, veterans of the Union cause, Irish and German immigrants, and in some cases Chinese coolies. The mixture of nationalities and races combined with the still-smoldering hatreds of the Civil War often led to bloodshed in the workers' settlements, the jerry-built "end-of-track" towns that moved westward along with the railroads. Robert Louis Stevenson was probably indulging in classic British understatement when he described these tent and shack settlements as "roaring, impromptu cities full of gold and lust and death." Eventually some of the laborers who laid the track—which brought five major east-west railroads into existence on the plains by the turn of the century—did settle down on land bought from the company or secured free from the U.S. government under the Homestead Act. Others helped turn end-of-track settlements into permanent towns. One of these towns became Bismarck, North Dakota, the capital of that state.

The railroads were not the only institutions to entice settlers to the plains with booster propaganda. Often rail company agents worked closely with promoters from the various Plains States governments who were interested in peopling the

THE GLIDDEN BARB

The men who fenced the plains

Joseph Glidden (above) and Jacob Haish (below), residents of Illinois, initiated a revolutionary change in plains life in the 1870s, when each introduced a commercially practical type of barbed wire. Before then, fence building on the plains had been impractical, for the region had little timber or stone and ordinary wire was easily trampled. With barbed wire, however, farmers could fence fields to protect them from wandering livestock herds, and ranchers could enclose parcels of land to create private spreads.

According to one account, both Glidden and Haish were inspired by seeing a crude form of barbed wire at a county fair in 1873. Within months, Glidden applied for a patent on his design (above), which had the barb twisted around one strand and held in place by a second. Haish soon applied for a patent on his design (below), in which the barb was twisted around two strands. Eventually both patents were bought by a large wire manufacturer.

THE HAISH BARB

empty prairie with voters and taxpayers. "Land for the landless! Homes for the homeless!" was the cry that attracted hundreds of thousands. But land alone was not enough to support all those newcomers. They needed water to nourish their crops and pastures. Few people, however, gave more than a passing thought to the occasional warnings of the scantiness and undependability of rainfall on the High Plains.

As early as the 1840s, optimists were waxing eloquent about the supposed virtues of prairie soil, despite the fact that most Americans still held to the myth of the "Great American Desert." In 1844 one Josiah Gregg, in a book entitled *Commerce of the Prairies*, wrote: "Why may we not suppose that the genial influences of civilization—that extensive cultivation of the earth—might not contribute to the multiplication of showers [on the plains]? Or that the shady groves, as they advance upon the prairies, may have some effect upon the seasons?" In the decades to follow, thousands adopted such optimistic notions, based entirely upon wishful thinking. A body of pseudo-science held that in some magical manner the mere planting of trees and tilling of the soil would persuade the sky to disgorge vast quantities of water. There is no reason to doubt that many land speculators and immigration promoters of the 1870s and 1880s who spread the slogan "Rainfall follows the plow" were quite sincere; in any event their message fell upon ears eager to listen. In the campaign to people the plains the promoters were aided by a freak of nature. During the early 1880s there were several unusually wet years on the normally arid trans-Missouri grasslands, a phenomenon that seemed to support the predictions of self-styled prophets.

Equally important to the farmers' optimistic frame of mind was the new technology that offered them the steel plow, barbed wire and more efficient windmills. But even these tools were of little use in the absence of adequate water for irrigation purposes. Thousands of homesteaders arrived on the plains believing that just beneath the sod lay a wealth of water in natural underground springs. More often than not the pioneers were disappointed and were left to depend on the uncertain rainfall. Settlement on the Western plains "rose and fell with the rain and drought," according to one observer, "like a mighty tide beating against the tremendous wall of the Rockies. And every such wave left behind it a mass of human wreckage in the shape of broken fortunes, deserted farms and ruined homes."

The problems raised by drought were compounded by government land policies. Thousands had come west to take advantage of the Homestead Act, with its prize of 160 free acres, but this legislation often offered much less than met the eye. Such a spread, which would have been considered extensive in Norway or even on the East Coast, was hardly large enough to support a single family on the more arid reaches of the plains.

There were, of course, methods by which a farmer could increase his holdings, either without cost or by the expenditure of a very small sum. The Preemption Act of 1841 and the Timber Culture Act of 1873 could sometimes be used by homesteaders to make additional claims on the public domain. But all too frequently the homesteader arriving on the grasslands in the 1870s and 1880s found that the best farming land was already in the hands of the railroads, whose prices, though low, were often beyond his means. Much other good land had been snapped up by ranchers who had their own hired hands file spurious claims to it. These claims were immediately put together into giant cattle spreads, thus defeating the very purposes of the Homestead Law and other acts designed to help the small farmer. And even when the farmer was lucky enough to find and hold a relatively fertile piece of land, he still faced the sometimes insurmountable problem of financing his venture. The tools he needed—special sodbusting plows, harvesting equipment, horses or oxen, seed to plant his first crop—all cost money, perhaps several thousand dollars. The Homestead Act made no provision for government loans, and the farmer had little choice but to borrow at the very high interest rates then charged by banks and merchants. Add to this the high freight rates charged by the railroads for hauling produce to market, and the wonder of it is that relatively few farmers gave up in disgust and headed back east with the slogan "In God we trusted, in Kansas we busted" painted on the sides of their prairie schooners

Many did leave, but many thousands stayed, and more followed them to try their luck on the soil. With eventual liberalization of the landholding laws, the shrewdest and hardiest of the immigrants began to add to their holdings until they had farms that covered many hundreds of acres— spreads big enough to justify the large capital investments needed to turn the Great American Desert into the world's most bountiful granary. By the turn of the century the day of the badman, the marshal, and the undisciplined cattle baron was drawing to a close. The Great Plains was being tamed; the age of the farmer had dawned.

LAWLESS DAYS ON THE PLAINS

CHRONICLING SOME EPISODES THAT MADE THE WEST WILD

As the nation drew closer to civil war, violence became endemic on the plains. Tension between proslavery forces and their abolitionist opponents provoked attacks by such guerrillas as the Red Legs of Kansas and Missouri's infamous Quantrill's raiders. Even after the war, the violence did not end. Many guerrillas found living by the gun more alluring than trying to plow the Western sod. Their talents suited the new towns growing wild on the frontier faster than lawmen could tame them. Cow towns, like Dodge City, made their living off cowpokes who drove their Longhorns to the Kansas railroads, then came into town looking for excitement. And gold-mining towns, like Deadwood, drew people looking for gold any way they could get it. Law and order eventually came to the plains, but not before an era had been made into legend by contemporary photographers, artists and journalists.

QUANTRILL'S BLOOD-SOAKED REVENGE

RUTHLESS GANGS of guerrillas in the 1850s and 1860s terrorized towns on both sides of the Kansas-Missouri border. Among the most notorious of the border brigands was William Clarke Quantrill, who on August 21, 1863, led his anti-Union raiders against the town of Lawrence, Kansas, in one of the most vicious attacks on civilians made during the Civil War.

Lawrence was a town long hated by Quantrill and his men. Home of the demagogic antislavery Senator, Jim Lane, it was also a stronghold of the Red Legs, Union guerrillas who had sacked much of western Missouri. An attack on this citadel of abolition would bring revenge for any wrongs, real or imagined, the Southerners had suffered.

With a gang of some 450 cutthroats, Quantrill stormed the sleeping town just before dawn. Shouting bloodthirstily, the riders galloped across the tents of sleeping Union soldiers, crushing the life from 17 young recruits. Then, as the town awoke to its danger, the atrocities began to mount. One group of townsmen, who meekly surrendered, were lined up and shot. A storekeeper, with hands bound, was thrown alive into the flames of his burning shop. After four hours, the gang fled as quickly as it had arrived, leaving behind 150 dead, all of them men.

"Kill! Kill!" shouted Quantrill as his crew butchered the citizens of Lawrence. Above, a raider lifts up his rifle to strike an old man.

When one poor woman pleaded for her husband's life, one of the brigands pressed his pistol against the man's head and killed him.

"COLONEL" QUANTRILL

To defend his murderous attacks as legitimate acts of war, Quantrill claimed the rank of Confederate colonel. Whether he was actually commissioned is not clear. His brutal tactics were condemned by military men of both sides, and one Confederate general even threatened to arrest him and all his men.

A HERO'S DEMISE

How Wild Bill Hickok Was Brought Down in Deadwood

"DIED, IN DEADWOOD, Black Hills, August 2, 1876, from the effect of a pistol shot, J. B. Hickok, (Wild Bill) formerly of Cheyenne, Wyoming. Funeral services will be held at Charlie Utter's camp, on Thursday afternoon August 3, 1876, at 3 o'clock. All are respectfully invited to attend."

With this short bulletin, friends paid final tribute to one of the West's truly authentic folk heroes, Wild Bill Hickok (*right*).

Wild Bill was born James Butler Hickok in 1837 in LaSalle County, Illinois, where his parents were operating a station on the Underground Railroad, smuggling slaves out of the South. It was there that Hickok had his first taste of hostile gunfire: he was chased by policemen who suspected him and his father of carrying more than just hay in their wagon. At 17 he was a towpath driver on the Illinois and Michigan Canal, and by 20 he was in Kansas with the Free-State Army of General James Lane.

But it was not until 1861 that the legend of Wild Bill Hickok really began to take shape. Weakened, so the story goes, from an attack by an angry bear, Hickok took up light work at a stagecoach way station at Rock Creek in Nebraska Territory. There, on a hot July afternoon in 1861, an angry settler named David McCanles went with his son and two neighbors to collect a debt from the stagecoach company. Some say, however, that McCanles was after Hickok for mak-

WILD BILL HICKOK

RAMSHACKLE AND RIOTOUS, Deadwood's Main Street in the late 1870s was a paradise for con men and prostitutes intent on separating Black Hills miners from their hard-won gains. Beneath these canopies were such soon-to-be legendary establishments as the Wide West Saloon. There "Madam Mustache," a bewhiskered French hag, held court over the faro tables, while, at The Melodeon, "Deadwood Dick" and his mistress serenaded the men at the bar. Another popular nightspot was the Bella Union, where miners vied, sometimes at gunpoint, for the affections of "ladies of the evening."

ing time with Sarah Shull, a local belle he had his own eye on when Mrs. McCanles was not around. Whatever the cause, by the time the fracas was over, McCanles and his two neighbors lay dead in the Nebraska dust and the West had a new hero.

Some years later, an account of the "McCanles Massacre" reported that by Hickok's own count "he slew McCanles and five henchmen with his only six bullets, cut four more to death in hand-to-hand combat, and walked away from the carnage in fair health except for eleven buckshot holes and thirteen stab wounds." Already Hickok was embellishing his own image.

Not long afterward, Hickok was said to have received the nickname he used for the rest of his life. Serving the Union as a scout and spy during the Civil War, he was in Independence, Missouri, looking for troops to chase down some Confederate guerrillas. Instead of soldiers he found an angry, drunken mob trying to lynch a bartender who had shot a hoodlum in a brawl. With

hardly a second thought, he fired two shots over the heads of the men, then stared them down until all had retreated and disappeared. After the cowed mob took to its heels, a grateful woman was allegedly heard to shout from the sidelines, "Good for you, Wild Bill!" She may have mistaken Hickok for someone else, but the name stuck.

Over the next few years Wild Bill's fame as a gunfighter, deserved or not, grew rapidly. Finally, in 1876,

THE COWARD'S ACT

ON HIS LAST TRIP down to the No. 10 Saloon, Wild Bill *(center)* ignored his cautious habit of sitting with his back to the wall. According to most accounts, his friends were already playing, and he took a seat that exposed his back to an open door—in the rear —and to the bar. Given the advantage of surprise, the killer slipped up from behind, shouted "Take that!" and fired. From Hickok's fingers fell two aces, two eights and another card, a combination known since then as aces and eights, the dead man's hand.

as both his eyesight and his career were fading, he headed into the Dakota hills to one of the last real wild West hellholes, Deadwood. Earning his keep by playing poker, he made a routine call one day at the No. 10 Saloon, joining some companions at cards. Without warning, Jack McCall, a drunken nobody possibly trying to make a name for himself, stepped away from the bar and with a single bullet, through the head, sent Wild Bill Hickok to his grave.

CALAMITY JANE

WILD BILL'S "ONE TRUE LOVE"

She was the "White Devil of the Yellowstone," "a woman low down, even in her class," but she was Calamity Jane and Wild Bill loved her —so the legend goes. But legend is all it was. Calamity Jane, pictured here on a visit to Hickok's grave, was often known to wear men's clothes and chew tobacco, swearing like a trooper. She was the most colorful woman in Deadwood, and what seemed more natural than a liaison with the most colorful man around, Wild Bill Hickok? No one knows how the rumor of their love affair started, but certainly neither of them bothered to scotch it. After Hickok's murder, Calamity drifted around the West, but the rumor of her one great affair never faded, and it is still said that her dying words were "Bury me next to Bill."

JAMES-YOUNGER FIASCO

MISJUDGING THE TOWN'S RAW COURAGE BROUGHT THE OUTLAWS TO THEIR DESERVED FATE

TEN SAVAGE MINUTES in the remote Minnesota farm town of Northfield on September 7, 1876, brought to a violent end the plains' most notorious outlaws, the James-Younger gang. For several years, the James brothers, Frank and Jesse, and the Youngers, Cole, Bob and Jim, had been robbing, pillaging and killing with reckless abandon. Across seven states, from Texas to Minnesota, they left 11 men dead and got away with loot estimated at nearly half a million dollars.

The end in Northfield really began early in the summer of 1876, when a new recruit, Bill Chadwell, joined the gang. Known as a horse thief, highwayman and all-around desper-

ado, Chadwell advised the others to try out their luck on the banks up Minnesota way. Bank robbery there was all but unheard of, he suggested. They eventually picked the small community of Northfield, reported to have one of the richest country banks (*right*) in the state.

On September 7, a few minutes before noon, the Jameses and gang member Charlie Pitts rode quietly into town. After lunch they strolled toward the bank, sat down and waited. At 1 o'clock, when the church bell struck, all hell broke loose. Bob Younger, Chadwell and Clell Miller, another gang member, roared into town from the south, guns blazing, shouting the Rebel yell. At the same

Northfield's First National Bank occupied the back of the two-story brick-and-stone structure above, known as the Scriver Block. Although the front of the building faced on the town's main square, the bank entrance was on a narrow street across from the Dampier House hotel. From the hotel a student, Henry Wheeler, had an unimpeded line of fire on the bandits as they tried to flee. To the right of the block was a hardware store where townspeople gathered rifles to fight the gang.

time Cole and Jim Younger swept in from the west, and the townspeople headed for cover. Spotting one young man who failed to move fast enough, Cole killed him with a single shot.

But Henry Wheeler, a student home on vacation, saw the shot from his father's drugstore. Interviewed later, he related, "I remembered suddenly that there was an Army rifle . . . in the Dampier House. I figured if I could get my hands on it that I could run upstairs to one of the front rooms of the hotel and start shooting from the window." He succeeded, and shot Miller out of the saddle, killing him, and a few seconds later got a bead on Bob Younger, shattering his right elbow. From a nearby corner, another man sent a slug ripping through Cole Younger's shoulder, then brought down Chadwell with a bullet through the heart.

Jesse, Frank and Pitts had, meanwhile, entered the bank. They did not enter the vault, however; hearing the shots from outside, they grabbed what money they could from tellers' counters and left. On reaching the street, they found Miller and Chadwell dead, Cole Younger drenched in blood, Jim's jaw shot away and Bob with one arm useless.

Somehow the survivors reached their horses and got out of town. But with so many wounded, they decided to break up into two smaller groups. Jesse and Frank traveled west, and eight days later escaped into Dakota Territory. Two weeks after the hold-up, Charlie Pitts was spotted and followed back to the hideout where he and the three Youngers were holed up. An hour later a hundred men descended on the camp, and after a short gunfight Pitts lay dead and the Youngers were taken captive. At their trial the three pleaded guilty so that, under Minnesota law, they would not be hanged. Although Frank and Jesse survived to rob and kill another day, the era of the despised and dreaded James-Younger gang was ended as the court sentenced the Youngers to spend the rest of their lives in a prison.

THE OUTLAWS' DESTINIES

Jesse James later recruited a new gang, but his luck ran out in 1882 when—at age 34—one of his men, Bob Ford, shot him from behind.

Frank James, later tried on another count and acquitted, held odd jobs, even that of a special policeman, until he died at age 72 in 1915.

Although all three Younger brothers were sentenced to life imprisonment, only one died behind bars. Bob (left), wounded in the lungs at Northfield, never completely recovered, and died of pneumonia in prison in 1889. Cole (center) and Jim (right) spent 25 years in prison and then in 1901 were given pardons through the efforts of a man whose life Cole had once saved. Barely a year later, plagued by depressions, Jim committed suicide. Cole lived until 1916 and at one time ran a wild West show with his old cohort, Frank James.

The bodies of the three men killed, Charlie Pitts (right), Bill Chadwell (center) and Clell Miller (far right), set up for the photographer, testify mutely to the gang's underestimation of the citizens of Northfield. Many townsmen were veterans of Civil War campaigns and so were not cowed by a little shooting.

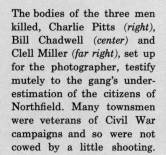

DARING ROBBERY

THE BIG JOB AT BIG SPRINGS, NEB.

A HUGE PRIZE

DESPERADOES' FIRST TRY
FOR WELLS FARGO'S GOLD

SAM BASS

AMONG THE MOST TEMPTING prospects for a gunslinger on the unruly plains was the chance to rob one of the Union Pacific trains that carried gold back east from the mining areas in special express cars. Sam Bass was launched on his road to fame—or notoriety—in such an operation, which was reportedly one of the most profitable train holdups in the Old West. His heist of a Union Pacific express at Big Springs, Nebraska, in 1877, temporarily made him richer by $60,000.

Formerly a two-bit stagecoach bandit, Bass had been driven from the saloons and bordellos of Deadwood along with the Joel Collins gang. With Jim Berry, Tom Nixon, Bill Heffridge, Jack Davis and Joel Collins, he now headed into Nebraska, hoping to make a killing knocking off some trains.

As it happened, the gang's first job

The Big Springs train station, seen in a photograph taken three or four years after the Collins gang made its raid, was one of many watering stops along the Union Pacific tracks, which stretched westward from Omaha across the plains. It was a likely spot for a robbery, as it was well isolated, 15 miles from the nearest large town, Ogallala, and on the outskirts of the little farm community of Big Springs.

The look of villainy was caught on film when *(from the left)* Sam Bass and Joel Collins posed with a friend and Joel's brother Joe.

Death caught up with Heffridge and Collins as they crept furtively across the Kansas plains. Captured by an alert sheriff, the two desperadoes drew their .45s, but before they could fire they were shot by the sheriff's men. In their saddlebags was found $25,000 in gold.

hit it big. Setting up camp near Big Springs, an isolated water station on the Union Pacific line, the robbers laid out their plans. Berry rode into nearby Ogallala for red bandannas to use as masks, and on Tuesday, September 18, they struck.

Guns drawn and faces masked, they stormed the train station, tore out the telegraph and held the agent prisoner. About 10 p.m., the express pulled in. The gang quickly captured the train crew, then sent the station agent to open up the Wells Fargo Express car that carried the gold. Inside the car, though, they ran into trouble. The safe, holding more than $200,000, had a time lock that even the company guard could not open. As a last resort, Bass tore open a small wooden box sitting beside the safe, and out spilled rolls of freshly minted gold coins. There were two more boxes just like it—a haul worth a total of $60,000. Counting the loot later, the men divided it, then paired off and scattered.

Unfortunately, they had made two mistakes. One of the passengers had recognized Collins. A few days later a merchant from Ogallala identified a piece of red bandanna found near the station as one he had sold Jim Berry. Collins and Heffridge got as far as Kansas before a sheriff and his posse caught up with them *(above right)*. Berry, who had been with Nix-

on, was in Missouri when the law reached him. He, too, died shooting it out. There was no sign of Davis, and years later he was reported living in Nicaragua. Nixon also got away, some say into Canada.

Bass, his name emblazoned on WANTED posters across the plains, made it all the way to Texas, where he got together another gang. Within a few months one of his partners turned traitor and told the law where Bass could be found. Then on July 19, 1878, two days before Bass's 27th birthday, the law closed in and brought him down in an ambush.

A FREQUENT OCCURRENCE ON THE RAILS

Train holdups were part and parcel of the West in the public's imagination, and the poster above was surely an effective drawing card for Buffalo Bill's Wild West and Pioneer Exhibition. Despite some exaggeration—such as the number of bandits involved—the details are realistic. Wells Fargo Express cars were indeed looted, safes blown open and passengers robbed of all their possessions.

A FRONTIER BABYLON

An Actress Shot in Bed

The killing of the actress Dora Hand climaxed one of Dodge City's most violent years, 1878. An attempted train robbery, three shootings and the rumor of an Indian attack that year preceded the October night when Jim Kenedy, son of a wealthy cattleman, rode past the house where Dora was sleeping and fired through a door, killing her instantly. Later caught by Sheriff Bat Masterson, Wyatt Earp, Bill Tilghman and others, Kenedy found out he had hit the wrong person. Intending to kill saloon owner "Dog" Kelley, Kenedy had instead shot Dora, who was staying in Kelley's house while he was away.

SOURCE OF MORE TALES of bawdiness and bloodshed than probably any other town on the plains, Dodge City, Kansas, was a railhead serving two Texas cattle trails, and was often called the Queen of the Cowtowns. Just out of town was the cemetery called Boot Hill, the last resting place for cowpokes who, it was said, died with their boots on. One story even suggests that Dodge City had the first red-light district, named for one bordello's red-glassed door that served as a "beacon in the night for the lusty cowboys off the lonesome trail."

Law and order meant little enough in Dodge. Of one marshal's career it was said, "his term of office [was] distinguished only by the fact that by looking the other way at the right time he had managed to survive." Many Dodge City lawmen, however, were notable enough to join the ranks of bigger-than-life heroes. Wyatt Earp and Bat Masterson are the best known, but Marshal Bill Tilghman was perhaps more successful than any other in keeping peace

Dodge City's deadline, marked by the railroad tracks (*foreground*), separated the lawless part of town from the law-abiding section shown above. No guns were allowed north of the deadline, where such respectable saloons as the Long Branch operated. But on the south side, "a hell-bent cowpuncher could get loaded . . . and then empty his six-shooter in the direction of some kindred soul's guts."

Bill Tilghman posing in Hollywood in 1915.

vivid accounts of his encounters. Typical is this one in the *Kansas Cowboy* in 1884 reporting his run-in with a cowpoke in a bordello:

"The city marshal brought up a six-footer of monstrous proportions [a cowboy called Colorado Sampson], who got into a dive, and was rattling up the establishment. . . . He was evidently starting out to paint Dodge City a fiery red, and very appropriately started in the darkest spot in town. . . . What he would have done if the city marshal had not arrived on the spot will never be known. As it was [Sampson] . . . was about as ugly a customer as need be seen anywhere. The marshal showed himself equal to the emergency and tumbled him into the cooler." By the time Marshal Tilghman brought him up before the judge, the *Kansas Cowboy* concluded, he was "as cool as if he had been in a refrigerator."

in the "Gomorrah of the plains." In 1878, Tilghman rode with Earp and Masterson after the killer of the popular local actress, Dora Hand *(opposite)*. Five years later he was appointed assistant marshal by the Dodge City Peace Commission *(below)* and a year later he became city marshal.

Newspapers of the time often gave

A TRUMPED-UP PEACE COMMISSION

The vagaries of politics in Dodge City were highlighted by the Peace Commission *(at right)*, which existed solely to make sure that one group of gamblers and saloon owners would not be run out of town by the mayor, who was in cahoots with another group. The trouble began when the mayor ordered his marshal to run Luke Short, co-owner of the successful Long Branch saloon, out of town. Short, eager to return, enlisted the aid of several of his close friends, including his business partner, Will Harris, and such noted ex-Dodge lawmen as Bat Masterson, Charlie Bassett and Wyatt Earp. They forced the mayor to let Short return, and, forming the Dodge City Peace Commission, demanded the appointment of a new marshal: Bill Tilghman. He was appointed, and an uneasy peace settled on the rambunctious city.

WILL HARRIS   LUKE SHORT   BAT MASTERSON
CHARLIE BASSETT   WYATT EARP   FRANK McCLAIN   NEAL BROWN

A TALE OF GOOD MEN WHO TURNED TO CRIME

FOUL PLAY ON A VERY FOUL DAY

Two Leading Lawmen on the Other Side of the Law

HENRY BROWN, MARSHAL

BEN WHEELER, DEPUTY

GOOD GUYS AND BAD GUYS were hard to tell apart in the Old West, and some gunslingers worked both for and against the law—occasionally at the same time. Nonetheless, the Kansas town of Caldwell was still shocked when its respected marshal, Henry Brown—who admittedly had once ridden with Billy the Kid—and his deputy, Ben Wheeler, were caught after holding up a bank in nearby Medicine Lodge.

Just the year before, Brown had been given a Winchester by the town fathers in appreciation for his services. Yet here was the telegram from Medicine Lodge: "The bank robbers were Brown and Wheeler, marshal and deputy of Caldwell, and [William] Smith and [John] Wesley. All arrested. Tried to escape. Brown killed. Balance hung." The full story was chronicled in the Caldwell *Journal* on May 8, 1884, under the fitting headline:

A TERRIBLE DAY!

"One week ago Sunday afternoon, Henry N. Brown, marshal of this city, and Ben F. Wheeler, his deputy, having obtained permission from the mayor to be absent from the city . . .

THE TOWN THAT WAS DISGRACED

Caldwell, seen here in a photograph taken four years after the bank holdup at Medicine Lodge, mourned the loss of its marshal and deputy, even though they had been guilty of robbery and murder. The Caldwell *Journal* paid tribute to the men's good deeds while in office:

"The tragic death of the robbers has already been told. That it was just, all know. . . . They had made many warm friends in this city, and while here had made two as good officers as the city has ever had. . . . That they have brought disgrace on the city, no one can help; and that they met their just deserts, all rejoice. But let the mantle of charity fall over their memory."

rode out of town. . . . They were joined, it is supposed, on Monday by Smith and Wesley, cowboys. . . . When Brown and Wheeler entered the bank, Payne [the bank president] . . . reached for his revolver. This was his death warrant. Brown shot him, and Wheeler immediately shot Geppert [the cashier]."

The group's attempted escape and final capture were reported in the Medicine Lodge *Cresset:* "The robbers . . . mounted and rode out of town, going south. It was but a few minutes until a score or more men were in hot pursuit.

"To those who remained, on going into the bank, a horrible sight was presented. George Geppert, the esteemed cashier, lay at the door of the vault

WELTERING IN HIS BLOOD, and dead. . . . Mr. Payne, the pres-

ident, lay near him

GROANING WITH PAIN.

"[The robbers] took refuge in a canyon some three or four miles southwest of town. . . . Every gun and horse that could be brought into service was on the road to the canyon. Before the reinforcements arrived on the ground, however, the robbers had surrendered.

"When the party were brought in they were surrounded by a crowd of exasperated citizens, and cries of

HANG THEM! HANG THEM! sounded on every side. . . .

"About nine o'clock the stillness of the night was broken by three shots. . . . A crowd of armed men advanced toward the jail and demanded the prisoners. . . . The sheriff and his posse were overpowered and the doors of the jail opened, when the prisoners who were in the inner

Captured within hours of the robbery, the outlaws were photographed in handcuffs before being thrown into jail. Henry Brown *(center, with light bandanna)* had had a shady past but was thought to have gone straight. His deputy, Ben Wheeler *(right, with unbuttoned vest),* had come from Texas after wounding a man in a gunfight. Of Wesley *(on Brown's right)* and Smith *(visored cap),* little is known other than that both had been Texas ranch hands.

◆

cell unshackled made a sudden

DASH FOR LIBERTY.

Brown ran a few yards from the jail and fell dead, riddled with a charge of buckshot, besides having a few stray Winchester balls in various parts of his body.

"Wheeler, Smith and Wesley were taken by the crowd to an elm tree in the bottom east of town . . . the ready ropes were fastened on the necks of the robbers, the end tossed over a limb, and in a moment more their bodies swung in the wind."

The Condon Bank, held up first by the Daltons, was hit by some 80 bullets fired by aroused citizens, who hid in the stores lining the other side of Coffeyville's main plaza.

THE "FOOLPROOF" PLAN THAT WENT AWRY

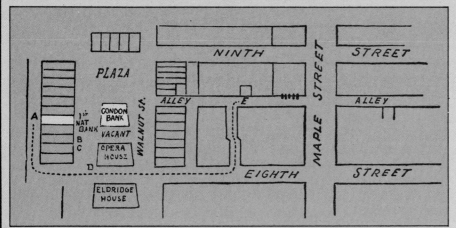

Leaving their horses (*oblong dots*) in the alley, the robbers made for the two banks. Two were spotted from Isham's store next to the First National. Fleeing the bank on his way back (*dotted line*) to the alley, Bob Dalton dropped one victim (*A*), then fired again (*D*) and got two more (*B, C*). Other killings occurred in the alley (*E*).

The gang's arrival.

Gunfire from Isham's.

DALTONS

Gang Demolished in Bloody Massacre at Coffeyville

CREATION OF A NEW LEGEND IN WESTERN OUTLAWRY

A BURNING DESIRE to "beat anything Jesse James ever did" led to one of the most reckless and disastrous robbery attempts in the annals of Western outlawry. The Dalton gang, unusual for the brevity of its existence—it lasted less than a year and a half—became a part of Western legend on October 5, 1892, when its members tried holding up two banks at once in their hometown of Coffeyville, Kansas.

Arriving in town early that day, Bob, Emmett and Grat Dalton, Bill Powers and Dick Broadwell hitched their horses in an alley not far from the center of town. They shuffled toward the central plaza, Bob and Emmett heading for the First National, the other three for the Condon Bank, a lone structure in the center of the plaza. They reached the Condon first. Inside, Grat leveled his Winchester at the cashier.

"Open the safe and open it quick!"

With cool nerve, the cashier faced the gunman. "It's a time lock. It doesn't open until nine forty-five," he lied, stalling the gang for three precious minutes. Later, Emmett would recall that the cashier's "shifty falsehood about the vault—which all the time was open to any hand—was to . . . cause the death of eight men within the next five minutes."

Across the street, Bob and Emmett were entering the First National. But a citizen had spotted them and was spreading the alarm.

The armed trio entering the Condon had also been spotted, and the word was out: "The Dalton gang—they're holding up both banks!" From inside Isham's Hardware Store and other establishments, the townspeople opened fire, sighting on the bandits through the bank windows.

Hearing the fire, Bob and Emmett ducked out the back door of the First National, hoping to escape unseen. There they met a clerk running up the alley from a nearby store, and with a shot Bob Dalton brought down the first victim. On reaching the plaza, he spotted two men near the front of the First National, one of them armed. He fired—"Bob Dalton's aim was fatally unerring," reported an eyewitness—and two more fell dead. Meanwhile, as fusillades shattered the Condon, Grat, Powers and Broadwell made a break for it. By some miracle all five bandits reached the alley near their horses. Just then Marshal Charles Connelly ran into the alley ahead of the gang to cut them off. With one shot Grat dropped him before he could fire. From behind a nearby fence, though, stable owner John Kloehr, "the best shot in town," was taking aim. One shot rubbed out Bob Dalton and another ripped fatally through Grat's neck. Powers, almost in the saddle, jerked backwards as a shot from Isham's tore a hole in his chest. Emmett and Broadwell reached their horses and headed down the alley; then, unbelievably, Emmett turned back in an effort to retrieve brother Bob's bloody corpse. Then he, too, fell, his arm shattered, his thigh broken, and a dozen buckshot in his back, critically wounded but still alive. Broadwell, nailed as he headed out of town, was found a mile away.

Several days later, a train was held up not far from Coffeyville, and rumors swept the anxious town that the Daltons' outlaw friends were there, ready to strike back in reprisal. But the attack never came, and law and order returned once more.

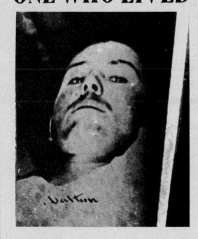

ONE WHO LIVED

Though badly wounded, Emmett Dalton survived the gunfight, and was sentenced to life imprisonment. Pardoned in 1907, Emmett is reported to have observed, "The biggest fool on earth is the one who thinks he can beat the law."

A HARD LESSON FOR THOSE WHO TRY TO LIVE BY VIOLENCE

When the smoke cleared, eight men lay dead on the streets of Coffeyville. Four were gang members Bill Powers, Bob Dalton, Grat Dalton and Dick Broadwell, laid out left to right after the shooting. Of the other victims, Bob Dalton alone had brought down three: Lucius Baldwin, who had intercepted him behind the First National, and George Cubine and Charles Brown, two shoemakers who had been posted as guards out front. The eighth victim, Marshal Connelly, was shot by Grat when he tried to stop the gang near their horses.

4

Taming
the Wild River

Like a monster skeletal tree, the Missouri River and its branches reach out across the plains, touching six of the seven states in the region and touching the lives of their citizens as well. Historically the Missouri has been a powerful arbiter of life in the plains region, and in a godlike fashion it has both given and taken away. Until the day of the railroad it was the primary travelway to the north and west, but its hidden sand bars, shifting currents and floating islands of debris exacted a high toll of Indian dugout canoes, flatboats and sturdy river steamers. Its waters have enriched thousands of acres of prairie, but its floods have periodically laid waste much that it made fertile. Today man's ingenuity has largely tamed the river and it is once again an artery of commerce. But even now, when the big river and its tendrils throb to life in the spring, plainsmen in town and country sit up and take notice.

"There is only one river that goes traveling side-wise," George Fitch, a 19th Century humorist, once commented with awe-tinged affection, "that

Under 20 feet of water, the industrial area of Kansas City, Missouri, suffers the devastating flood of July 1951. Disaster occurred when the Kansas *(bottom)* and Missouri Rivers, which meet at the city, overflowed their banks after several months of heavy rains.

interferes in politics, rearranges geography and dabbles in real estate; a river that plays hide and seek with you today, and tomorrow follows you around like a pet dog with a dynamite cracker tied to its tail. That river is the Missouri." This erratic waterway begins its 2,466-mile course placidly enough, and through its long upper reaches in Montana it runs between stable banks; only when it enters the grasslands does it become unpredictable. The distance between restraining bluffs then grows wide—so wide that in some spots it is difficult for a man standing on one side to see the other, even on sunny days—and between the banks the water is free to wander every which way.

The Missouri's source is in an 800-foot-wide Montana valley. From there it flows through canyons, forms rapids and dramatically drops three times over high waterfalls before entering the Plains States. The last great descent is the most precipitous—the rushing water cascades down a 90-foot cliff at Great Falls, Montana. Along its course to its junction with the Mississippi, just north of St. Louis, the Missouri is joined by scores of tributaries. The Cannonball and Heart, the Grand and Moreau, the Cheyenne and White all find union with the Missouri in the Dakotas; the Niobrara and the Platte empty into the main stem in Nebraska; and the Kansas (also known as the Kaw), after swallowing the Republican River, is itself gulped down by the Missouri at Kansas City.

The first white man to see the Missouri and record his impressions was Father Jacques Marquette, who canoed down the Mississippi in 1673 to its junction with the Missouri. The sight of Big Muddy pouring into the comparatively placid Mississippi left the cleric shaken and appalled. He recorded in his journal that he had seen "nothing more frightful, a mass of large trees entire with branches, real floating islands. . . ." The turbulence of the Missouri as it thundered debris into the Mississippi was, according to Marquette, "so impetuous that we could not without great danger expose ourselves to pass across. The agitation was so great that the water was all muddy, and could not get clear."

Marquette's remarks have been seconded and expanded upon countless times in the three centuries that have passed since his epic journey. George Fitch, who found in the Missouri an endless source of wry humor, wrote of its greedy ways and varied appetites: "It is eating all the time—eating yellow clay banks and cornfields, eighty acres at a mouthful; winding up its banquet with a truck garden and picking its teeth with the timbers of a big red barn. Its yearly menu is ten thousand acres of good, rich farming land, several miles of railroad, a few hundred houses, a forest or two and uncounted miles of sandbars."

The mud to which Marquette referred is noticeable throughout most of the river's length on even the calmest of days, giving the Missouri its nickname, Big Muddy. "Its muddiness," wrote Horace Greeley, "is beyond all description; its color and consistency are those of thick milk porridge; you could not discern an egg in a glass of it." Others have described the sometimes viscous, sometimes roaring mass of brownish liquid as "too thick to drink, too thin to cultivate."

Most of the mud comes, not from the Missouri itself, but from its tributaries, which disgorge two basic types of sediment into the river in vast quantities: (1) lightweight soils (silt) such as loam and marl that float along near the surface and (2) heavier sediment such as gravel and sand that falls to the river bed and shifts with the deep water currents. An expert on the Missouri once said that it is "essentially a moving sand bottom river," with sediment constantly shifting, not only downstream but sidewise and up and down in elevation. This mass of muck in motion affects the river's flow so radically that the channel may move from one side to another between morning and afternoon. Nor is it just the channel that moves; large sections of the river bed are sometimes abandoned by the Missouri, which then settles down in a new and presumably more comfortable spot.

Doniphan, Kansas, for example, was once a thriving river port, but in 1870 the Missouri suddenly changed its bed, leaving the town high and dry. As a parting gesture, the river tore away railroad tracks and demolished the train station and other municipal buildings before settling down in its new channel some distance from the town. With its primary source of income gone, Doniphan suffered a swift decline in fortune and population. Brunswick, Missouri, is another community that lost its position on the banks of the river when, in 1875, the wandering stream moved some miles away. During the 1952 flood the channel shifted to relocate part of the border between Kansas and Missouri, and the St. Joseph, Missouri, airport, originally built on Missouri territory, suddenly came under the jurisdiction of Kansas.

With such an inconstant river at their doorsteps, plainsmen have developed a mystique about Big Muddy. They take pride in its rapaciousness and speak affectionately of its capriciousness. They not only attribute human qualities to the river but often refer to it in terms that one might employ in discussing a powerful yet playful god. They castigate it for the damage it causes, yet exult in its capacity to scour one of its more rocky banks "as clean as a Thanksgiving turkey . . . as flat as the side of a skyscraper." A century ago the Missouri Valley was described only half humorously as a place "where all the steamboats are aground, and all the houses are afloat."

Year after year the river demonstrated its destructive power. The stretch from St. Louis to St. Joseph, just across from northeastern Kansas, was in general more subject to bank-jumping than any other; the two Kansas Citys, hugging the oxbow bluffs where the Missouri turns sharply east, have suffered heavily from flood damage. The 1903 flood took out 16 of 17 bridges and caused more than $22 million in damage; scores of people were drowned. Nor have the smaller communities and farmlands been spared. The willful Missouri and its tributaries for years have distributed disaster throughout most of the Plains States region. A list of the Missouri's depredations could be endless, for if there is one thing certain about the river it is that during any year it will flood somewhere and bring grief to many.

On their way to join the rampaging Missouri,

the waters of the Republican and Kansas Rivers in a single flood inundated 57,000 acres in Nebraska and 200,000 in Kansas. Plainsmen near St. Francis, Kansas, still talk of that 1935 Memorial Day deluge on the Republican's south fork, recalled by one landowner as "a 15-foot-tall walking wall of water" before which cattle could be seen running in desperation. "By flashes of lightning," the farmer said 30 years later, "we could see our house was surrounded by a sea of water. There was no dodging it. All our family saw the black water come creeping in under the door, then slowly rise in the room, while there was nothing we could do but wait—which is awfully hard when the water starts lapping at the legs of your piano."

Of all the floods of recent years, those of 1951 and 1952 stand out in the memories of plainsmen as events of unparalleled destructiveness. In both years a combination of extreme weather conditions, freakish even by plains standards, was responsible for the onslaughts of water and mud that drowned whole sections of cities and submerged millions of acres of farmland.

In 1951 Kansas experienced an exceptional amount of early spring rain, and through April and May, residents had reason to believe that there would be considerable, though manageable flooding. What they could not anticipate, however, was that the rains would continue with increased intensity throughout the normally dry month of June and well into July. By mid-June the soil was like a sponge, each step producing a puddle of muddy water, and by late June the ground was saturated; it could no longer absorb the continuing downpours that now began to run off freely into the swelling rivers of the area: the Kansas, the Blue, the Osage, the Neosho, the Marais des Cygnes and the Missouri itself.

On June 29 the first major flood disaster hit at Manhattan, Kansas, near the junction of the Blue and the Kansas. A crest of water, 10 feet above flood level, spilled into the town of 17,000 to smash stores, office buildings and restaurants and cause $20 million worth of damage. But that was nothing compared with what happened at the two Kansas Citys on July 12.

A magazine article of the time described the scene: "The [Kansas] flows into the Missouri River at the Kansas Citys. There the low-lying industrial districts are protected by flood walls as high as 22 feet, built to cope with high water equal to that of the previous record flood in 1903. The flood of '51 roared over the levees, covered the Santa Fe's great transfer yards and shops, inundated the

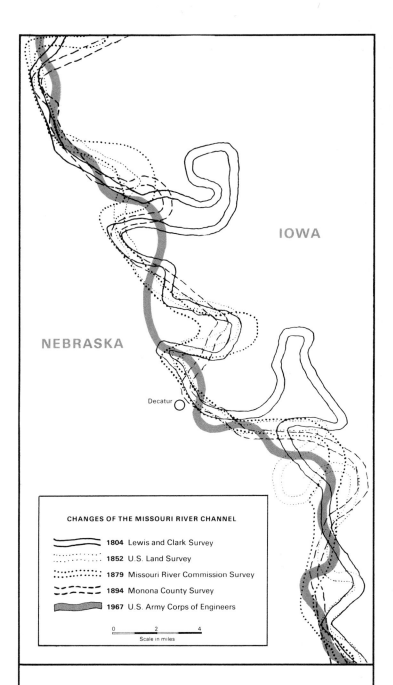

CHANGES OF THE MISSOURI RIVER CHANNEL

——— 1804 Lewis and Clark Survey

············· 1852 U.S. Land Survey

:::::::::::: 1879 Missouri River Commission Survey

– – – – 1894 Monona County Survey

▬▬▬ 1967 U.S. Army Corps of Engineers

0   2   4
Scale in miles

The wanderings of a restless river

The meanderings of the Missouri River, charted above along an approximately 30-mile stretch that forms part of the Iowa-Nebraska border, challenged mapmakers for a century after Lewis and Clark first surveyed the river in 1804. By constantly undercutting and carrying away the soft soil of its banks, the Missouri had created a broad trench—10 miles across in some places—through which it flowed as it pleased. Whenever mud or debris blocked its path, the Missouri swung around the obstacles, occasionally forming huge loops. The river might later fill in the loops to form shallow lakes, or cut them off by creating shortcuts across their narrow necks. Old-time river pilots had to rely on information from other rivermen and their own intimate knowledge to navigate. Today, restricted by a series of dams, levees and dikes, the river has been forced to flow along a gently curving course.

Two kinds of stern-wheelers

The two steamboats shown here, diagramed from builders' plans, were among the last to sail the Missouri, and represent a triumph of riverboat design of their day: stern-wheelers that could operate fully loaded in water less than five feet deep. Most Missouri steamboats were stripped of all possible weight to keep them afloat in shallow water. Their remarkable buoyancy was achieved at the cost of durability; the flimsily built craft usually wore out within five years.

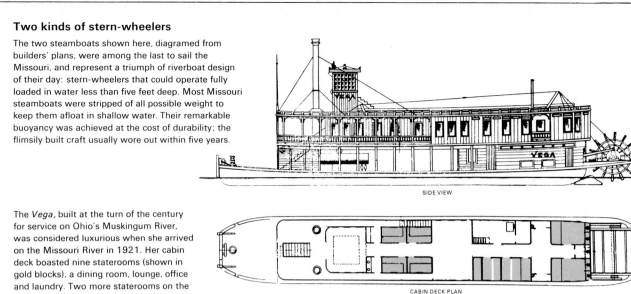

SIDE VIEW

The *Vega*, built at the turn of the century for service on Ohio's Muskingum River, was considered luxurious when she arrived on the Missouri River in 1921. Her cabin deck boasted nine staterooms (shown in gold blocks), a dining room, lounge, office and laundry. Two more staterooms on the main deck separated the coal-burning boilers from the steam engines. The wood-plank hull *(cutaway)* was 104 feet long, 17.5 feet wide and drew only 30 inches of water. Above the water line, however, the *Vega* towered 39 feet to the top of her smokestacks. Used mainly as a towboat, she plied the Missouri until 1926, when she capsized during a sudden squall.

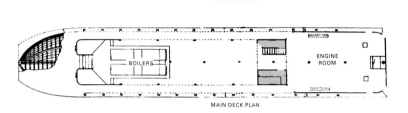

CABIN DECK PLAN

BOILERS   ENGINE ROOM

MAIN DECK PLAN

spreading stockyards, coursed through factories. Rescue workers had a hard time convincing some oldtime residents to leave, so sure were they that the flood would be no worse than in 1903. . . . [Later these] workers heard cries of the trapped as their houses floated away. Water covered 1,384 square blocks of the two cities. It flooded the pumping station which furnishes water to about two-thirds of Kansas City, Missouri.

"Then fire was added to water. The flood ripped up a crude oil storage tank and hurled it against a high tension wire in Kansas City, Missouri. The flaming tank drifted into more gasoline and oil storage tanks. Flames shot up 500 feet into the air as the tanks exploded. Flaming oil and gasoline raced on top of the flood, while firemen in boats vainly poured flood water back on to the fire. The blaze, fed by more than one million gallons of oil, demolished seven square blocks. The [Kansas City] *Star* called it [the town's] 'most disastrous day.' "

All together more than 100,000 people in Kansas and Missouri were driven from their homes, and 28 persons were killed. A million and a half acres were inundated, and the chief of the Army Engineers estimated damage at $870 million. It was the costliest flood in U.S. history.

In some respects, however, the flood that took place the following spring was even worse. Unlike the 1951 disaster, it affected only the upper Missouri Basin and was caused by ice jams in the river and by mild winds melting the winter's accumulation of snow. In March and April of 1952 the winds were warmer than usual, and the snow was much deeper than normal; nighttime temperatures rarely fell below freezing and daytime readings rose into the 70s. As a consequence of this mild weather, the melting of the snows, which generally took several weeks, was accomplished in one. But the ground itself was still hard and frozen, in no condition to receive and store moisture, which instead flowed quickly into the rivers of the High Plains and from there into the Missouri.

Meanwhile, on the tributaries, the warm weather was breaking up the ice that had formed during the winter. Massive chunks now floated into the Missouri itself to collide with the ice already there. Bottlenecks were created, impeding and then halting the flow of water. Unable to continue on its normal course, the water built up quickly behind these ice jams and then cascaded over the banks.

Thousands of people were forced to move to high ground to save themselves, while others attempted to avert disaster by joining brigades of volunteer workers raising dikes against the anticipated on-

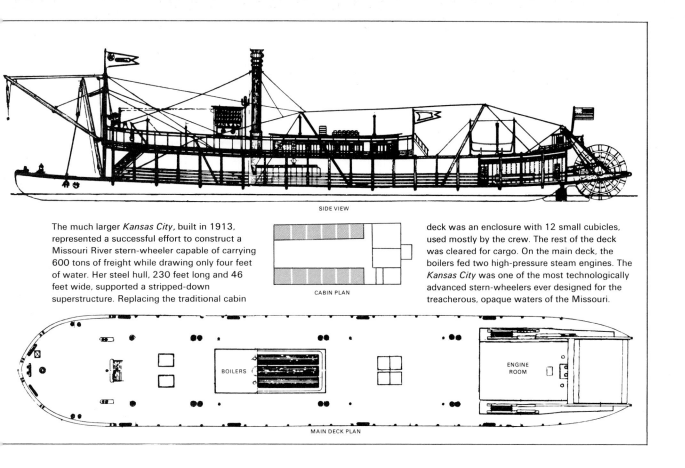

SIDE VIEW

CABIN PLAN

MAIN DECK PLAN

The much larger *Kansas City,* built in 1913, represented a successful effort to construct a Missouri River stern-wheeler capable of carrying 600 tons of freight while drawing only four feet of water. Her steel hull, 230 feet long and 46 feet wide, supported a stripped-down superstructure. Replacing the traditional cabin deck was an enclosure with 12 small cubicles, used mostly by the crew. The rest of the deck was cleared for cargo. On the main deck, the boilers fed two high-pressure steam engines. The *Kansas City* was one of the most technologically advanced stern-wheelers ever designed for the treacherous, opaque waters of the Missouri.

BOILERS

ENGINE ROOM

slaught. At the sister cities of Omaha, Nebraska, and Council Bluffs, Iowa, separated only by a narrow waist of the river, 24,000 men worked round the clock filling 3.5 million sandbags to reinforce the dikes. While the unskilled—factory hands, clerks, businessmen, lawyers, dentists and the like —filled the sandbags, a team of 700 construction workers—carpenters, plasterers and masons—performed a minor miracle by building, in just three days, a 23-mile-long wooden temporary dike to hold back the waters. Such monumental efforts saved the two cities from extensive destruction. Other sections of the upper Missouri Basin were not so fortunate, however. Though property damage was held down to $179 million, mostly because the waters hit few densely populated areas, more than two million acres of farmland were flooded and 130,000 residents of Iowa, Nebraska and the Dakotas were forced to flee their homes.

It might seem surprising that even as late as the middle of the 20th Century, man had done so little to control the Missouri and its tributaries or to protect the people who live along their banks. In fact, for most of the century and a half between the Louisiana Purchase in 1803 and the great floods of the early 1950s, the federal government's involvement with the challenges of the Missouri was generally limited to uncoordinated efforts to improve navigation on the river. Shortly after the Louisiana Territory came under the sovereignty of the United States, President Jefferson authorized the Lewis and Clark expedition and the two explorers set out to chart the Missouri's course. Although they found the river to be the "most direct and practical water communication [to the West] for the purposes of commerce," more than a decade passed before the government tested this assertion, and 35 years went by before it began really serious efforts to clear a channel.

The meagerness of government attention at that time did not seem to matter very much. Fur traders had braved the tempestuous Missouri with keelboats, proving that with determination and skill they could make it serve them. But it was the introduction of the steamboat in 1819 that ushered in the golden era of Missouri River commerce.

Many people were astonished that any steamboat could master the Missouri, and one river buff set down his prescription for a proper vessel to subdue Big Muddy. It "should be shallow, lithe, deepchested and exceedingly strong in the stern wheel, hinged in the middle and . . . fitted with a suction dredge so that when it cannot climb over a sandbar it can assimilate it. The Missouri River

The *General Meade,* a Missouri stern-wheeler, takes on cargo in 1885. Cargo handling was generally a difficult job performed by deck hands without machines. Because the Missouri had few graded wharves, workmen often had to scramble up and down steep riverbanks as they carried freight to the boats.

steamboat should be able to make use of a channel, but should not have to depend upon it. A steamer that cannot, on occasion, climb a steep clay bank, go across a cornfield and corner a river that is trying to get away, has little excuse for trying to navigate the Missouri."

During the steamboat age (approximately 1845 to 1870), an average of 60 boats a year plied the Missouri to transport settlers west and carry freight to the burgeoning river towns. Vessels designed specifically for the Missouri would charge about $150 for cabin passage from St. Louis to Fort Benton, near the foot of the Rockies—a rather large sum for those days when even a physician's weekly income might be only $20. The returning steamboats carried as much as $100,000 worth of furs or more than a million dollars in gold dust.

In the early days of steamboating on the Missouri, life aboard the ships was simple and informal. Passengers who paid for a cabin received exactly the same food as those who slept on deck—usually beans, fat pork and more beans. From time to time, all passengers were expected to disembark along the banks to help crewmen cut wood for the engines. By the late 1850s, however, a few amenities were being added to riverboat life on the Missouri. Captains began hiring marksmen whose

duty was to shoot down game during the voyage, thus providing the passengers with a variety of meat. Though the Missouri boats were never as sumptuous as the floating palaces of the Mississippi, many were at least very comfortable. If there were no storms, if the ship did not hit a snag, and if Indians did not attack from the shore, a trip up the river could provide delightful relaxation.

One such voyage, up and down the river, was recalled in 1924 by a passenger, Charles P. Deatherage, a lumber executive and amateur historian, 60 years after it took place. Deatherage's reminiscences of life aboard the *Sioux City* evoke a bygone period of lazy days and nights on the river:

"The pleasure of a ride upon [the Missouri's] unruffled . . . waters was . . . a delight, and was not taken without a desire to repeat the invigorating trip, with its quiet gliding down near the banks, with the mighty forests which lined it at that time . . . making every day an enjoyable one as the passengers sat upon the cabin deck, touched by the gentle breeze as the fast receding trees and objects on the bank [seemed to be] swiftly gliding by.

"At Lexington, Dover and the small villages then lining the river, it was customary for the gay young parties to board these river steamers, and after the evening meal had been served, the tables and chairs removed from the cabin salon, the music maker, at that time an old-time fiddler, soon tuned the strings and rosined the bow, and the . . . gallant young men [and their sweethearts] were ready to execute the most intricate evolutions in the Virginia Reel. . . . It took but a few minutes for these revelers to persuade the captain . . . to tie up at Waverly, Missouri, and the gay young people were in for an all-night dance.

"At the break of day the bell is sounded, the roustabouts, Negro deckhands, heave-ho with the great stage plank. . . . Captain Woolford is at the wheel and the *Sioux City* slides out from her moorings. . . ." After many stops, loading and unloading cargo, getting wood and making repairs, the *Sioux City* was passing the town of Hermann on her return trip. "When about three miles below, we found the river spread out, until there was no water that would carry us over, so we returned to Hermann and unloaded the heavy freight, such as hogsheads of tobacco, and the next day again tried to cross the bar, without success, and we again returned to Hermann and unloaded practically all the freight on the boat, and again tried the bar, only to find the only hope the captain had of landing his overcrowded boat of passengers was impossible, so he again returned to Hermann and tied the boat up . . . and sent the passengers on the Missouri Pacific railroad to St. Louis. . . . We arrived in St. Louis about midnight, and the *Sioux City* came down about two weeks later."

Not all trips on the Missouri were as placid. One passenger, a Frenchman, left this alarming account of his journey upriver: "The river is so tortuous and the current so strong, that it took us four hours to pass the Sioux River junction, although making all possible steam. Our boat shuddered from stem to stern; the decks were awash and the bows sometimes vanished completely under water. We would make a few inches headway, only to drop back again, as the current appeared to redouble its strength. The captain was beside himself. He ordered a barrel of resin thrown into the fire-box—a solemn moment for us passengers, who were torn between fear and excitement." The reader is left hanging at this perilous moment, for the writer fails to relate the result of the incident, which he and the ship presumably survived.

The turbulent and unpredictable nature of the Missouri put a high premium on the skills of the men who could guide a steamboat through the shifting channels, over sand bars, and around the snags and innumerable bends that are characteristic of the river. A pilot in those days, according to Mark Twain, who had been one himself on the Mississippi, "was the only unfettered and entirely independent human being that lived in the earth." Technically it was not the pilot but the captain who was the ship's commanding officer. In reality, however, the captain's duties were generally limited to the overseeing of cargo loading and unloading, attending to the needs of passengers and cutting a fancy figure in the main salon, while the safety of the ship, its passengers and its freight rested with the pilot. In *Life on the Mississippi* Twain tells of the brief moments of authority enjoyed by the captain before necessity forced him to bow, often with ill-concealed chagrin, to the superior technical competence of the pilot. The minute the boat was underway, the pilot became, in the author's words, "a king without a keeper," in absolute control while afloat—a power that also made him vain as a peacock when ashore.

But even a proud and proficient Mississippi pilot was considered a neophyte when he tried to transfer over to the Missouri, at least until he had proved that he could extend his river sense to the unique challenges of Big Muddy. Those who could master the river were paid as much as $1,200 a month, a magnificent salary in those days, while the captain of the same vessel was likely to draw only $200. Occasionally the positions of captain and pilot were combined in one person, and for such a paragon a monthly stipend of $2,000 was neither unheard of nor unwarranted. Until the problems of Missouri River navigation were eased by construction engineers, owners of steamboats and freight barges were utterly dependent on the skills of the pilots to keep their investments afloat.

The coming of the railroad train, with its speed, relative safety and adherence to schedules, proved the deathblow to passenger traffic along the Missouri, and many thought that even freight barges could not compete in the age of rails. Indeed, for many years it seemed that the day of the Missouri River as a throughway for commerce was done. Government efforts to deepen the channel were condemned as "pork barrel" legislation, makework projects intended only to win votes for favored congressmen. During one period, in fact, Army engineers were operating three snag boats to keep the channel clear for only 15 commercial vessels. River enthusiasts of the time delighted in a joke that recounted the bewilderment of a visitor when he saw one of the Army ships on the Missouri. "What's that?" he asked a friend. "It's a government snag boat," came the reply. "Its job is to clear the channel so that other government snag boats can run up the river." Despite such mockings the dredging work went forward and today an eight-foot-deep channel extends from St. Louis to Sioux City, a distance of 735 miles.

Partly because of these efforts, the Missouri has once again become an important route for commerce. Barges of all descriptions, carrying grain, animal feeds, molasses, fertilizer and chemicals, ply its muddy waters. In 1967 Missouri River craft carried 2.6 million tons of commercial freight, 16 times the amount they had handled just 14 years earlier. Ironically, it is now the railroads that suffer because of competition from riverboats, for with a deep channel free of snags these craft are able to maintain tight schedules and haul freight cheaply and safely. In 1967 barges on the Missouri were actually carrying more grain south than were the railroads whose lines run through the plains.

Present-day efforts to improve navigation on the Missouri are part of an overall regional development scheme known as the Pick-Sloan Plan, which is aimed at harnessing the rivers of the Missouri Basin for a variety of purposes: irrigation, electric-power generation, conservation, recreation and, perhaps most important of all, flood control. Although Congress authorized the Pick-Sloan Plan as far back as 1944, it was not until the floods of

1951 and 1952 that work on the project began in earnest. The delay was caused primarily by disputes among competing pressure groups. Public power enthusiasts fought private power interests; conservationists debated with flood-control engineers; railroad lobbyists contended with barge line owners. Not even plainsmen who lived along the Missouri and its tributaries could agree on the proposal. Some upper basin dwellers long held the notion that the water they needed for irrigation and power would be drained away to keep the downstream navigation channel full. On the lower river, however, the cry was: "You're going to drown us out if the river isn't controlled." Given the acrimony of the debates, it seemed for a time that the Pick-Sloan Plan would never advance beyond the drawing boards and the debating forums. But the disasters of the early 1950s were a sobering influence, and since then much has been accomplished. The Missouri, if not yet entirely domesticated, has at least been caged and exploited.

Six major multipurpose dams are now in operation along the Missouri River's upper reaches, from Montana down to the South Dakota-Nebraska line. One of these, Oahe in South Dakota, which began producing power in 1962, is the world's largest rolled-earth dam. A reporter has written of Oahe that it is "so big that it seems less a dam than a reshuffling of geography. It rises 245 feet—higher than a 20-story office building—from the river bed. It is 9,300 feet long; underwater, from upstream heel to downstream toe, it measures more than a mile."

Oahe and the other dams along the upper river made an immediate impact upon the lives of plainsmen, many of whom suddenly found that electric power was available to them. As one observer wrote in 1962: "The result [of the damming of the upper Missouri] is most obvious in a night flight over the Dakotas. Formerly the plains below were a black void; now lights sparkle in nearly every farmyard. A decade ago the rural Dakotas were the nation's power 'desert,' with only 2 per cent of the farms electrified. Today more than 90 per cent of the area has electric lights."

Oahe Dam alone can generate more than half a million kilowatts of power, enough to meet the commercial, industrial and residential needs of a city of 500,000 people or the electric energy requirements of many thousands of farms; the reservoir behind the dam can hold 23.6 million acre-feet of water. From this reservoir will come water to irrigate 190,000 acres of farmland.

When the Pick-Sloan Plan is completed the six major dams on the upper Missouri will be complemented by about 125 smaller dams on the river's tributaries and 1,500 miles of levees and flood walls will protect some three million town and farmland acres that have been particularly susceptible to flooding. Though the original design called for irrigation projects that would affect five million acres, this work has progressed very slowly, and it now seems unlikely that more than a fraction of the land slated for irrigation will ever benefit from the Pick-Sloan Plan. Faulty research and overoptimistic reports by government engineers had created the impression that millions of marginal acres could be improved by irrigation. Only now is it becoming apparent that water alone would do little to enhance their fertility. Nor will the Pick-Sloan Plan completely forestall the threat of floods. "America never will be able to stop all flood damage," declares James R. Smith, an expert on the Missouri. "But thanks to the dams we can't have another major disaster like the last one in '52. What's impossible is protection against flash floods—where you get eight or more inches of rainfall in a few hours." Professionally involved in plains problems for many years, Smith echoes a widely held view that even greater progress in controlling the river could be achieved "if people's memories regarding floods weren't so notoriously short."

Shortness of memory has some advantages, however. It is an important ingredient in the persistent optimism in the Plains States region, the same optimism that helped plainsmen in former years challenge the "Great American Desert" in the hope that they might make it, in the Biblical words, "blossom as the rose." The grasslands rivers have in the past caused much suffering, but in the 20th Century, with the help of new control techniques, the Missouri and its tributaries are changing the pattern of plains life—and changing it radically for the better. In the Missouri Basin even normally taciturn people become enthusiastic when the subject of the river comes up.

They talk not simply about the minimization of flood damage, or those thousands of tons of freight that can now be hauled profitably by water, or the jump in industrial potential that inexpensive hydroelectric power makes possible. Each of these things is, of course, important in itself; of far greater import is the combination of all of them, for together they add up to a new opportunity for the plainsman. The harnessing of the Missouri River system promises a life in which less time need be spent in scratching out a living from the land and more can be spent in enjoying that living.

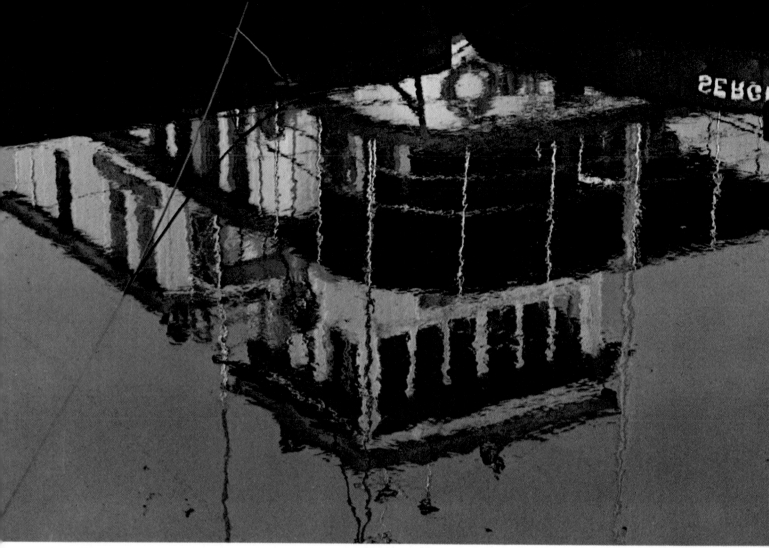

A mooring line cuts through a Missouri riverboat's shimmering reflection.

An old way of life on Big Muddy

Evoking a bygone era when the riverboat was king and the Missouri River was the highway to the West, the reflected image of the *Sergeant Floyd* dances on the surface of Big Muddy *(above)*. The *Floyd* is a modern diesel-powered vessel used by Army engineers who keep the Missouri navigable. But from its shallow-draft hull, drawing only four feet of water, to its boxy pilothouse, the *Floyd* is a descendant of the paddle-wheel steamboats that mastered the Missouri, from its mouth near St. Louis to Fort Benton, Montana—some 2,285 miles—more than a century ago. In the sturdy utility of its gear and the skillful work of its crew, shown in the photographs on the following pages, the *Floyd* is a reminder of the days before the railroads came, when steamboats carried settlers and adventurers on their historic journeys westward.

Photographs by Larry Nicholson

In the pilothouse the captain manipulates a rudder control to steer the ship.

A pair of speed control indicators dominate the engine-room instruments.

Well-used brooms and mops of a tidy boat are hung in a locker.

A deck hand prepares to cast off as the *Floyd* gets underway.

The port engine fuel valve.

A mop-filled porthole.

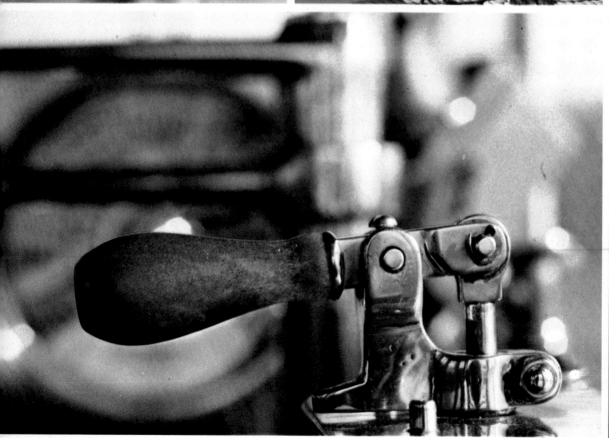

A searchlight control handle.

The emergency anchor.

A spare propeller and winch wheel.

The engine-room speaking tube.

The emergency fuel pump.

The whistle release valve.

Spare rope is always neatly coiled and stored.

A polished cuspidor is part of the pilothouse brass.

Binoculars hang ready for use by the captain.

Its lights twinkling at dusk, the *Sergeant Floyd* rides peacefully at a mooring.

The huge grain elevator above, owned by the Farmers Cooperative Commission Company in Hutchinson, Kansas, holds more than 15 million bushels of wheat. After harvest, grain is brought from local elevators to major markets such as Hutchinson or Minneapolis.

5

America's Breadbasket

For a few blistering hot days in August 1955, a dozen Russian agronomists were escorted around a number of Plains States farms. They admired cornfields, grunting hogs and the processing techniques of a meat packer and marveled at the efficiency of the American farmer. And on an elm-shaded lawn framing a farmhouse in Rice County, Minnesota, they met a U.S. Senator who won them, they said, because he had the rough and calloused hands of a farmer. The lawmaker came by the distinction honestly. No gentleman landowner like Thomas Jefferson, Ed Thye, a descendant of a Scandinavian immigrant, had tilled his own fields, wringing prosperity from the land and becoming a highly respected member of the community. Eventually he served the people of his state as deputy commissioner of agriculture, lieutenant governor and governor before being sent to the Senate in Washington, where he represented Minnesota for 12 years.

Few Americans would share the Russians' surprise in finding a man of prestige whose hands were calloused, but the story illustrates an abiding truth about the plains region. The fact that it is predominantly agrarian in no way limits the array of opportunities it offers. A farmer who exchanges his overalls for a lawmaker's toga is not at all uncommon; nor indeed is his neighbor who makes it big in money as well as prestige. They say in Hyannis, Nebraska, out in the Sand Hills of Grant County, that they have more retired millionaires per capita than any other American small town. These Nebraskans have made their fortunes raising cattle and some call their county "Cadillac and

Jeep country," because four-wheel drive is a necessity for negotiating the sandy backlands and a luxury car proclaims a man's status when he takes to the highway.

The significant role of crops and livestock in the plains economy extends through all seven states. In four states more than 90 per cent of the land is devoted to crops or animal husbandry. Acreage yields for wheat and corn are so high as to make the plains not only the primary agricultural resource of the nation, but a supplier of food to much of the world as well. Time and again, grain from the plains has saved hundreds of thousands in India, Southeast Asia, Africa and the Middle East from starvation. And in the years just after World War II, produce from the Plains States played a vital role in the emergency relief programs that helped feed Europe's millions.

Kansas alone produces almost one fifth of the nation's winter wheat, more than any other state in the Union; and North Dakota tops the country in spring and durum wheat. Illinois, it is true, sometimes outproduces Iowa in the total amount of corn harvested, but the latter state, year in and year out, leads the plains region in annual yields. Land is rich in much of the region, particularly in the portion east of the 100th meridian (25 per cent of the best topsoil in the U.S. is within Iowa's boundaries), and this factor, combined with the sturdy yeomanry of its settlers, helped to develop the efficient, successful farms that today make this region the nation's breadbasket.

So efficient, in fact, is agriculture in the Plains States that some farmers have become victims of their neighbors' success. The growing of grains to feed the nation requires fewer and fewer farmers, and competition, despite the host of subsidies that the federal government offers, is becoming ever more severe. The trend on the plains, seemingly irreversible, is toward highly capitalized farms. Those farmers who cannot raise the money to buy and maintain the expensive equipment necessary to compete are finding their occupation less and less rewarding, particularly in light of the opportunities available in the nearby small and large cities. But those farmers who have successfully negotiated the financial barriers, who have learned to use the most advanced farm machinery and techniques, who are exploiting the fertile soil to its fullest potential, are continually ringing up record acreage yields and prospering.

The natural richness of much of the plains is due to the combination of topography and the specific properties of the local soil. Some scientists believe that the plains were once submerged beneath the sea. According to this theory thick layers of erosional debris were carried by the waters and spread out along the bottom. When the waters receded, great deposits of marine organisms were left behind, their skeletons eventually forming chalk and calcium, which are valuable soil nutrients. Retreating glaciers left still more rich material for soil formation on the northern portion of the plains region and smoothed the surface of the land as well.

Climate, weather and drainage factors also affect the soil, helping to determine just what forms of vegetable life are suitable to a particular area. On the plains these factors combined to produce conditions unfavorable to the growth of forests but favorable to the growth of grass, one of the richest of all possible soil nutrients. The thickness of the grass cover in the region has been limited only by the amount of rainfall: the more rain the more luxuriant the cover. Thus in humid areas of the plains —mostly in Missouri, Iowa and southern Minnesota—grass can grow luxuriantly and the land is ideal for farming. Conversely, the chief drawback for agriculture in the more arid reaches of the plains, where the grass cover was never as thick, has been the difficulty farmers have had in irrigating their holdings.

Even in the supposedly well-watered areas, the pioneer farmers had to learn how to guard against drought and how to manage the soil properly, though sometimes the land was bountiful enough to foster dangerous delusions of grandeur. In 1853 a Minnesota farmer grew a rutabaga weighing 19.5 pounds, and not far away an onion measuring five and a half inches in diameter was reported. Although such things are freaks of nature, the fact that vegetable giants came out of the heretofore unplowed sod encouraged many an early plainsman in his mistaken belief that the soil would never wear out.

During the great era of settlement, few farmers gave much thought to soil management, or for that matter to anything besides feeding their families and turning a big profit as quickly as possible. Wheat was the crop that promised the greatest rewards, and by 1874 a farm editor was cautioning: "Don't risk your *all* on wheat. Raise corn and hogs, oats, barley, hay, flax, potatoes, sheep, cattle, poultry, bees—anything that is profitable so that if any . . . calamities befall you as they have thousands of wheat growers in the west . . . you may have some other reliance to depend on." Advice of this kind generally fell on deaf ears. In Minnesota and the Dakotas in those early days, wheat was considered the get-rich-quick crop, the best choice for a farmer trying to establish himself. And for some the prescription worked. Beginning in the middle 1870s, in the wide Red River Valley shared by western Minnesota and the eastern Dakotas, an experiment in large-scale mechanized farming got under way. The rich valley land was so vast, a speaker told an Eastern audience, that were it not for the Red River cutting it in two, a man could plow an uninterrupted furrow that would equal the distance between Boston and Philadelphia.

Nothing had a bigger, wider, Western-style sweep than these monster holdings, which were popularly known as bonanza farms. One of these wheat plantations had 40,000 acres under cultivation, and several others encompassed more than 10,000 acres of prime agricultural land. On many bonanza farms 40 to 50 multiteam plows in formation broke the sod in the fall; months later, after harrowing, 20 or more seeders or grain drills moved across the fields to plant the wheat; and at harvesttime the cutting and binding was done by machines that covered several hundred acres a day. Often hundreds of field hands were hired by a single employer during the harvest season.

Like other bonanzas, the giant Red River farms were gambles that paid off for a few but in the end proved impractical. The Eastern financiers who put up much of the capital for these enterprises were interested only in a high return on their investment; when the droughts of the late 1880s resulted in several years of poor harvests, the capitalists, in an effort to cut their losses, began selling off the land in small parcels to local farmers. Neither the science of agriculture nor the technology of farming were as yet far enough advanced to sustain these extensive wheat operations for very long. Nevertheless, the size of the bonanza farms presaged the giant wheat and corn spreads that now dot the Plains States and are today among the most efficient—and most scientific—of all American agricultural enterprises.

In Kansas and Nebraska as well as in Minnesota and the Dakotas, many plainsmen limited themselves to a single crop, but unlike their neighbors to the north they planted corn instead of wheat because many had moved west from Ohio, Indiana or Illinois, where corn was already the staple crop and the farmers were familiar with the planting and harvesting procedures for this grain. In addition, corn had a number of advantages over wheat, especially for the subsistence farmer who was less interested in a cash crop than in raising food for his family and his livestock. Corn required consid-

erably less soil preparation and was a better animal fodder. Furthermore, though the market price was often less than half that of the finer grain, high acreage yields from cornfields might make up the difference, and price was often relatively unimportant to the farmer who consumed much of his own produce and who lacked transportation facilities to get his product to market.

During the last half century, there has been a change in land-use patterns on the plains. A greater understanding of the capabilities of the land and a wider experience with the techniques of scientific agriculture have persuaded farmers to alter their planting practices. Some areas that once produced corn almost exclusively—such as Sedgwick County in southern Kansas—are now leading centers of winter-wheat production, while other areas once dominated by wheat now produce a variety of crops. But a long process of trial and error was necessary before farmers learned which crops were best suited to their own parcels of land. Minnesota wheat enthusiasts only gradually discovered that diversified farming, with emphasis on corn, was much more profitable for them than a reliance on wheat. By the 1960s, Minnesota farmers were growing only one thirteenth as much wheat as corn and many were finding such crops as oats and alfalfa highly profitable.

Carefully controlled experimentation has been even more important than trial and error. Alfalfa, for example, was a crop infrequently planted in the northern plains until a 19th Century German immigrant, Wendelin Grimm, determined to develop a strain hardy enough to weather the harsh winters of Minnesota. Starting with a bag of seed brought over from his homeland, and then sowing and resowing from plants that had survived the subzero winter months, Grimm gradually brought into existence an alfalfa strain suitable to the climate of the plains. In due course this crop became a staple in the region.

Hybrid corn is another grain that has benefited greatly from experimentation carried on by plains agronomists, even though the earliest varieties were developed in other regions. Work on many strains of hybrid corn has continued under the direction of government and agricultural college scientists, such as the Iowa State College researchers who for many years maintained a center in Guatemala for studying corn variants dating as far back as pre-Columbian civilizations. In years past, the U.S. Department of Agriculture has sent agronomists to Argentina, Ethiopia, the Middle East and even the Kirghiz Steppes of central Asia to bring back

Dust Clouds Rolling Over The Prairies

A menacing cloud of wind-whipped dust blackens the sky only moments before engulfing Hugoton, Kansas, during the worst days of the Dust Bowl of the 1930s. For many decades, plains farmers had plowed up the moisture-conserving sod and neglected soil conservation measures. When a prolonged period of drought occurred, the loose and all but weightless topsoil simply blew away.

wheat seed that might improve the yield of crops on the dry High Plains farms.

Even before plainsmen began to concern themselves with such sophisticated matters as hybrids, many were forced to deal with the more immediate problems of insufficient rainfall and frequent dangerous windstorms. Homesteaders in western Nebraska, for example, rather than give up their claims to the deep, fertile loam of the North Platte Valley, struggled to devise workable irrigation systems; as a result, the valley—where rainfall can be as little as 10 inches a year (compared with 20 to 40 inches in Iowa)—now produces hundreds of thousands of tons of sugar beets and thousands of tons of potatoes and dry beans.

Contributing mightily to the prosperity of the Plains States agriculture will be irrigation made possible by the new Missouri River dams. A quarter of a million acres in eastern North Dakota will be brought into more profitable use by the Garrison Dam, and the Oahe Dam near Pierre, South Dakota, will similarly affect an area almost as large. Irrigation for Dakota cattlemen means more home-grown corn with which to fatten livestock, so that fewer head need to be sent out of state for fattening on their way to market.

These vast irrigation projects, financed by the federal government, represent a triumph for the farmers of the semiarid portions of the plains. Until recently the farmers had to rely solely on individual or cooperative efforts to guarantee sufficient water for their crops. In some instances, local cooperatives attempted small-scale projects to divert streams for irrigation, but in general the practice was for each farmer to look to his own water supply. Most plainsmen dug deep wells and set up windmills to pump the water. In this sense, wind has been made to serve the plainsman, for without windmills—drawing water from great underground depths—it would have been impossible for many of the pioneers to irrigate even small plots or to slake the thirst of livestock. The skeletal profiles of windmills remain characteristic of the horizontal landscape. More often than not, however, the wind in itself has been a menace to grassland agriculture. Dry, burning summer winds are destructive. During one Kansas summer 10 million bushels of corn were flattened by the wind. The author Walter Prescott Webb wrote that "the economic disaster occasioned by these hot winds is terrible. Everything goes before the furnace blast. . . . It is not uncommon for fine fields of dark-green corn to be destroyed in two days. The hope of the farmer is to mature the corn before the hot winds begin to blow." Many of today's plains-men lived through the dust storms of the 1930s, and they recall that in 1934 they had some of the lowest yields in the country. The dry, loose soil simply blew into the air, and hundreds of miles away, in cities like Minneapolis, Dakota earth covered the floors of houses, while thousands of miles away, in the Atlantic Ocean, ships reported that they were being lightly coated with dust that clearly had come from the plains. A contemporary report describes the November day in 1933 when the farms of South Dakota first began to blow away:

"By mid-morning a gale was blowing, cold and black. By noon it was blacker than night, because one can see through night and this was an opaque black. It was a wall of dirt. . . .

"When the wind died and the sun shone forth again, it was on a different world. There were no fields, only sand drifting into mounds and eddies that swirled in what was now but an autumn breeze. There was no longer a section-line road 50 feet from the front door. It was obliterated. In the farmyard, fences, machinery and trees were gone, buried. The roofs of sheds stuck out through drifts deeper than a man is tall."

Drought had piled on drought, and disaster had struck because so much of the sod that had held the plains soil intact had been plowed under. Methods have since been devised to help keep the soil in place, but some experts say that dust-bowl cycles on the plains are probably inevitable. "They are as much a part of that region," a leading soil conservationist wrote after more than a score of years of study, "as tumbleweed and devil-dusters. The climatic pattern of recent decades is a continuation of a long past of erratic behavior which is recorded in every aspect of the landscape."

Dust storms may never be completely eliminated, but the damage they do can be minimized. Soil conservation measures, such as terracing and fallowing (the plowing of fields left unplanted), husband the moisture that comes naturally to the ground, helping to hold the soil in place. Increased irrigation also helps the earth resist the howling winds. And other afflictions that once harassed the farmer have been either eradicated or greatly alleviated by modern scientific techniques. The millions of grasshoppers that once swooped down upon the plains to strip the wheat and cornstalks bare have been held in check by chemical sprays, thus saving untold millions of dollars worth of crops. Many other insect pests have been dealt with in a similar fashion.

While scientific agriculture has made tremendous contributions toward easing the plainsman's lot, equally important have been the political and economic actions taken by the farmers themselves against powerfully entrenched forces that had profited from their misery. Most of these militant activities arose out of radical movements that for many years flourished on the plains.

Almost from the moment that immigrant farmers began to flood into the plains they found themselves squeezed in an economic vise that seemed to tighten year after year. For one thing, the farmers were caught between the rising cost of things they needed—implements, machinery, household furniture and the like—and the falling prices they received for their produce. Between 1870 and 1897 the price of wheat, for example, plummeted from $1.07 to 63 cents per bushel, while corn in the same years fell from 43 cents to 30 cents per bushel.

Beyond this, the farmer had to pay freight charges for transporting his produce to market, and in his view these fees were excessively high and discriminatory. In 1897, for example, the Pennsylvania Railroad charged only 56 cents to haul a ton one mile along its tracks east of Chicago. The Burlington Railroad, however, charged 78 cents per ton-mile between Chicago and the Missouri River and $1.28 per ton-mile west of the Missouri. The railroads, for their part, tried to justify these rates with the plea that operating expenses were higher in the West. The sparseness of the population contributed to these costs but even more important was the one-way traffic across the prairies. During those times of year, especially in the spring, when the farmers needed supplies, fully loaded freight cars headed west on the plains and returned east either empty or with very small cargoes. During the harvest season, the process was reversed, with westbound trains empty and eastbound trains filled with wheat and corn. Less easy to explain, however, were certain other practices that gouged the farmer. It was not unusual for the railroads to lower their rates during periods when farmers could use river transport to send their produce east, only to raise the rates again when the rivers froze over or flooded. Another favorite device was the system of "transit rates" by which the railroad billed the farmer for the full distance to the line's eastern terminus, no matter how far the shipment went. Thus, if a farmer in Nebraska was shipping grain to a point 100 miles away, he would be charged as much as a neighboring farmer who was shipping grain all the way to Chicago. Sometimes the railroad would refund a portion of the "transit rate," but the amount returned to the farmer was set by the company.

Other practices were equally outrageous and unethical. The roads commonly scheduled stops at only one loading point in each town. There a businessman favored by the railroad would set up a grain elevator. The elevator operator bought grain from the farmers at prices somewhat related to those paid at big city markets. But it was the operator who graded the grain, and since the railroad would stop for loading only at his establishment, his word was law. Farmers had little choice but to accept the elevator owner's assessment of their grain's worth. They were often forced to sell their grain at prices below the amount they would have received had they had access to a truly free market. As a result many farmers found that their expenses far exceeded their cash return.

As the farmers' incomes fell, their anger rose. They began to suspect that they were the victims of a conspiracy hatched by Eastern capitalists, a conspiracy to depress their standard of living by keeping their income artificially low and their costs artificially high. In the United States the last half of the 19th Century was an age of runaway economic expansion, of combinations of great wealth and of trusts and monopolies. Economic practices were based on the old formula of high profits and low turnover. Industrialists found it to their mutual advantage to suppress competition by forming tremendous trusts that could gouge the hapless consumer, forcing him to pay outrageous prices for his needs. The farmers, pushed until their backs were against the wall, had no choice but to organize and hit back. Agrarian discontent became agrarian revolt as farmers attempted to roll back the tide of high prices and low returns. The highhanded tactics of the railroads and their friends lit a spark on the plains that flared into a raging fire during hard times, only to be dampened by good times and to blaze forth anew, again and again with each economic recession.

The first organized expression of the farmers' discontent was the National Grange of the Patrons of Husbandry, better known as the Grange. This organization was originally established in 1867 by a Department of Agriculture clerk to provide farmers and their wives with facilities for social gatherings that could relieve the monotony of their lives. By 1874, membership in the Grange had soared to 1.5 million and the major purpose of the organization had become political and economic. Throughout the Plains States as well as in other regions of

the nation, the Grange offered the farmers meetinghouses in which they could discuss their mutual problems and propose remedies. On the political level the farmers hit upon a way to reward their friends and punish their foes by supporting rurally oriented candidates for the state legislatures, men who would enact laws to regulate freight rates and oversee the operations of grain elevator owners. On an economic level the farmers, with Grange support, began organizing consumer and producer cooperatives to lower the prices of equipment. By 1874, legislation had been passed in Iowa and Minnesota, as well as in some nearby states, setting freight and grain elevator rates within their borders. Although a number of these laws were later repealed as a result of overwhelming pressures exerted by the railroads, they led eventually to the modern system of state and federal regulation of public-utility rates.

On the economic front the farmers met with varying success. Their consumer cooperatives often did force prices down, and one major U.S. mail-order house, Montgomery Ward, was founded with the explicit purpose of selling goods to these cooperatives to "meet the wants of the Patrons of Husbandry." But when the farmers attempted to operate cooperatively owned factories to produce plows and reapers, they generally met with failure, for private manufacturers quickly lowered their prices and drove the fledgling enterprises out of business. In the end most of these early cooperatives foundered, though not before they had proved that farmers could and would form combinations of their own to get the things they needed at reasonable prices. The day when manufacturers of plows could, with impunity, combine into a monopoly and then raise the price of their product by 100 per cent was fast drawing to a close.

Although the Grange was successful in mobilizing farmers, particularly in Minnesota, Iowa and Missouri, it was not to remain a powerful weapon of social reform. The farmers were much too individualistic to submit for long to even the minimal discipline that a political and economic program requires. When, in the late 1870s, the nation began to enjoy a brief period of general prosperity and commodity prices began to rise once more, the plainsman quickly abjured militancy and returned to his plow to cash in on the boom. In fact, the tillers of the soil suddenly found themselves courted and flattered by Eastern financiers looking for a place to invest their funds. Throughout the plains, agents of Eastern mortgage companies ranged far and wide literally begging the once-despised farm-

Bitter feelings aroused by the Populist movement of the late 19th Century led to the occupation of the Kansas legislature's Hall of Representatives by these armed Republicans in 1893. The troubles began after a disputed election in which both Populists and Republicans claimed a majority in the Hall of Representatives. When attempts at compromise failed and dialogue degenerated into riot, the Populists took control of the legislative hall. Soon rifle-carrying Republicans smashed down the door, drove out the Populists, then barricaded themselves inside the chamber. After the recently elected Populist Governor directed the militia to eject the Republicans, a truce was called and the dispute was taken to the Kansas Supreme Court; it upheld the Republican claim to a majority.

ers to take out loans secured by their chattels (equipment) or homesteads, and few plainsmen could resist the temptation. A mood of rampant optimism had seized the nation, and both farmer and moneylender believed that no finer investment could be made than in plains acreage. Kansas farmland that sold for $15 per acre in 1870 sky-rocketed to $270 per acre less than a decade later, and small-town building lots soared 1,000 per cent in value. The country in general and the plains in particular went on a financial binge, and even many sober-minded citizens allowed themselves to be swept up in the heady climate and began counseling the virtue of debt.

Like every other binge, this one ended in a monumental hangover. The droughts and freezes that destroyed thousands of plains cattle in 1886 and 1887 brought a full measure of grief to the farmers. Suddenly they could not meet their obligations, and the 10 per cent chattel mortgages and 8 per cent homestead mortgages so lightly entered into a few years earlier now became dead weights to drag them down to ruin. Debt-ridden and hounded by poor harvests, the plains farmers could see no solution to their predicament except to give up their farms or go even more deeply into the red in the hope that a sudden turn in the economic cycle

would bail them out. But Eastern lenders, once so liberal with their money, now turned the farmers away and loan sharks moved in, charging usurious interest rates. The inevitable result was repeated foreclosures. Between 1889 and 1893 about 11,000 farmers in Kansas lost their holdings and were forced either to leave the land or become tenants. Similar events were occurring throughout the plains, and the dream of the independent yeoman harvesting his own crop was fading fast, to be replaced by the nightmare of tenant farming and sharecropping. Suddenly militancy was awakened, but this time it was directed not just at the railroads and the manufacturers, but at the most sacrosanct of all capitalist institutions, the monetary system based on gold.

The farmer now saw his plight more and more in terms of currency. There was just not enough money coming in to meet his obligations, and he reasoned that this was because there was not enough money in circulation. This state of affairs would continue, so he thought, as long as every dollar had to be secured by that relatively scarce mineral, gold. But if silver became a partner with gold as a backing for the currency, more money could be minted. The inevitable result would be inflation, enabling the farmers to receive higher

Turn-of-the-century spokesman of the Western farmer, William Jennings Bryan examines wheatstalks near his Nebraska home. His fiery oratory in favor of economic reform made him a paragon to plains farmers and an anathema to Eastern financiers. In 1896, 1900 and 1908 he was the Democratic candidate for President.

prices for their crops and thus pay off their debts more easily. In other words, obligations contracted when the currency was "hard" would be discharged with newly debased coin. Leading the agitation for reform were such crusaders as Mary Elizabeth Lease of Kansas, who told farmers to "raise less corn and more hell," and "Sockless Jerry" Simpson, a one-time Great Lakes sailor, who vigorously denounced the railroads and called for government ownership as the only adequate solution.

In 1892 the People's Party (better known as the Populists) was formed and on July 4 of that year it nominated for President of the United States James B. Weaver, a spellbinder from Iowa. Weaver's platform included the "free and unlimited" coinage of silver, a graduated income tax and the establishment of a postal savings system. Although he campaigned extensively, Weaver received only one million votes and carried but four states, including Kansas. But despite this disappointing showing the Populists had proved themselves to be a force to be reckoned with. During the next four years, as the agricultural depression deepened, their influence grew apace.

In 1896 the Democratic Party, in a dramatic political upheaval, nominated William Jennings Bryan, the "boy orator" of Nebraska, who stampeded the convention with one of the most famous speeches ever delivered by an American. "If they [the Republicans] dare come out in the open field and defend the gold standard as a good thing," Bryan shouted to the sweltering delegates in Chicago, "we will fight them to the uttermost. Having behind us the producing masses of the nation and the world, supported by the commercial interests, the laboring interests and the toilers everywhere, we will answer their demand for a gold standard by saying to them: 'You shall not press down upon the brow of labor this crown of thorns, you shall not crucify mankind upon a cross of gold.' "

Here then was a challenge to the rulers of America. One of the two major parties had been taken over by people whom the moneyed interests of the nation must have considered to be at best foggy-minded visionaries and at worst revolutionaries bent on the complete destruction of the prevailing social and political order. William Allen White, a Kansan and the longtime editor and publisher of the *Emporia Gazette*, recalled in his autobiography the fear and disdain that the nomination of Bryan roused in conservative breasts. "To me, he [Bryan] was an incarnation of demagogy, the apotheosis of riot, destruction and carnage. A little group of us were standing around the ticker as the story came in, and I can remember someone . . . cried out as the drama climaxed in Bryan's nomination: 'Marat, Marat, Marat has won!' "

Certainly White and his fellow conservatives shared this view of Bryan as the spiritual descendant of Jean Paul Marat, one of the most radical leaders of the French Revolution. In their eyes Bryan represented the destruction of all the great American virtues: thrift, hard work, hard money and free enterprise. In anger White sat down and composed an indictment of his fellow Kansans, and, by implication, all other Plains States farmers who supported the Democratic cause. This editorial, entitled "What's the Matter with Kansas?", was distributed by Republican politicians and their conservative allies around the U.S. to aid their candidate, William McKinley. White quoted Bryan as saying, "There are two ideas of government. There are those who believe that if you legislate to make the well-to-do prosperous, this prosperity will leak through on those below. The Democratic idea has been that if you legislate to make the masses prosperous their prosperity will find its way up and through every class."

Then White heaped scorn upon the Democratic formula for prosperity. "That's the stuff!" he wrote. "Give the prosperous man the dickens! Legislate the thriftless man into ease, whack the stuffing out of the creditors and tell the debtors who borrowed the money five years ago when money 'per capita' was greater . . . that the contraction of currency gives him the right to repudiate.

"Whoop it up for the ragged trousers: put the lazy, greasy fizzle, who can't pay his debts, on the altar, and bow down and worship him. Let the state ideal be high. What we need is not the respect of our fellow men, but the chance to get something for nothing."

Though some Republican politicians credited White's blast with helping to provide the 600,000 margin that McKinley gained over Bryan in the election, it is more likely that the economic threats from employers and creditors were even more decisive. As White himself wrote, "McKinley won because the Republicans had persuaded the middle class, almost to a man, that a threat to the gold standard was a threat to their property. Incidentally, labor as a class was persuaded to the point of coercion, that if McKinley was defeated industry would shut down."

The 1896 Bryan campaign marked a high-water point for the tide of rural discontent. From there the tide quickly receded, not to rise again in any really powerful and nationwide movement for more than three decades.

Soon free coinage of silver ceased to be a major preoccupation of the plainsman, partly because newly discovered gold mines in Alaska, Africa and Australia loosened the supply of that precious metal and increased the amount of currency in circulation. More important, however, was the return of good times to the U.S. as a whole. By the turn of the century, farmers of the plains were benefiting from a period of general prosperity and rising prices. A decade and a half later, World War I contributed to the farmers' renewed sense of optimism —and to their false sense of security—as government purchases of agricultural produce and exports to a war-torn and food-scarce Europe sent commodity prices skyrocketing.

Contributing to the decline of rural radicalism was the fact that many Populist demands were slowly being met. Railroad regulation, the direct election of U.S. senators, and the graduated income tax were all becoming either the law of the land or the accepted practice of many states. Proposals that had seemed dangerously radical in the 1890s came to be accepted as reasonable and necessary reforms before the 20th Century was two decades old.

By the end of World War I many a plains farmer probably believed that prosperity would go on forever, but soon he was to be roughly disabused. Europe was beginning to produce enough food to feed itself once again, thus reducing the export market. Agricultural abundance in America was quickly becoming agricultural glut, and grain prices tumbled in the wake of the federal government's removal of wartime price supports. Almost a decade before the cities of the nation fell into the Great Depression, the farming regions were beginning to hurt badly. When the Depression of the '30s finally struck the entire country, the plains farmer was thrown even deeper into hard times. Not only were prices low, but the farmers were hit by a series of crop failures. The old dolorous cycle of debt, default and foreclosure reasserted itself and the plainsman's radicalism was reawakened from its long slumber. No longer would he accept his ill fortune with mere verbal protests and electoral maneuverings. There were plenty of protests, of course, but this time there was direct action, as well.

Reformist political organizations like Minnesota's Farmer-Labor Party and North Dakota's Non-Partisan League were swept into power on a tide of rural militancy. In 1933 Governor Floyd Olsen of Minnesota declared a moratorium on mortgage foreclosures, and North Dakota's Governor William Langer actually called out the state militia to prevent the forced sale of farms. And throughout the plains, farmers were taking matters into their own hands. Foreclosure auctions often turned into tense encounters between the authorities charged with selling properties at the highest possible prices and local farmers determined that their neighbors not lose their holdings. Various tactics were employed to thwart the bankers and tax collectors at these sales. One of the most popular was the one-cent bid. A group of farmers would gather at the auction site and put in a penny bid. Their menacing looks, accompanied perhaps by a rifle or two, effectively silenced other would-be buyers. Upon acceptance of the single bid, the deed to the property was turned over to the about-to-be dispossessed farmer.

Even in so rich a state as Iowa the hard-pressed farmers struck back against the system that had laid them low. They engaged in militant action to force up the price of grain by withholding it from wholesalers, and they terrorized truckers bringing produce into market.

Although violence on the plains was sporadic during the early years of the Depression, the plight of the farmer stood as a constant reproach to America. One of the first items of business for Franklin D. Roosevelt's Administration in 1933 was to find some solution to the farm problem. Out of the fertile brains of New Deal bureaucrats and their successors have come proposal after proposal to alleviate the farmers' distress. The Commodity Credit Corporation, acreage allotments, subsidies, price supports, conservation measures and a host of other remedies have been tried with varying degrees of success. On the one hand, the nation's agriculture has responded to Washington's efforts. Harvests grow bigger and bigger, and many farmers who are able to take full advantage of government programs have become rich men. On the other hand, however, many farm problems remain unsolved. Government programs have been most effective in helping the already efficient to become even more efficient, the already well-off to become more wealthy. The marginal farmer, with 160 or 200 acres, has had neither the acreage nor the capital to benefit fully from Washington's largess, and the result has been the slow but steady decline of the small family farm in favor of increasingly large spreads.

The sophisticated machinery necessary to operate a farm at peak efficiency can sometimes cost more than the land itself; a single combine, or harvesting machine, sells for about $11,000, and many farms on the plains use about $60,000 worth of equipment. The trend is toward still higher investments, and the governor of the Farm Credit Administration, which lends several billion dollars a year to help farmers take advantage of the new technology, has predicted that by 1980 the typical family-owned farm will require a total capitalization ranging from $100,000 to $250,000.

The problem is that on the plains, as almost everywhere else in the nation, the small farm is no longer an economically viable institution. "I've almost paid off my mortgage now," one Minnesota dairy farmer said recently, adding that he is "very nicely set up" to milk 25 cows. "Trouble is," he went on, "to make a living I should be milking thirty-five cows now. Which means I need ten cows, a bigger barn, a bigger silo, more crop land, more pasture, a bigger tractor—so on right down the line. If I borrow money to do these things, I won't be half paid back before I'll probably need *fifty* cows to keep up. Sometimes I think, if my wife and I were paid fifty cents an hour for the time we spent working this farm, we'd come out ahead."

The plaint of this man is not unusual; it is echoed throughout the region on every kind of farm. But if some plains farmers have doubts about the future, there are many for whom tomorrow holds no dread. For the farmer who combines high intelligence, a thorough knowledge of his land and its capabilities, and access to the capital needed to buy the most up-to-date equipment and more land, the future never looked brighter. As one successful corn grower put it: "Agriculture is perfectly sound —at least around here it is. I'm buying land. I say that this land is worth whatever you have to pay to get it." In South Dakota the average size of farms increased from 439 acres in 1930 to 917 in the mid-1960s. In Hughes County in that same state, farms at the turn of the century averaged less than 300 acres; recently the trend has been toward combined wheat and cattle farming, and the average holding today encompasses 1,700 acres.

Even with intelligence, knowledge and capital, a farmer needs a measure of luck, for the uncertainties of weather make farming in many parts of the region at best a calculated risk. A wheat farmer in western North Dakota, for example, may make a killing one year when the spring starts early and there is sufficient rain to water his crops, but for the next two or three years his acreage may produce next to nothing. Of course, it is the man with a large farm who is in the best position to withstand the vagaries of nature, for he can fall back on secondary crops and at the same time continue to receive government checks for hundreds of acres left fallow. Still, in spite of fickle weather, income earned by North Dakota farm products, for example, jumped about $200 million in a four-year period in the 1960s. The state not only led all others in the production of durum and other types of spring wheat, but in barley, rye and flaxseed as well.

Such gains reflect an immense rise in the use of self-propelled farm machinery. Agronomist Edward Higbee dramatically summed up the revolutionary effects of farm mechanization when he wrote: "From the days of the Pharaohs to the year 1800, two men with sickles were able to cut, bind and shock one acre of wheat per day. Between 1800 and 1830, two men with cradles could cut, bind and shock two acres of wheat. In 1896, two men with three horses and one mechanical binder could cut and shock ten acres of wheat a day. In 1930, two men with one 12-foot combine and one tractor could cut and thresh 25 acres of wheat per day. In 1956, one man with a 16-foot self-propelled combine could cut and thresh 30 acres. Between 1800 and 1956 efficiency in harvesting wheat multiplied 60 times because of machines." The resulting ef-

Juggernaut of the wheatfields

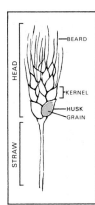

The machine in the cutaway drawing below is a combine, or self-propelled combined harvester-thresher, the latest in a long line of labor-saving devices that have virtually automated the huge wheat harvests of the Plains States. Performing the six operations described on this page, the combine devours its way across the wheatfields, separating grain from the wheat plant *(left)* in a matter of minutes. The one-man combine, which is often owned and shared by a group of wheat farmers, can harvest 50 acres in a day—a task that would have required scores of men in the days before machinery.

1 REAPING

The four wooden bats of the reel push the standing wheat against the serrated cutter bar, which cuts a swath up to 22 feet wide. Two cylindrical feeders pick up the cut wheat and deliver it to a conveyor belt, which carries it to the threshing unit. The cutting apparatus is similar to that of Cyrus McCormick's reaper, the machine that began the agricultural revolution in 1834. Before then, the scythe was the traditional cutting tool.

2 THRESHING

The cut wheat is pushed under the thresher, a revolving cylinder, which rubs the grain-bearing kernels from the straw and at the same time loosens their protective husks. The kernels then fall through the kernel separating grate onto the kernel conveyor belt, which carries them to the cleaning area. Meanwhile, the unwanted straw is guided from the thresher by the straw separator. Farmers of ancient times had to thresh their wheat with a flail.

3 CLEANING

To separate the grain from the husks, the kernels are passed over the chaffers, a series of oscillating sieves and screens. The agitation shakes off the husks—which become powdery chaff; the cleaned grain drops into the grain elevator. Meanwhile, a fan blows the chaff out in a spray of dust. In the old days, cleaning was usually done by hand. Using sieves, farmers tossed the kernels into the air until the chaff blew away or fell to the ground.

4 STORAGE

Clean grain from the chaffers, ready for the market minutes after being part of a living plant, is lifted by the grain elevator to a grain storage tank that holds from 50 to 100 bushels. When the tank is full, the grain is transferred to a truck or trailer through a high-speed grain unloader, which can empty the tank in little more than a minute. Sometimes, trucks and combines move together, the tanks being emptied as the combines continue to harvest.

5 RETHRESHING

Although up to 90 per cent of the wheat kernels entering the combine are processed into grain, the machine also seeks out stray kernels that it might have overlooked. One source is tailings, or unthreshed kernels, which once were left for gleaners. The tailings fall out of the chaffers because they are bigger than other kernels. They drop into the tailings elevator, which takes them back to the threshing cylinder for rethreshing and cleaning.

6 STRAW REMOVAL

Another source of stray kernels is the straw that is discarded after the threshing process. The straw passes beneath the straw separator, a roller that guides it onto the straw walkers, a series of oscillating racks that pitch the straw rearward and out onto the mowed field. The straw walkers also sift out any remaining kernels. These fall through small openings into the kernel return pans, which drop them onto the chaffers for cleaning.

fect of such advances on American life has, of course, been tremendous.

One major result is that increasingly large numbers of farmers, on the plains as elsewhere, are fleeing the land. The trend has been illustrated by a recent Iowa State University study of an eight-county area in south-central Iowa. In 1960 about 81,000 people lived there, many of them farmers and almost all of them in one way or another dependent on the land for their livelihoods. By 1970, the study predicted, the population would fall to 67,000, and if the projections are correct, by 1980 only 54,000 people will live in the eight counties. Already the average farmer in the area is past 50 years of age, and no one expects massive infusions of young blood to replace the elderly.

Another result is that in some places hired help is harder to find than ever before. "I plead with young high school graduates . . . to go the farm hand route," an Iowa rural employment expert told a reporter in 1966. "They tell me they absolutely will not work as hired hands. They take factory jobs instead." In a sense the youngsters who show such reluctance to rent out their labor on a farm may well be acting in their own best interests, for after they have served their apprenticeship they could find that starting their own farm requires more money than they can ever hope to raise. Of course such sentiments do not help the successful farmer meet his need for labor, and in a desperate effort to entice youngsters to their farms, many landowners are now trying to compete with factories in matters of pay, working conditions and fringe benefits—a trend unique in the history of agriculture. Some farmers offer free insurance, paid vacations and a percentage of the profits; others even pay for overtime. There is a wide range in the salaries of farm employees, but in Iowa the average wage is about $290 per month and housing and electricity are provided free of charge. At these rates more than 20,000 men are regularly employed as hired hands in the state.

But in Iowa, as in the rest of the region, the labor shortage is acute, and women are increasingly observed driving the tractors. Many wives are willing volunteers for outdoor work when their husbands find it impossible to find adequate help or when there is a chance to save money this way. Their world has been revolutionized in countless other ways as well. The "old homestead" look of the countryside is almost impossible to find on the plains these days. Today's farmhouses are likely to be split-levels, colonials, or ranches and many resemble dwellings in modern suburban develop-

ments. The kitchens are filled with all the gadgets —blenders, mixers, rotisseries and the like—that one would expect to find in suburbia, and the housewife herself is much more likely to appear in skintight slacks than in a faded flower print and sunbonnet. Each year fewer women keep a dooryard garden or put up vegetables and fruits; instead they hop into the family car for a trip to the supermarket. In fact, there is little to distinguish them from the city women, for they wear the same fashions, read the same magazines, and belong to the same churches and clubs. Today, more and more farm women are college educated, and they are sharing the burdens of management with their husbands, participating in decisions that are changing and improving the economic potential of many farm families.

Changes in the agricultural scene are not limited to farms that raise crops. Today the raising of chickens and turkeys has become as specialized as that of beef and pork. Hogs contribute much to making agriculture big business in Iowa, Minnesota and Nebraska, and the world's largest producer of country hams is located in a Missouri county-seat town named California. Cattlemen, of course, are the lords of the western third of the Plains States region. Here on the High Plains a ranch as small as 2,000 acres will barely produce a living for a man and his family. But a spread like the Flying A in Nebraska's Sand Hills totals 40,000 acres of grassland and annually readies more than 2,000 head of beef for market.

Livestock, poultry and more than 50 different kinds of harvested crops earn plainsmen more than $11 billion annually in cash receipts. At the same time, Kansas farmers by themselves spend almost a billion dollars a year on farm machinery and equipment, oil products, tires, fertilizers, chemicals, feeds, seeds and fencing material. The revenue from these sales helps support a host of small-town businessmen and their big city suppliers. The farmer has thus become a fully integrated member of the American economic system. Gone is the isolation of rural life; gone the pitchfork-armed, old-before-his-time plainsman immortalized in painter Grant Wood's *American Gothic*. There may be fewer farmers now than there were a decade ago; there will certainly be fewer farmers a decade hence than there are today, but those who still cling to the land they love, to the broad trans-Mississippi prairies and grasslands, are better prepared than ever before to help feed a national population that may well pass the 300 million mark by the turn of the century.

The wheat cycle: high-stakes gamble

Wheat, one of man's primary sources of nourishment, is nowhere in the U.S. more assiduously cultivated than in Kansas and North Dakota. Few crops require such continuous care, and for the farmer, the seasons fade almost indiscernibly into each other, for as one crop is harvested the wheat grower is already preparing fields for the new sowing. The cycle of soil preparation, seeding, growth and harvest is never-ending, and only during the dead of winter, when the land lies dormant, can the farmer rest. But even then his mind is not at ease, for his thoughts turn to the myriad troubles that may befall him. In few places is nature more unpredictable than on the plains, where flood, drought, cold snaps, blight and insect infestation can destroy a crop overnight. Each golden kernel brought to harvest thus becomes a victory for the farmer in his game of chance with nature.

Kansas farmer George Meeker *(top)* and a professional wheat cutter examine ripening heads to determine the precise moment to harvest. A miscalculation of a day or two could mean a poor grade of wheat and low market prices.

Photographs by A. Y. Owen

After a heavy rain, a farmer in western Kansas plows his
recently harvested fields to check weed growth.

The pampered land

Two basic types of wheat are planted in the Plains States, winter wheat and spring wheat. In Kansas, as in most of the southern parts of the region, the winter varieties, used for high-quality bread flour, predominate. Planted in September and October, winter wheat grows to a height of three to four inches before cold weather sets in. The stalks then lie semidormant until spring, when they resume their growth; by June or early July the crop is ready to harvest. In North Dakota, however, wheat planted in the fall will not survive the bitter winters, and farmers in that state therefore plant spring wheat, seeding their fields in April or May and harvesting in August or September.

Techniques used to grow and harvest these two types of wheat differ in some respects, but there are also many similarities. Of major importance to growers of both varieties is the careful and constant working of the land to make it suitable for sowing. Even acres that are lying fallow must be plowed and replowed, to insure that rainfall will seep into the soil rather than run off and to kill weeds that soak up valuable moisture. Thus fields that will not be sown for a year or more receive the same care as acres scheduled to be planted during the next growing season.

A large cultivator, called a spring-tooth harrow, rips weeds from the soil where they have threatened moisture reserves.

Seeding the soil

When his fields have been prepared and the season for sowing has arrived, the farmer must tackle the problem of deciding when to plant. A mistaken decision could cost him his crop before it is even fairly underway. Here, a wheat grower's experience and his "feel for the land" are vital assets. By fingering samples of the soil, he estimates the moisture content to find out whether the ground is ready to receive the

It takes about four minutes for these three drills, pulled by a tractor, to seed an acre of Kansas earth with winter wheat.

seeds. If the earth is too wet the seeds will rot; if it is too dry they will quickly die of thirst.

Until the mid-19th Century, wheat growers seeded their fields by hand. The farmer reached into a bag at his side, scooped up a handful of seeds and scattered them on the freshly turned earth. Today, most wheat farmers use a grain drill, a tractor accessory that mechanically deposits seeds at preset intervals.

In a close-up of a grain drill in action *(below)*, metal disks cut into the soil. Behind each disk is a tube through which the seeds are dropped into the newly opened earth. Even the covering of the seeds is done mechanically; a chain at the rear of the drill drags soil over each seed after it is planted.

Sprouts of Kansas winter wheat stand several inches high in mid-September. In winter, growth will temporarily cease.

The waiting period

During the months between the sowing and the harvest, the wheat grower endures a frustrating period of watchful waiting. So much depends upon the weather that the farmer is hostage to its capricious whims.

A few days after planting, the farmer walks out to his fields and gently digs in the earth. If hungry worms have not already gotten to his seeds, and if the soil has remained warm and moist, he may discover that beneath the earth his wheat has begun to sprout. As he proceeds, he looks ever skyward, watching for a storm cloud on the horizon. If the previous days have been hot and dry, he seeks these signs of rain with a hope born of despair. If, on the other hand, the clouds have already been pouring water down on his fields, a black thunderhead in the distance bespeaks the ominous threat of an inundation that may well drown all life from the seeds and destroy his hopes for the year.

About one week after the earth has been seeded—if all has gone well—the farmer discovers the first green shoots poking up from the soil. One stage in the wheat's growth has passed and with each succeeding day of good weather it becomes taller and riper, unless, of course, disease or an infestation of insects should destroy the crop. But until the moment of harvest, uncertainty is the farmer's constant companion.

Cattle graze on winter wheat during its semidormant period. This impedes stalk growth and holds back the growth process until the return of warm weather. If the plants were to mature too early, a sudden cold snap might kill the crop.

Ripe heads of winter wheat in Kansas await the onslaught of the
combine, sometimes called the "Cadillac of the wheat fields."

Winter-wheat harvest

For the Kansas winter-wheat farmer, the long days of June and early July are a time of tension tinged by high hopes. The wheat is now waist-high, its heads are ripening to a rich golden hue under the hot sun, and the moment of harvest is approaching. Considerable money rides on the farmer's decision about when to harvest, for if he can bring his crop in at just the right moment, the grain will have precisely the degree of hardness and moisture needed to make the finest flour for bread and cereals. If his educated guess is correct, he will receive a high price per bushel for his wheat. But even if he should begin the harvest at the grain's peak of ripeness, he still remains at nature's mercy. Heavy rain or hail, which can appear out of nowhere on the plains, can leave the farmer with acres of ruined wheat. To bring the harvest in quickly, many farmers in Kansas hire custom-cutting teams whose skilled members, armed with combines, can harvest hundreds of acres of wheat a day, their monster machines cutting and threshing in a single operation.

Doug Meeker, 19, checks the blades of his father's combine. Dull or improperly set blades can waste bushels of wheat.

George Meeker lifts some kernels on his tongue to test them for hardness—one gauge of the quality and maturity of wheat.

Meeker breaks open a head of wheat and extracts a few kernels. By handling the grain he can estimate its moisture content.

After a long day in the fields, a combine unloads harvested grain into a truck that will carry the wheat to a storage elevator.

Spring-wheat harvest

After following the harvest north through the plains, the custom cutters finally arrive in North Dakota for the gathering each August of spring wheat, grains used generally in the making of flour for bread and noodles. Unlike winter wheat, which is cut and threshed in a single operation, spring wheat is usually harvested in two steps. First the wheat is cut and the stalks are left on the ground in long rows—called

Windrows of freshly cut wheat are left to dry by a North Dakota farmer as he finishes cutting a sloping field.

windrows—for three to five days. This is done because spring wheat, when cut, usually contains too much moisture for safe storage and must be permitted to dry out. After drying, the stalks are collected and threshed by the combines.

Although the harvest is the high point in the continuing cycle of plowing, planting and reaping, it marks no pause in the labor of either winter- or spring-wheat farmers. Kansas wheat growers must plow under the stubble left by the combines, for this nourishes the soil and makes it highly absorbent during the year or more it will rest. In North Dakota, however, crop rotation is often used. Recently harvested fields are made ready to receive corn, potatoes or beets that will enrich the acres upon which bushels of spring wheat will eventually grow once again.

Shaded by a large umbrella, a North Dakota wheat farmer
watches carefully as the wheat feeds into the cutter.

Two combines scoop up windrows of wheat, separate the
grain from its husks and spray out the straw and chaff.

OSKALOOSA, IOWA

PALMYRA, MISSOURI

OSAGE CITY, KANSAS

EMPORIA, KANSAS

The familiar, repetitive look of yesterday's Main Street, as it is remembered by millions of Americans, was captured in the early 1940s by a photographer from LIFE magazine, who covered towns in the Plains States for a report on the U.S. during World War II.

6

The Small Town in Decline

OTTAWA, KANSAS

OSAWATOMIE, KANSAS

The center of the plains for every plainsman is his own hometown. And more than in any other region, the hometown is likely to be a community with a population of fewer than 25,000. The "city," as the word is understood by the New Yorker, Californian or even the Ohioan, remains something of a rarity on the plains, for communities that boast more than 25,000 people are highly untypical of the region.

There are, of course, small towns throughout the nation, but those on the plains are, in some important particulars, unique. In the past the very scarcity of large urban centers in the region gave the small town an economic importance far greater than its size alone would have warranted. It was as farm service centers—buying produce and sell-

ing seed, equipment and implements—that many towns and villages of the plains made their mark. Had more cities been easily accessible to the farmer, fewer rural towns would have blossomed and waxed strong.

The towns of the plains are unique in another sense as well. Many were founded not in response to economic or social needs but in anticipation of such needs. This was particularly true in the western tier of the Plains States region, which was settled during the railroad boom of the late 19th Century. In that era, when there was so much optimism concerning the suitability of the plains for large-scale exploitation, the railroads laid more track than the region could easily absorb. Those competing lines with public lands at their disposal

Taken at my desk thereway we moulding public opinion and governing a sovereign people. W A W.

William Allen White (1868-1944), shown at left at his desk in Emporia, Kansas, was one of the best known and most quoted journalists in the nation. He first achieved fame during the 1896 election when he wrote an editorial entitled "What's the Matter with Kansas?" for the *Emporia Gazette,* the newspaper he owned. A diatribe against the Democratic candidate for President, William Jennings Bryan, the editorial gave eloquent voice to conservative viewpoints. Although White later became more liberal, he remained a spokesman for middle-class Americans, occasionally turning his brittle humor upon their foibles. The note above, written in his own hand on the back of this photograph, is an example of his dry tongue-in-cheek wit turned upon himself.

sold off large stretches of prairie to real-estate speculators who in turn laid out more towns than could be economically sustained. Consequently, upon the wide prairie hundreds of settlements came into existence in places where they served no useful function. Intense competition for survival and a stubborn resistance to the facing of economic realities were the results of such overbuilding. To this very day scores of plains hamlets, villages and towns continue to suffer from their birth defects.

At a glance most of the towns of the plains seem very much alike. Few of them are nestled in natural amphitheaters or protected by gently sloping valleys. Most seem superimposed; they are intruders upon the land. Their buildings appear almost as separate from the flat landscape as pawns from a chessboard; stores and residences are lined up on dusty grids divided by railroad tracks or by an unbending, monotonously level highway.

Although they may look alike, the towns of the plains have provoked widely different reactions, ranging from nostalgia to downright loathing. Among most Americans there has been a tendency to romanticize all small towns and particularly the farm centers of the plains as repositories of thrift, hard work and the other Puritan virtues that we like to think have made America great. Here on the endless prairie, according to the legend, a near-perfect society of small farmers, artisans and merchants arose to breathe life into the Jeffersonian dream—the dream of a real grassroots democracy in which all men are truly equal and each man's voice and views can be heard. Looking back upon his boyhood in Hannibal, Missouri, Mark Twain described his hometown as "a little democracy . . . full of liberty, equality and Fourth of July." In our own time Eric Sevareid, the television commentator, who grew up in Velva, North Dakota, has echoed the great humorist's views. "No man lived in fear of another," Sevareid wrote of Velva. "No man had the power to direct another to vote this way or that. . . . This was an agrarian democracy, which meant that there was no concentration of capital goods, which meant in turn, since we had no all-powerful landlords, that no class society based upon birth or privilege had a chance to develop." Still others would agree with William Allen White, the late editor of the *Emporia Gazette,* that the small communities of the plains "house their citizens more satisfactorily, give them more breathing space, provide more of the physical and spiritual blessings of life . . . for the average citizen than any other kind of human habitation."

Such idealizations do contain elements of truth,

but they ignore many facets of small-town life that are less than ideal. Sinclair Lewis, whose novel *Main Street* was an attack upon the values he believed were represented in his hometown of Sauk Centre, Minnesota, described the communities of the prairies as strongholds of contentment, "the contentment of the quiet dead, who are scornful of the living for their restless walking. It is negation canonized as the one positive virtue. It is the prohibition of happiness. It is slavery self-sought and self-defended. It is dullness made God."

The fact that one man of discernment can see the small town of the plains as "an agrarian democracy," while another sees it as "slavery self-sought and self-defended," is perhaps not so paradoxical as it seems. Within the framework of narrowly defined middle-class values and ethics, the small town of the past was indeed a friendly, democratic place. So long as a man shared the common, everyday ambition to rise financially and socially, the local banker might be pleased to wave him a friendly greeting as they passed on the street. So long as he worshiped God in an acceptable church, went hunting and fishing with "the boys," and damned labor unions with sufficient fervor, Main Street on the plains could be a cheery and comfortable environment. But if the Main Street merchant suddenly ceased going to church and began to wear bohemian clothing and raised his voice to challenge the conventional wisdom of his era, then the small town could become a cold and comfortless place. Soon the banker would greet him with a fishy stare and turn down his application for a loan, the ladies of the sewing club would spend their afternoons gossiping about him and his family, and trade at his store might suddenly drop off precipitously. Nor has the narrowness of the small-town mentality yet disappeared. Recently a California photographer, whose wife had died, was denied custody of his son by the Iowa Supreme Court, which cited the photographer's lack of "concern for formal religious training" as well as his political liberalism. The court went on to characterize the photographer's household as "unstable, unconventional, arty, bohemian, and probably intellectually stimulating." In granting custody of the child to his mother's parents, the court spoke with approval of the "stable, dependable, conventional, middle-class, Middle West background" they could provide. Thus, after almost five decades, Sinclair Lewis' jibe about "dullness made God" still has a ring of truth.

Obviously then, for some people, the country town on the plains has been more of a nightmare than a realization of the American dream, while for others it has seemed the best of all possible worlds. But these extremes of sentiment obscure the real nature of the life that has existed in the prairie hamlets, villages and towns over the last century. For most, they have offered a satisfactory, if constraining, environment for a private pursuit of happiness, and this in itself is not an accomplishment to be dismissed lightly. Now, however, these societies of small merchants dependent on the trade of small farmers find themselves deep in a period of crisis.

In 1958 Carl Rowan, recently Director of the United States Information Agency, then a reporter for the *Minneapolis Tribune*, made an in-depth study of the economic and social conditions of the small towns in western and southwestern Minnesota, the richest agricultural area in the state. He found that the technological revolution on the farms was threatening to destroy the economic organization of many of these communities. As farms became larger and more efficient, and the number of farm owners decreased, the typical small-town resident was forced to the realization that his primary source of income was rapidly disappearing. Subsequent surveys have borne out Mr. Rowan's analysis. Even the farmers who have remained on the land—generally the successful and the well educated—have tended to make their major purchases in large cities, where the selection of goods is larger and the prices cheaper. Slowly the economic underpinnings of many farm marketing centers have been withering away, and with them have gone thousands of residents who could no longer find an opportunity along Main Street to satisfy their ambitions for secure and comfortable lives.

The continuing plight of the small town is reflected in demographic studies that reveal the steady depopulation of once prosperous farm marketing centers. In Nebraska in the 1950s, for example, some 68.1 per cent of a group of 407 small country villages registered population declines. And of 76 larger Nebraska towns, with populations of 1,000 to 2,500, more than 59 per cent lost ground during the same decade. Nor is this trend merely a postwar phenomenon. It parallels the rise of mechanized and high-yield agriculture that has made possible increased food production by an ever-decreasing number of farmers. One example is the town of Hope, North Dakota. In 1910 the population of this farm marketing center was 900, but each succeeding census revealed a decline in the number of residents, and by 1960 Hope could claim only 390 citizens. And Omemee, in the

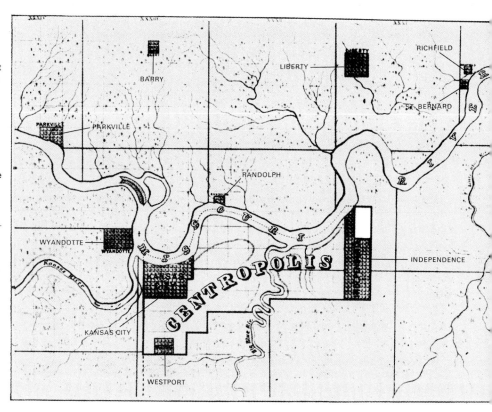

"Centropolis," a projected "central city of the Basin of the Mississippi," appears on this 1859 map issued by an imaginative land speculator named William Gilpin. Predicting that a great city would rise at the junction of the Missouri and Kansas Rivers, Gilpin drew its boundaries to include the Missouri towns of Kansas City, Westport and Independence, where Gilpin-owned land is shown as a white block. Although nothing came of this consolidation scheme, nor of an earlier plan to make Independence the core of a 100-square-mile Centropolis, Gilpin's prediction is in a way being fulfilled today through the continuing growth of Kansas City. The city's metropolitan area, which covers both Centropolis and Wyandotte—now Kansas City, Kansas—is one of the nation's major urban centers, with a population of more than a million.

same state, dropped from a population of 332 to a mere 11.

For towns like Hope and Omemee the road to oblivion has been a long one; for others the path was much shorter. The historian Lewis Atherton has written that during the 19th Century the "rapid occupation of rich, western lands encouraged dreams of great cities, extravagant speculation in town real estate, and the creation of country villages in excessive numbers. Many towns advanced no further than the planning stage; others grew feverishly, only to join the long list of ghost towns when new rivals, changes in transportation or unexpected complications blighted them. . . . Although the death struggle of midwestern country towns was on the whole . . . prosaic, they . . . battled to survive in an atmosphere which spawned them in reckless and fickle optimism."

An example of a town that rose and then fell is Marine on St. Croix, Minnesota, on the eastern rim of the Plains States, which began its history with a better economic base than many other communities. In the 1840s—it was then known as Marine Mills—the town was already a bustling lumber center, and because of its delightful river location it soon developed a lively society of its own. Formal dances highlighted the busy round of so-

cial activities in which townsmen engaged. By the 1870s the little city's future as an industrial and cultural center seemed secure. Less than a decade later, however, Marine on St. Croix began a precipitous slide downhill. Severe log jams on the St. Croix were followed in 1884 by a disastrous tornado that damaged nearly every building in town and laid waste to the lumber mill. By the time the mill reopened, the lumber industry had moved farther north, shattering the economy of the recently prosperous town. As the 19th Century closed, the cotillions and other stylish events had become only memories, and the community settled into the rut of an insignificant farm marketing center.

The rise and decline of Marine on St. Croix was a typical experience for the plains region. In the first flush of optimistic town-building, many small communities even saw themselves as the future Washington, Paris or Athens of the prairie. Mark Twain caught the prevailing spirit of boosterism in his novel *The Adventures of Colonel Sellers*, in which a speculator, Colonel Eschol Sellers, writes to his friends back East: "Come right along to Missouri. Don't wait and worry about a good price, but sell out for whatever you can get, and come along, or you might be too late. . . . You'll never regret it. It's the grandest country—the loveliest land—the purest atmosphere—I can't describe it; no pen can do it justice. And it's filling up every day—people coming from everywhere. I've got the biggest scheme on earth—and I'll take you in; I'll take in every friend I've got that ever stood by me for there's enough for all, and to spare. Mum's the word—don't whisper—keep yourself to yourself. You'll see! Come!—rush!—hurry!—don't wait for anything."

In such an atmosphere of feverish real-estate speculation, towns fought each other fiercely for the honor of being named the county seat (some partisans even going so far as to steal county records for their own communities) or to secure a small slaughterhouse or factory or to be made a scheduled stop by the railroad. Anything that would bring in new people and increase land values was eagerly sought. Optimism about the future of the region in general and about one's own hometown in particular was rampant. Intellectually inclined speculators wrote elaborate philosophical treatises to prove that this town or that was destined for urban greatness. One William Gilpin, later to become the first territorial governor of Colorado, declared in the 1850s that Independence, Missouri, was immutably destiny's child; that one day it might even replace Washington as the nation's capital. Gilpin went so far as to prepare a map of "Centropolis," the city he envisioned growing out of Independence, and included in it a new national capitol. Like other promoters of his time, Gilpin revealed a strong inclination toward the mystical and pseudoscientific. Readers of his visionary writings were confidently assured that the plains region was to become a great population center because North America was a "symmetrical and sublime" continent with "the Great Basin of the Mississippi [as] the amphitheatre of the world . . . the most magnificent dwelling marked out by God for man's abode." Independence and the more easterly city of St. Louis, which he also admired, "stand out upon the face of the continent like eyes in the human head. . . . The peculiar configuration of the continent and its rivers and plains make these *two* natural *focal* points."

While men like Gilpin and Colonel Sellers built their castles in the sky, ensnaring themselves and hundreds of other land-hungry citizens in evanescent webs of gold thread, the little towns of the plains slowly took shape and developed character. Few were to become more than farm market centers, but many townspeople found it impossible to abandon the illusions of the past. Dependent upon the farmer for economic sustenance but scorning

him as a rube and an illiterate, the small-town merchant often had an inflated view of himself. He tended to identify his own interests with those of his suppliers rather than with those of his farmer customers. The farmer, for his part, often believed —with considerable justification—that the merchant was little more than a "tollgate keeper" for the "vested interests," the monopolies and trusts.

Given this atmosphere, it is not surprising that tension between townsman and countryman was endemic on the plains. It boiled over into out-and-out hostility during the Granger and Populist eras when farmers began to organize consumer and producer cooperatives to bypass small-town businessmen. Mutual suspicion was also fostered by the fact that in many areas of the plains the townspeople were of old Yankee stock while the farmers were often recent immigrants from northern and central Europe.

Willa Cather in her novel of late-19th Century Nebraska, *My Ántonia*, described the attitude of townspeople toward their farmer neighbors in a passage that told much about the rigid, bourgeois provincialism of the townsmen themselves. "The daughters of Black Hawk [actually Miss Cather's hometown of Red Cloud] merchants had a confident, unenquiring belief that they were 'refined,' and that the country girls . . . were not. . . . I thought the attitude of the town people toward these girls very stupid. If I told my schoolmates that Lena Lingard's grandfather was a clergyman, and much respected in Norway, they looked at me blankly. What did it matter? All foreigners were ignorant people. . . . The Black Hawk boys looked forward to marrying Black Hawk girls, and living in a brand-new little house with best chairs that must not be sat upon, and hand-painted china that must not be used. . . . The country girls were considered a menace to social order. Their beauty shone out too boldly against a conventional background. But anxious mothers need have felt no alarm. They mistook the mettle of their sons. The respect for respectability was stronger than any desire in Black Hawk youth."

In the constricted environment of most small towns it was indeed "respectability" that mattered. Wealth also was well regarded, of course, for wealth brought—and bought—the tokens of respectability: the three-story frame house on the best street in town and membership in socially acceptable clubs and, by the 1920s, in the local country club. Yet, for all that, there was a rough frontier feeling for equality. Though there were rich men in many towns, few felt free to flaunt their wealth beyond acceptable limits that were narrowly defined. Certainly there were no rigid class lines, and the son of a clerk would hardly be stretching the limits of reasonable ambition if he hoped one day to become mayor. There was, however, a price for this leveling. Without an organized wealthy class there were few people with the leisure to develop such artistic instincts as they may have had, or to lead the rest of the town toward an appreciation of literature, paintings and music. It was a small businessman's society that gauged progress primarily in terms of the practical and immediately useful and scorned all else as effete. Though the small towns of the plains have produced their share of artists, writers and composers, few of them achieved fame in their hometowns. Even William Allen White, who built a career on his reputation as a small-town sage, often left the dust of Emporia behind him in favor of long sojourns in New York, Washington, London and Paris, where his well-honed rustic horse sense could be displayed in sophisticated company.

Sinclair Lewis, perhaps more bitter than most of the authors whose roots were in the small towns of the prairies, expressed his scorn through the thoughts of Carol Kennicott, the heroine of *Main Street*. She saw Gopher Prairie (really Sauk Centre) as a sinkhole of greed and prejudice. Lewis has her charge with a fine disdain that Main Street's "conception of a community ideal is not the grand manner . . . the fine aristocratic pride, but cheap labor in the kitchen and the rapid increase in the price of land. It plays cards on a greasy oil cloth in a shanty, and does not know that prophets are walking and talking on the terrace."

If Carol Kennicott were suddenly to return to Sauk Centre, she would certainly be awed by the new technology that includes radio and television, superhighways and jet planes. The local merchant is now likely to spend his evenings watching news and entertainment programs emanating from New York, Washington and Los Angeles television studios, and inevitably this window on the world broadens his views on politics, race relations, manners and morals. His wife can now drive to Minneapolis-St. Paul in less than three hours along a new four-lane superhighway. This gives her easy access to the latest styles in clothing and home furnishings, as well as the opportunity to acquaint herself with the Twin Cities' many cultural attractions: museums, art galleries, theaters, a symphony orchestra and the like. Such effects of the technological revolution have brought a patina of sophistication to many Sauk Centre residents and

are clearly evident in some aspects of town life.

But as significant as these developments are, many things in Sauk Centre have remained virtually unchanged over the decades. In almost 50 years, population has risen only slightly, and the general prosperity that has prevailed throughout much of the country has passed the town by. Sauk Centre still appears somewhat run-down at the heels, and the average family income is only about $3,600 a year, just a few hundred dollars above the poverty line established by the federal government.

But for all its problems, Sauk Centre is more fortunate than many small towns on the plains, for at least it is holding its own—if just barely. There are hundreds of communities, however, like La Harpe, Kansas, that are slowly crumbling to dust. About 500 people still live in La Harpe, but long ago the town's reason for existence, as a farm service center, began to disappear, as the farmers' trade drifted to a somewhat larger community a few miles away. The depressed nature of life in La Harpe is shockingly evident at the quickest glance. About half the buildings on the one-block-long main street stand vacant; many of them have not had a tenant for years. A blacksmith, one of the few left in Kansas, still plies his trade in La Harpe, and two grocery stores hang on, but the town's brick sidewalks are now overgrown by grass. Incredibly, La Harpe still supports a high school (a three-story red brick building) and four churches. But how much longer these services can be sustained is anybody's guess. Bereft of all economic purpose, La Harpe nevertheless does struggle on, touchingly attempting to deny its irrelevance. In the middle of the main street the town fathers have had a crosswalk painted; an unnecessary expense in view of the light vehicular traffic.

La Harpe's dwindling automobile traffic is significant, for the widespread use of automobiles has been an important contributing cause of the decline of such towns. Farmers, once restricted by horse-and-buggy transportation and muddy roads to shopping within a few miles of their homesteads, can now get into their cars and drive to moderate-sized urban centers, where prices may be cheaper and the selection of goods greater. Compounding the small towns' trials is the fact that there are fewer and fewer farmers every year. Half a century ago, towns on the plains had to be closely spaced and a community that served about 900 farmers within an area of 72 square miles was economically viable. Even in those days, there were too many towns in terms of the rural population they served. But today, when a farmer can travel at least 50 or

Posing with his wife and child in front of their sod house in Custer County, Nebraska, in the late 1800s, George Golden looks the very image of a prosperous homesteader. The glass windows of his dwelling reveal his relative affluence, even though he, like many pioneers in the treeless plains, had to build his first house by laying up hundreds of squares of sod cut from the lush grassland. Even the roofs were covered with sod. These structures were generally dark and dirty; in wet weather the walls oozed moisture. Sod houses, however, had one advantage. The earthen blocks were superb insulators, keeping the houses warm in winter, cool in summer.

60 miles in an hour, a marketing community must serve a 3,200-square-mile area that has a population of at least 26,000 in order to be economically successful.

Until the third decade of this century, many plains towns were important rail shipping centers for farm produce. But with the increase of highway traffic, even this function has all but disappeared. And the businessmen who once depended almost wholly on the trade of farmers now have no dependable source of income. For small-town residents and tradesmen, the one hope of revival—albeit a dim one—rests with industrialization. Industry means a new and younger population, people with money to spend. But even when industry comes to a town, local merchants can attract new trade only if they provide a higher standard of service than their big city competition and a better selection of goods keyed to local needs and desires.

How then can industry be attracted to the towns of the plains? Most economists and government officials agree that the very small town—the country village or hamlet—is doomed to continue its slow and painful decline. Only those communities with populations of more than 2,500 have a chance of survival as independent entities. The larger towns at least offer a prospective employer a pool of labor

and local capital reserves that can be called upon to finance plant construction. Nebraska census figures, for example, reveal that while the really small towns are withering away, the somewhat larger communities are, on the whole, gaining population. But few towns can merely sit back and wait for industry to arrive. On the contrary, they must energetically court prospective industrialists. Often they must be prepared to offer financial incentives that require the investment of the townspeople's money. A key figure in the struggle to attract industry is the local banker. If he is a venturesome sort, he will make the necessary loans to encourage industry. If, on the other hand, he views his bank merely as a check-cashing institution or a placid custodian of certain local properties, then the town may find itself at a disadvantage in the competition with its neighbors for new business ventures.

Many towns on the plains are taking the necessary steps to insure their survival and enhance their prospects for prosperity. Young businessmen in McCook, Nebraska, for example, a town of 8,300 residents, formed the McCook Corporation in the mid-1960s in an effort to bring new industry to town. By selling shares at $25 apiece to almost every family in town, as well as to local banks and retail stores, they raised about $125,000 and built

An example of a town suddenly erected on the plains, Sargent, Nebraska, was prosperous enough in the 1880s to have its own bank. During the drought years of the 1890s, the bank failed, and the town, like so many others, went into a long period of decline. Today, Sargent is a small marketing center for ranchers, upon whom local tradesmen depend for a modest income.

a modern factory structure. Meanwhile, they got in touch with officials of the TRW corporation, a diversified concern that is one of the nation's largest manufacturers of electronic equipment. TRW, needing to expand its facilities, agreed to lease the plant, and then even asked for additional space—which the McCook Corporation was happy to provide. Since that time McCook has been running advertisements in major newspapers of the region to attract other prospective industries.

Sometimes, of course, towns will benefit from a stroke of good fortune. Citizens of Northfield, Minnesota, did nothing more than make space available to a North Dakota inventor in which to develop a highly efficient machine for making plastic bags. The result was an enterprise of several divisions, one of which makes meteoroid detectors for Pegasus satellites and high-altitude balloons for atmospheric research. More than 1,200 people in Northfield are now employed by this company and the town is booming.

It would be folly, of course, for any town to put its trust in sheer good luck. For most towns, hard work and a realistic outlook offer the best hope for survival. Atchison, Kansas, is a prime example of what can be accomplished, even under the most trying of circumstances. In 1958 the town was hit by two disastrous floods in the space of two weeks. The first sent 10 feet of water coursing through the center of town, causing almost five million dollars in damage and destroying 14 buildings in the dilapidated and economically depressed downtown area. The second flood, while not so severe, was perhaps psychologically even more devastating to the townspeople because it happened so soon after the first. But their response was magnificent. With the help of federal and state funds, but mostly through their own efforts, the people of Atchison rebuilt and modernized their 12-block business district within seven years, and at the same time they constructed new dams to hold back future floods. Their renovations so enhanced the town's trade facilities that retail sales jumped almost 20 per cent the year the project was completed. Most surprisingly of all, Atchison set a jewel in the center of its achievement by turning the most severely damaged area into a two-and-a-half-block-long mall of tree-lined walks. The sides of the mall are shaded by a pair of concrete canopies under which shoppers stroll, looking into the attractive store fronts. Weary visitors can rest on benches in the mall's sunlit center and watch fountains spill cascades of water into a reflecting pool. Today, Atchison is one of the most envied towns in Kansas and has pointed the way for other communities seeking to modernize their own facilities.

Many communities have indeed followed Atchison's example. The fact remains, however, that in terms of the problem's magnitude a great deal remains to be done. Outside of such big cities as St. Louis, Minneapolis, St. Paul, Kansas City, Des Moines and Omaha, opportunity is still intermittent on the plains. Bright young men and women continue to find the pull of large urban areas strong, for only there can they be assured of finding the economic, recreational and cultural advantages that they demand. Sauk Centre, for example, sends about 35 per cent of its young people to college and 15 per cent to advanced trade and technical schools, but relatively few college graduates return home. The very people the small town loses are the ones it can least afford to lose—the young with the intelligence, training and energy to lead movements of revitalization.

Even under the best of circumstances, few small towns on the plains are able to diversify their economy and roll back the tide of economic and population decline. But many of the villages and hamlets have an option that is too often ignored: consolidation.

The case for consolidation was summed up by Dwight A. Nesmith. As director of the Community Survey Program at Kansas State University, he wrote: "While it may be foolish to suggest that small towns which have been fighting one another for a hundred years should get together, combine resources and make sacrifices for their mutual good, that seems to be the only way to revitalize the declining rural towns." One area in which consolidation has been successfully attempted is education. Not long ago even the idea of a consolidated school system was anathema to many small-town residents. Townspeople gloried in the athletic exploits of local high-school teams, which brought distinction to the town as a whole, and they insisted upon direct control over the hiring and firing of teachers. Too often ignored was the fact that many qualified teachers were shunning the small towns because of low salaries and inadequate facilities. While parents debated the question of consolidation, thousands of plains children were allowed to grow up receiving substandard educations. Often they graduated from high school unqualified even to be farmers—though for many years successful farming on the plains has depended, in large measure, upon a basic understanding of many branches of science and technology.

Gradually the idea of consolidated schools has gained acceptance, at least in some parts of the plains. Between 1957 and 1962 the number of school districts in Iowa, Minnesota, Missouri, Nebraska and North Dakota decreased by more than 1,000. In Kansas, and in Nebraska as well, the trend is toward fewer and larger school districts; only in South Dakota, one of the most sparsely populated states in the nation, has there been little change. A major stumbling block is scattered population. One authority has pointed out that in some areas the population is so sparse that to provide a high school with an enrollment of at least 400—which experts consider a minimum—would require a geographical area so large that many students would spend more hours going to and from school than they would in the school itself.

In other fields, however, where consolidation would be salutary, and perhaps relatively easy to achieve, there has been a lag. Certainly such services as volunteer fire departments, police and libraries could be more efficiently coordinated and equipped if the resources of several neighboring towns were pooled. Perhaps even more important, consolidation replaces the climate of rivalry with one of cooperation in the struggle to diversify the economy. But like his counterpart in other regions of the U.S., the plainsman is proud of his hometown and is loath to take any action that might further undermine or destroy its identity. Too often it seems that he would rather see his community die slowly than help it to revive and prosper as part of a larger urban complex.

The continuing depopulation of some of the rural reaches of the plains poses a problem not just for the communities and states involved, but for the entire nation as well. The federal government recognizes this, and in cooperation with state and university officials it has begun to plan for a new era for the region. Hubert Humphrey, a plainsman who grew up in the small town of Dalton, South Dakota, and went on to become a professor at the University of Minnesota, mayor of Minneapolis, Senator from Minnesota and Vice President of the United States, is vitally interested in the future of his home region. Referring to demographic projections that indicate that the population of the United States may double in the next half century or so, Mr. Humphrey acknowledges that the already densely settled portions of the nation will experience a population explosion. But the plains, he says, offer a "vast expanse of unused, or at least unoccupied, land [that is] a potential asset because it offers great opportunity for growth." This potential can only be realized if the nation "can influence the movement of population into the area." Out on the oceanic expanses of the prairie there is room to settle millions upon millions of people, who, under the right circumstances, could find ample scope there for both self-fulfillment and economic prosperity.

Because the Plains States offer so much space for population expansion, the region is likely to become a major testing ground for new ideas in urban planning. Already taking shape on drawing boards at the University of Minnesota is a design for a preplanned "Experimental City," which may be built in the western part of the state. Both the federal government and private corporations have shown their interest in the idea by contributing a total of $300,000 to finance the project's early planning stages. Conceived by Athelstan Spilhaus, until recently Dean of the University of Minnesota's Institute of Technology, Experimental City is viewed by some urban planners as a prototype of an ideal urban complex. In this city of 250,000 people, many essential services—transport, garbage disposal, power generation and the like—would be placed underground, with wastes carried off to processing plants; major sources of air pollution would thus be eliminated. The aboveground streets would be for pedestrians only, and there is even talk of enclosing parts of the city under plastic canopies to permit climate control, thus mitigating one of the least attractive elements in plains life: the harsh extremes of weather. Bordering Experimental City would be a broad swath of open country, reserved for recreation, cultural activities and agriculture.

What would such a city cost to build? Estimates range from two to four billion dollars. Dr. Spilhaus believes that part of the money might be secured from the federal government, which would make long-term low-interest loans. Sections of private industry might also be interested in contributing to the growth of the city, for here new ideas in communication, construction and transportation could be worked out. But in the final analysis, communities like Experimental City must be able to stand on their own, without constant subsidy from public and private funds. A broad range of industrial and commercial enterprises must be attracted in order to make such cities economically viable and offer their citizens multiple opportunities for self-fulfillment. It has been shown time and again that industry gravitates toward areas where the educational facilities are most impressive; but many decades are normally required before a top-quality educational institution can be established. With the continuing revolution in communications, however, it may be possible to create from scratch excellent universities in a matter of years instead of decades.

Hubert Humphrey puts it this way: "Communication satellites are going to upgrade all of the universities. The monopolistic claim of excellence a few schools now have will soon be dissipated. If you can televise a ski-jump from Grenoble, France, you can telecast a lecture from the University of Paris, from Cambridge or Oxford or even from a New Delhi lecture hall. It can be done, and it is much cheaper to put up a space satellite and tap in with the great minds of the world than it is to try to attract the great professors to this or that school. The day may not be far off when a small university in Minnesota or South Dakota will be able to have the most eminent scholars projected right into its classrooms." Microfilm and computers can also be used to build up instant libraries, permitting students at brand-new schools to have access to the same books that students at Oxford or Yale find in their library stacks.

Many people may object that planning implies the subordination of the individual to a bureaucracy. Mr. Humphrey, however, sees in the prospect of preplanned cities on the plains a chance to involve the individual more than ever before in the shaping of his own destiny. "I view the perfect city," he says, "as a cluster of neighborhoods. I think the great mistake in the past has been that the American city has become overwhelmed by the problem of dealing with masses of people. The city of tomorrow . . . will be a confederation of neighborhoods. It will be decentralized even in its government."

By emphasizing neighborhoods, rather than the city as a whole, Mr. Humphrey believes that the best aspect of small-town life—the sense that each man has a unique and important contribution to make to community affairs—can be preserved and the anonymity of urban life can be avoided. In other words, the new cities of the plains may well be groupings of small towns that share such major attractions of urban life as libraries, theaters, universities and fine restaurants. Thus a wholesome synthesis of town and city may develop, and the day may yet come when the phrase "small-town mind" will no longer stand for the prejudice and narrowness excoriated by Sinclair Lewis. Instead it may come to mean a liberalness of mind, a sophistication of taste and a sense of unlimited opportunity to match the unlimited expanses of the plains themselves.

Fur trader Pierre Laclède *(hand extended)* greets Indians gathered at the site of St. Louis in 1763. The tiny French settlement that Laclède established there the following year quickly became the center of the Western fur trade.

St. Louis: the plains' cosmopolis

St. Louis is a city of many faces. To Westerners it is an outpost of Eastern culture; Easterners regard it as a provincial Western town; Southerners, remembering its support of the Union, think of it as Northern; and Northerners, mindful of the city's river connection with New Orleans, often associate it with the South. In fact, St. Louis is all of these things, a mid-American cosmopolis drawing its heritage from a blend of French, German, Irish, Italian and regional American cultures.

From its earliest days as a fur-trading post to its current role as a leading manufacturing and cultural center, the city has experienced periods of runaway boom and stultifying stagnation. Today, busily erasing the scars of urban blight, St. Louis is more than ever justifying the vision of its founder, Pierre Laclède *(above)*, who said that his little community would become "one of the finest cities in America."

Boomtown of the steamboat era

On July 27, 1817, the *Zebulon M. Pike* chugged into St. Louis, ending a six-week voyage from Louisville and beginning the fabulous steamboat era on the upper Mississippi and Missouri Rivers. The *Pike* was the first of thousands of steam-driven paddle wheelers that by 1870 would help transform St. Louis from a frontier town to the third-largest city in the nation.

Located at a strategic point near the best overland and river routes to the West, St. Louis had begun to serve as a funnel for trade and migration in the early 19th Century. With the advent of the steamboat, the

A fleet of steamboats fills almost every bit of space along the St. Louis levee in 1858, at the height of the riverboat boom. Many buildings seen here were built after 1849, when fire (started on a boat) devastated the riverfront.

trickle of people and goods became a torrent. From as far away as Pittsburgh and New Orleans the boats came. They brought not only settlers on their way west, but luxury goods for the city's merchants and raw materials for its new industries.

When steamboating's golden age began around 1830, St. Louis had a population of only 4,977. By the end of the era, 40 years later, the city had grown to 310,864, almost a third of whom were German and Irish immigrants. Proud St. Louisans predicted that their city would one day be the nation's capital.

A wedding of railroads and industry

The completion of the Eads Bridge *(below)* across the Mississippi in 1874, linking St. Louis to Illinois by rail, signaled the doom of the steamboat era. In fact, St. Louis had begun to turn its back on the river during the Civil War, when north-south trade had been interrupted by both Federal and Confederate blockades. The city, however, enhanced its prosperity as a major industrial center by supplying goods to the Union Army in the West. The value of St. Louis-made products tripled between 1860 and 1870, and many reached their destinations on rail lines that radiated from the city to ever more distant points. At the turn of the century, St. Louis was renowned for such diverse items as beer, shoes, stoves, clothing, wagons, paint and even automobiles *(right),* which it exported to distant parts of the nation. St. Louisans basked in a climate of optimism as their city approached its zenith of affluence.

The workshop of the St. Louis Motor Carriage Company, one of the nation's first automobile manufacturers, turned out 65 cars in 1901 at $1,200 each.

Pioneering locomotives, such as the Pacific Railroad's *Charles H. Peck,* helped open the run between St. Louis and Kansas City in 1865.

A marvel of its day, St. Louis' mile-long Eads Bridge is shown under construction. Completed in 1874, it was the world's first steel-truss bridge.

A pretty visitor poses on a gondola used at the fair.

A glittering monument
to the city's pride

"Meet me in St. Louie, Louie. Meet me at the fair . . ." ran the words to the popular song, and millions of Americans accepted the tuneful invitation to visit the glittering Louisiana Purchase Exposition of 1904, a spectacular monument to the wealth, culture and pride of St. Louis. It had taken more than two years and $40 million to convert 1,240 acres of Forest Park into the majestic setting of the biggest and most extravagant fair the world had ever seen. Such wonders of modern technology as the electric stove, the dial telephone and the wireless telegraph were exhibited in block-long plaster palaces. Shimmering lagoons traversed by Venetian gondolas *(above)*, rippling cascades and formal gardens added a sumptuous note to the grounds. But the favorite attraction for many visitors was the mile-long amusement area called the Pike. Here, where the ice-cream cone is said to have been invented, Hagenbeck's Wild Animal Show and the Temple of Mirth vied with vivid re-enactments of Boer War battles, staged by English and Afrikaner veterans of the recent conflict.

The huge Palace of Machinery *(background)*, seen from
the center of the grounds, supplied power for the fair.

A reverie of schmaltz and baseball

It was after World War I that St. Louis, with more than 150 years of dynamic growth and prosperity behind it, began to doze. In the words of unofficial city historian Ernest Kirschten, "St. Louis turned in on itself [and] contemplated its communal navel." Wealthy and complacent, the city stopped building and relaxed in an aura of lethargic provincialism. When Prohibition closed their beloved beer gardens and crippled the city's vital brewing industry, St. Louisans grumbled—but also embraced the huge, schmaltzy outdoor musical-comedy productions staged each summer by the Municipal Opera *(below).* And the 1930s are remembered in baseball-loving St. Louis not so much for the Depression and the spread of slums, but more for the fabulous Gas House Gang *(right).*

Big-league baseball has been a tradition in St. Louis since 1876, and the city has at one time or another been represented in every major league since then. But of all the teams that have worn St. Louis uniforms, the best-known was the World Champion Cardinals of 1934 *(above)*. Called the Gas House Gang because of their antic aggressiveness, they included *(left to right):* Dizzy Dean, Leo Durocher, Ernie Orsatti, Bill DeLancey, Rip Collins, Joe Medwick, player-manager Frank Frisch, Jack Rothrock and Pepper Martin. A typical bit of Gas House Gang action came in the 1934 World Series when Medwick slid hard into Marvin Owen of the Detroit Tigers *(left)*. After a fight with Owen and a barrage of garbage from Detroit fans, Medwick was removed from the game for his own protection.

The Municipal Opera, seen here in a 1919 performance, still attracts nightly audiences of up to 12,000 persons with a steady summertime diet of time-tested musicals.

Rising in front of the St. Louis skyline, the legs of Eero Saarinen's Gateway Arch are shown during construction. The arch is part of the 82-acre Jefferson National Expansion Memorial along the old levee.

Soaring symbol of a new claim to greatness

"You might ask why anyone would be proud of such a dump," wrote an English author during a 1951 visit to St. Louis. After more than three decades of neglect, the city was in terrible shape. Its streets were snarled with traffic, and its ancient public buildings were in various stages of decrepitude. Fully half its homes were slums or near-slums. Much of the middle class had fled to the suburbs, to be replaced largely by poor Negroes from the South.

On the brink of civic disaster, St. Louis began to awaken in 1953 and fought back with bulldozer, wrecking ball and ambitious renewal plans. Entire slum blocks vanished, and in their place rose apartment and office buildings, motels, parking garages and a handsome, 50,000-seat sports stadium. St. Louis had embarked on a long-range campaign that called for more than 20 per cent of the city's 61 square miles to be rehabilitated, at a cost of almost two billion dollars.

The soaring symbol of St. Louis' renaissance is the 630-foot-high Gateway Arch *(right),* which dominates the riverfront area. The strikingly modern arch is a unique expression of a revitalized city proudly reasserting its claims to greatness.

Like a rainbow of stainless steel, the Gateway Arch—tallest man-made monument in the nation—links symbols of St. Louis' past and present: the historic Old Courthouse and the brand-new Gateway Tower.

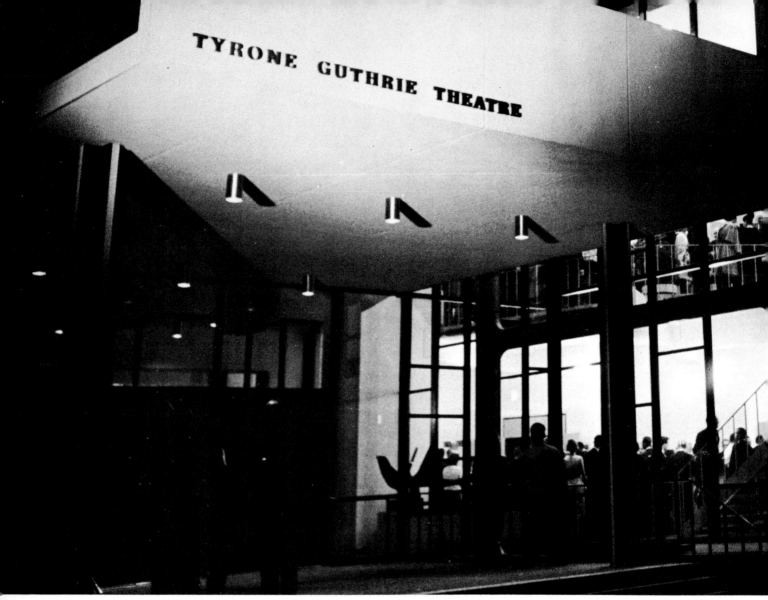

A thousand miles from Broadway, playgoers gather in the lobby of
the Tyrone Guthrie Theatre in Minneapolis for a production of
Hamlet. The theater, designed by architect Ralph Rapson, houses
one of the nation's leading repertory companies.

7

The Arts
in Full Blossom

The nation's most important theatrical news of 1963 came from neither Broadway nor Hollywood but from Minneapolis, Minnesota. That was the year the $2.25 million Tyrone Guthrie Theatre was opened under the command of Sir Tyrone, one of the world's most famous directors and a brilliant light of London's renowned Old Vic repertory company. Press agencies, national magazines, numerous newspapers, including *The New York Times*—all had critics, reporters and photographers on hand to assess and record the event.

There was a curious note of disbelief in some of the dispatches written before opening night. Why would a repertory company—one that aspired, in time, to become the American counterpart of the Old Vic—start up in the Plains States? Was there really an audience for Greek drama, Shakespeare, Shaw and Strindberg on the wind-swept prairies? "It seems strange," one New York newspaperman had said en route to Minneapolis. "It's as though the center of opera in this country were shifting from New York to Jackson, Mississippi."

The theater building, everyone agreed, was beautiful, a graceful, well-designed glass-walled structure overlooking a wide expanse of grass and trees. The 1,437 seats, covered with luxurious multicolored material, formed an arc on three sides of the large "thrust" stage. The lighting and other stage equipment were the finest available.

The opening night production of Hamlet, on May 7, 1963, proved that one of the most ambitious theatrical projects in American history was an artistic success as well as an architectural one. The people of the Plains States and beyond gave it rousing support. In the first year the 20-week summer season brought in nearly 200,000 patrons. The following year, attendance topped a quarter of a million, and in 1965 the figure was nearly 280,000. Nor was it only the audiences that responded to this exciting theatrical experiment. Actors with worldwide reputations, such as Hume Cronyn and his wife, Jessica Tandy, George Grizzard and Zoe Caldwell, were equally enthusiastic. Despite the relatively meager salaries the repertory company offered, these stars and a host of other experienced actors were delighted by the opportunity to perform at the Guthrie Theatre in the kinds of play infrequently seen in the commercial theater. Today, the Minnesota Theatre Company, the producing organization, is one of the most firmly established repertory companies in the nation. It enjoys a worldwide reputation and is the model for a number of other theatrical enterprises that have come into existence in recent years.

The Tyrone Guthrie Theatre is a glittering symbol of the vigorous revolution that is taking place in the arts throughout the Plains States, in small towns as well as in large cities. Professional, semi-professional and amateur acting groups are popping up all over the region like spring dandelions. There are now 50 symphony orchestras in the seven states and an astonishing number of chamber music groups, choral societies, ballet troupes, civic opera companies and similar organizations. Although many small towns in the region were once about as barren of culture as Sinclair Lewis portrayed them, the Plains States as a whole have never been an intellectual desert—in music, literature and education, in particular, the heritage is rich. But only recently has the growth of the arts been luxuriant.

There are a number of interrelated reasons for this blooming, and some of them are purely economic. Because of unprecedented and prolonged national prosperity, there are currently more rich people than ever before to help meet a symphony's deficit, underwrite a museum's purchase of an important painting or subsidize a producer who wants to start a professional theater. On a lower but still quite comfortable financial level, there are now large numbers of citizens who have the money to attend concerts and plays.

But equally important to the success of the cultural revolution has been the growing sophistication of taste in the Plains States. Travel has become a part of the lives of more and more residents of the region, and New York's theater, London's ballet, Paris's Louvre, Milan's opera and Berlin's symphony are likely to be familiar experiences. Also, national periodicals, metropolitan newspapers, television and other mass media focus popular attention on the arts. People in Fargo, North Dakota, are likely to learn of the newest "black comedy" to open on Broadway, the latest electronically produced concert or the most recent trend in sculpture almost as soon as the residents of Manhattan. Such homogenizing influences do bring penalties—regional flavor is inevitably diminished—but the mass media have provided a powerful stimulus to the arts in the Plains States.

Perhaps the most important factor in preparing and maintaining an atmosphere in which the arts can flourish has been the high quality of the region's many colleges and universities. Although there was only a handful of colleges, most of them denominational, in the Plains States before 1850, today there are nearly 140 accredited public and private institutions of higher learning. Outstanding among them are the region's internationally renowned state universities. What brought about the creation or expansion of these public universities was Congressional passage of the Morrill Act of 1862, which gave the states 17 million acres of public lands; the land was to be sold and the proceeds used for the establishment of colleges and universities offering programs in agriculture and the "mechanical arts." Now a great dream could be realized and a remarkable experiment in mass higher education carried out.

The frontier society of the Plains States was strongly egalitarian. There was a belief that a college education should not be a privilege of the wealthy class but the right of every citizen who had the proper academic qualifications. Tuition in public colleges could be kept at a minimal level because of state and federal subsidies. There was a thirst for education in the region, and the institutions grew with astonishing speed. By the late 1960s, for example, the University of Minnesota had a total of nearly 60,000 students on its four campuses. With expansion has come a broadening of educational focus. Once mainly concerned with technical training—for teachers, farmers, engineers and others—the schools now place major emphasis on scholarship in the humanities and the sciences. The impact of these federal- and state-subsidized colleges and universities on the region's culture has been enormous. Today the percentage of Plains Staters who have attended college nearly matches the figure for New England, which had institutions of higher learning as early as the 17th Century. Thus the Plains States have been well prepared for an artistic blossoming.

In this flourishing of the arts, music in particular is receiving imaginative attention. The University of Kansas, in Lawrence, for example, celebrated its centennial in 1966 with the world première of Pulitzer Prize winner Douglas Moore's opera *Carry Nation*, a work the university had commissioned for the occasion. (The career of Carry Nation, an ardent temperance crusader who lived in Medicine Lodge, Kansas, was an apt choice of subject matter for presentation in a state that was almost the last to repeal laws forbidding the sale of liquor.)

Nebraska also turned to opera—and to Douglas Moore—for the 100th anniversary of its statehood in 1967. Moore's work, *The Ballad of Baby Doe*—a rousing account of the days when the West was swarming with get-rich-quick prospectors in search of silver—was a highlight of the centennial celebration. About the same time *Carry Nation* was being set to music, the Performing Arts Foundation of Kansas City commissioned the famed Missouri composer Virgil Thomson to create an orchestral suite for its "Celebration of Henry Purcell," a tribute to the great 17th Century British composer.

The modern idiom also receives serious attention in Kansas City. In 1966 the world première of the jazz opera *Without Memorial Banners* was held there. The work, composed by Missourian Herb Six, was produced in honor of the outstanding Negro saxophonist Charlie "Bird" Parker, one of the most influential jazz musicians of our time.

Music, however, is no newcomer to the Plains States. St. Louis has the nation's second-oldest symphony orchestra (after the New York Philharmonic). Founded in 1880, the orchestra has consistently ranked among the best in the country. Of equally great contemporary reputation is the Minneapolis Symphony, which was established in 1903. People from all over the region, and from as far west as Billings, Montana, flock to Minneapolis to hear this excellent orchestra. There is a local observation that if audiences came from as far east as they come from the west, the accents of Boston Brahmins would be heard during intermissions. But audiences in Boston, New York, in fact, in cities all over the world, *do* turn out to hear the Minneapolis orchestra when it makes its tours.

Serious music is heard in the towns as well as the cities of the Plains States. Huron, South Dakota, for example, with a population of about 15,000, has a resident 60-piece symphony orchestra that plays not only the standard classical repertoire but the works of modern composers as well. In the neighboring state of North Dakota, Grand Forks (population 40,000) has its own orchestra that gives four concerts annually. Mark Twain's Hannibal, Missouri (population 20,000), supports a professional choir, the Mark Twain Men's Chorale, and regularly plays host to the St. Louis Symphony and the St. Louis Opera Company.

Omaha, Nebraska, with a population of some 300,000, not only has a resident symphony orchestra but one of the region's most interesting collections of paintings, in the Joslyn Art Museum, which opened in 1931. The museum building, a gaudy three-million-dollar structure of varying shades of pink marble, was the gift of Sarah Joslyn, the widow of a millionaire purveyor of patent medicines. Although some architectural critics have blanched at the ostentatious housing for Omaha's art, there is little caviling about the major items in the collection, which includes such works as Titian's *Man with a Falcon* and canvases by Corot, Van Dyck, Goya, El Greco, Monet, Renoir, Rembrandt and Rubens.

Half a century before the Joslyn Art Museum opened its doors in Omaha, the St. Louis Museum of Fine Arts was an established institution. In 1907, another local museum, the municipally supported City Art Museum of St. Louis, was founded, and five years later the two organizations merged under the name of the latter. Usually rated among the top half a dozen art museums in the nation, the St. Louis institution is visited annually by about 600,000 people, who come to see works by artists like Rembrandt, Titian and Gainsborough.

Missouri's other museum of note is the Nelson Gallery of Art in Kansas City. Established in 1933 with an $11 million trust fund set up by William Rockhill Nelson, founder of the Kansas City *Star*, the Nelson Gallery has an impressive collection of Renaissance paintings as well as one of the finest assemblages of Oriental art to be found in the United States. No mere repository for old and "safe" works of art, however, the Nelson also encourages modern experimentalism. In 1965 Howard Jones, a pioneer in electric-light painting, drew enthusiastic audiences, and the following year the gallery itself staged a show titled "Sound Light Silence," which included, among other attractions, African music, moving sculpture and the continuous projection of an abstract movie. The assistant director of the gallery, Ralph T. Coe, reported that most of the patrons were young and liked the show, but he said that he "was amazed that members of the older generation tried as hard as they did to ex-

Minnesota-born Sinclair Lewis, shown above at a picnic when he was 20 years old, set many of his novels in the Plains States. Such works as *Main Street, Babbitt* and *Dodsworth* contained sharp criticism of plainsmen for their materialism and conventionality.

amine the exhibits . . . and did not simply scoff at what they saw."

In neighboring Iowa is an even younger museum —the handsome $700,000 Des Moines Art Center, designed by Eliel Saarinen and opened in 1948. In 1953 the center scored a coup by acquiring Goya's *Don Manuel Garcia de la Prada* for $130,000. Commenting on the purchase, Emily Genauer of the New York *Herald Tribune* wrote: "That so distinguished and costly a work should have been bought by a small Iowa museum not yet five years old, focuses attention on a significant phenomenon of recent years—the increasingly important role being played in America's cultural life by museums away from great art centers like New York and Chicago. . . . Acquisition of the Goya would, in truth, be a major event for *any* museum."

The flourishing health of the Plains States museums, reflected in the major acquisitions they have made during recent decades, has brought about a great change in America's art world. "New York museums used to condescend on occasion to send their treasures out on tour for the pleasure of art lovers in the hinterlands," said the New York *Herald Tribune* in 1957. "Now traffic goes the other way. Museums in 'provincial' cities send their prize pictures and sculpture to New York where

we may, for a fee, have the privilege of looking at them."

What prompted this newspaper article was a traveling exhibition from The Minneapolis Institute of Arts, a show that included works by Rembrandt, Goya and El Greco. John Canaday of *The New York Times*, who visited the institute in 1962, pointed out that the museum is not interested in acquiring "second-rate examples of impressive names." The policy, he said, "is to have nothing but first-rate examples of anything." In the permanent collection are such works as Fra Angelico's oil-on-wood *St. Benedict*—one of the few paintings by that artist to have been brought across the Atlantic—Picasso's bronze *Monkey and Her Baby*, and a number of canvases by top 19th and 20th Century French painters.

Also serving culture in Minneapolis is the Walker Art Center, which one critic described as "this country's most vigorous outpost of in-art." Jan van der Marck, Walker's former curator, explained his concept in an interview in 1967: "I think of a museum as a place of experiment, a proving and testing ground. . . . I am interested in giving people a jolt, putting them on their toes and making them think. Most people have mental arthritis by the age of twenty-five. I want to conduct a course of yoga for the mind."

Among the yoga exercises prescribed have been "spatialist" exhibits in which showings of paintings and sculptures are combined with performances in which dancers move, according to one observer, "to the accompaniment of electronic sounds, smoke effusions, and what looked like a flame thrower." In 1966 the Walker Art Center staged an exhibit of works by the Italian artist Lucio Fontana and, for the occasion, constructed an "environment" from the artist's design. According to a *New York Times* reporter, "One reached this environment through a short, dark tunnel. . . . One's feet sunk, not unpleasantly, into a foam rubber floor. Tiny lights, defining a regular rectangle along the floor, walls and ceiling, created the curious illusion of a wall, where, in fact, there was only empty space."

One of the most important functions of the Walker Art Center is its Midwest Biennial, a regional show open to all artists of the Plains States as well as those from Illinois and Wisconsin. Thousands of works are entered, and some 400 are selected for showing; many are sold. There has been, however, little or no regional flavor to the show in recent years. The curator explained that "the kind of regionalism we had twenty years ago

—the regionalism of Grant Wood, Tom Benton and [John Steuart] Curry—doesn't exist in the Midwest any more. Our young artists are much more conscious today of what is going on in New York and in Paris and, in fact, all over the world."

Oddly enough for a museum with such modern ideas, the Walker Art Center dates back to 1875; at that time it was probably the only art gallery between Pittsburgh and the West Coast. But before residents of the Plains States began to collect art, organize symphony orchestras and establish repertory theaters, the region had an intellectual center of international importance. In January 1866 seven residents of St. Louis founded the St. Louis Movement to "encourage the study and development of Speculative Philosophy, to foster an application of its results to Art, Religion, and Science, and to establish a philosophical basis for the professions of Medicine, Divinity, Law, Politics, Education, Fine Arts and Literature." A year later the group began publication of the *Journal of Speculative Philosophy*, the first periodical in America specifically dedicated to philosophy. Even the haughty Transcendentalists of New England, an assemblage that included Ralph Waldo Emerson and Henry David Thoreau, hailed the *Journal* as an important addition to America's intellectual life, and several of their number became contributors. During its 25 years of publication, the *Journal* had a wide audience among philosophers in the United States and Great Britain, and it became an important influence among many intellectuals.

William Torrey Harris, the editor of the magazine for most of its life, attracted national attention, and in 1889 newly elected President Benjamin Harrison appointed him United States Commissioner of Education. "For seventeen years his would be a strong Washington voice for moral and spiritual values in education," says Robert C. Whittemore in his *Makers of the American Mind*. Harris urged a tough educational schedule on America's schools. A basic high-school course, for example, should include "algebra, geometry, trigonometry, physical geography (comprising ethnology, zoology, botany, geology, meteorology and astronomy), physics and chemistry, Latin, Greek, one modern language, English literature." Harris also suggested that to this list might be added "some general or special study of the history of the fine arts . . . for the aesthetic side of man." Not all of his ideas were adopted throughout the nation, but enough were to make him a powerful influence in American education.

While the St. Louis Movement was functioning

Willa Cather, whose novels of pioneer life in the West were to make her famous, reads to her brother and sister in the yard of their Red Cloud, Nebraska, home around the turn of the century. Among her most famous works are *My Antonia, O Pioneers* and *One of Ours*.

as a major force in philosophy during the last third of the 19th Century, another Missourian of a wholly different genre was at work establishing one of the greatest reputations in American literature. Calling himself Mark Twain, this sometime newspaperman, itinerant printer and riverboat pilot named Samuel Langhorne Clemens captured on paper the lusty frontier life with all its broad humor and mindless brutality as no other writer before or since has been able to do. He first came to wide public attention in 1865 with the publication of a humorous short story, "The Celebrated Jumping Frog of Calaveras County." The appearance of *The Adventures of Tom Sawyer* in 1876 established him as one of the most impressive writing talents in American history.

With the publication of *Life on the Mississippi* in 1883 and the *Adventures of Huckleberry Finn* in 1884, Twain rounded out his magnificent tribute to his own boyhood and the river he loved. *Huckleberry Finn*, generally regarded as Twain's finest novel, has probably been the most influential book in American fiction; Ernest Hemingway voiced the viewpoint of many authors and critics when he said that all modern American literature derives from that work. "In its darker aspects," says critic Jay B. Hubbell in *The South in American Literature*,

"Twain's picture recalls not only [George Washington] Cable's Louisiana but also the Yoknapatawpha County of William Faulkner's Mississippi." Historian Dixon Wecter documents this observation about *Huckleberry Finn:* "We are shown the sloth and sadism of poor whites, backwoods loafers with their plug tobacco and Barlow knives, who sic dogs on stray sows and 'laugh at the fun and look grateful for the noise,' or drench a stray cur with turpentine and set him afire. . . . Death by violence lurks at every bend of road or river."

Although Twain continued to be thought of chiefly as a humorist, this darker side of his nature was considerably more manifest in such later works as *The Tragedy of Pudd'nhead Wilson* and *Personal Recollections of Joan of Arc.* Perhaps the author himself best explained his comic-tragic view of life: "Everything human is pathetic. The secret source of Humor itself is not joy but sorrow. There is no humor in heaven." But Irish playwright George Bernard Shaw best summed up the lasting qualities of Mark Twain's writings. "I am persuaded," Shaw wrote to Twain, "that the future historian of America will find your works as indispensable to him as a French historian finds the political tracts of Voltaire."

About the time of Mark Twain's death in 1910, another Plains States writer, Willa Cather, was beginning her literary career with poems, short stories and such novels as *O Pioneers!* (1913). This Virginia-born author, who had come to Nebraska when still a small child, wrote of the harsh lot of immigrants trying to wrest a living from the prairie and to adjust to the unfamiliar demands of small-town life. Writing with the disciplined skill of a true artist, Miss Cather continued to add to her literary reputation with *The Song of the Lark* (1915), *My Ántonia* (1918) and *One of Ours* (1922), which won a Pulitzer Prize.

Overlapping the career of Willa Cather was that of Sinclair Lewis, first the shame and later the pride of Sauk Centre, Minnesota. Few first novels have ever evoked the wildly enthusiastic acclaim and violent outrage that greeted the publication of *Main Street* in 1920. Using Sauk Centre as his model and calling it Gopher Prairie, Lewis unleashed a barrage of scorn, ridicule and satire on the smug, materialistic, intellectually sterile small towns of the Plains States. The book and the time were perfect for each other. A generation of Americans bitterly disillusioned by World War I and eager to destroy the false gods of their society found in *Main Street* an effective expression of their anger, frustration and contempt. In their eyes, Gopher Prairie was not just a Midwest community but a microcosm of all that was wrong in America. More conventional Americans loudly protested that the book was a vicious, unwarranted attack on everything that was sacred in the nation.

In 1922 Lewis published *Babbitt,* a far sounder novel than *Main Street,* and one that mixed compassion with a vitriolic assessment of the small-city businessman and booster. Again, Sinclair Lewis stirred up a great debate among his readers as he cast scorn upon values held sacred by many Americans. Soon "Babbitt" entered the language as a word characterizing the desperately conforming businessman.

Still another literary meteor rose from the Plains States in the 1920s when F. Scott Fitzgerald of St. Paul, Minnesota, made his professional debut with the publication of *This Side of Paradise* (1920). Like Lewis, Fitzgerald was in tune with the era, but his beat was completely different. Fitzgerald wrote of the "Lost Generation," the gay, uninhibited, cynical, live-for-today people who made the 1920s the "Jazz Age." Fitzgerald was an immediate success; his powerful *The Great Gatsby* (1925) made him a kind of national monument. But with the coming of the Great Depression of the 1930s, Fitzgerald lost his vogue. *Tender Is the Night,* which appeared in 1934, was one of his finest novels, but it was out of touch with the dark mood and elemental problems of the times. Depressed by financial worries and personal problems, Fitzgerald went to Hollywood to work as a screenwriter. A failure at that task, he nonetheless continued to work on serious fiction, completing a sizable portion of *The Last Tycoon* before his death in Hollywood in 1940.

Although the Plains States were not the setting for most of Fitzgerald's work, his native region was always manifest in his writing; he was forever the man from the hinterlands in awe of, and never quite comfortable with, the rich cosmopolites he so admired. Many of the protagonists of Fitzgerald's novels were transplanted Midwesterners and reflected the author's sense of inferiority when confronted with the sophisticated denizens of New York, London, Paris and the Riviera.

The Plains States produced yet a third towering literary figure who came into prominence during the 1920s. Although St. Louis-born poet and Nobel Prize winner Thomas Stearns Eliot spent most of his adult life in England, his wit retained a strong American flavor and some of his imagery reflected his youth in the Plains States. Almost certainly Eliot must have been thinking of the Mississippi or Missouri River when he wrote:

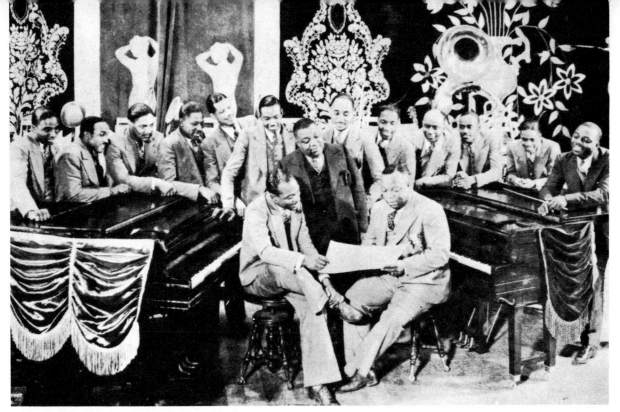

The Bennie Moten band was the leading group in the jazz-conscious Kansas City of the 1920s and 1930s. With its large Negro population, which supported numerous dance halls, Kansas City attracted jazz musicians from all over the country during this period, among them Moten *(seated at right)*, pianist Count Basie *(seated at left)*, and blues singer Jimmy Rushing *(standing between Basie and Moten)*. After Moten's death, some of his bandsmen formed the nucleus of the original Count Basie Band.

*I do not know much about gods; but I think
   that the river
Is a strong brown god—sullen, untamed
   and intractable,
Patient to some degree, at first recognized
   as a frontier;
Useful, untrustworthy, as a conveyor
   of commerce;
Then only a problem confronting
   the builder of bridges.*

The Plains States' capacity for producing outstanding writers did not end with Lewis, Fitzgerald and Eliot. Nebraska's historian and novelist Mari Sandoz and Missouri's novelist and poet Josephine W. Johnson, for example, were among those who made their appearances on the literary scene in the 1930s. Mari Sandoz, who was a regional writer in the best sense of that term, and who wrote, as one critic observed, "with a savage fury that almost raises blisters on the paper," made her debut in 1935 with *Old Jules*, a biography of her father, a hot-tempered, gun-toting farmer who came to Sheridan County, Nebraska, from Switzerland in the 1880s. Two years later *Slogum House*, a vivid, brawling novel about Plains frontier life, was published and was promptly banned in Nebraska

public libraries. (Twenty years later her home state was to honor her by declaring an official "Mari Sandoz Day" when *The Cattlemen* was published.) Of the score or so books she wrote before her death in 1966, *Crazy Horse, The Tom-Walker* and *Cheyenne Autumn* were among the most notable.

Josephine W. Johnson, a native of Missouri, began writing short stories while still a student at Washington University in St. Louis. Her first novel, *Now in November*, published in 1934, won the Pulitzer Prize. Although the author was only 24 when the book came out, this story of a Plains States farm during a drought was obviously the work of an artist—tough-minded and keenly observant. In the years that followed, Miss Johnson wrote such beautifully wrought novels as *Jordanstown, Wildwood* and *The Dark Traveler*, two volumes of short stories and one book of poetry, *Year's End*.

In the decades since the 1930s the Plains States have continued to be the source of some of America's finest writing talent. Novelist Wallace Stegner of Iowa, for example, established a solid reputation in the 1940s with *Fire and Ice* and *The Big Rock Candy Mountain*, while Nebraska's Wright Morris won the National Book Award with his novel, *The Field of Vision*, in the mid-1950s.

Iowa-born Paul Engle created a stir with his first

book of verse, *American Song*, in 1934. In *Corn*, a book of poetry published in 1939, he celebrated the simple life of Iowa farmers. William Inge, a frustrated actor from Independence, Kansas, shot to fame as a playwright in 1950 when his drama *Come Back, Little Sheba* opened on Broadway. It was a tender yet powerful play of a middle-aged couple and their shattered marriage. *Picnic*, his next big success, opened for a long run in 1953 and won a Pulitzer Prize for the author. *Bus Stop*, which appeared two years later, was equally acclaimed by the critics and public and, like his other two plays, was made into a highly popular motion picture.

Much of the continuing vigor of writing and the other arts in the Plains States is supplied by the region's colleges and universities. These institutions, which were vital in establishing a healthy atmosphere for culture, have been contributing directly to the arts through both on- and off-campus activities. The State University of Iowa is fairly typical in exercising this dual influence.

For graduate students with writing talent, the university operates the famed Writers' Workshop, which offers not only the guidance of professional writers on the staff but the counsel and criticism of such visiting authors as Herbert Gold, Philip Roth, Hortense Calisher and Nelson Algren. Off campus, the university cooperates with the Iowa Arts Council by sending chamber music groups and theatrical companies to all parts of the state.

The University of Missouri runs a community-wide program in music and theater. The Kansas City campus, for example, operates a children's theater and stages winter and summer seasons of plays for adults, while the Kansas City Conservatory of Music, which is a part of the university, gives public concerts and sends an orchestra on regular tours.

In Kansas the state universities are active in bringing music and art to the public. The Wichita Symphony Orchestra is a joint enterprise of Wichita State University and the city. Kansas State University helps to maintain interest in art through its Rural-Urban Art Club, which works through the state's County Extension Service.

Private institutions also do their part in the Plains States' cultural life. Creighton University, a Jesuit-run school in Omaha, Nebraska, for instance, operates a program to encourage high-school students from low-income families to remain in school. With room and board paid and materials furnished, students live on the campus for a seven-week period and attend sessions in writing, dramatics, music and other subjects.

Another Catholic institution, St. Louis University, in St. Louis, made an enormous contribution to scholarship, not only in the region but in the nation as well, with the opening of the Pope Pius XII Memorial Library in 1959. American scholars had long been handicapped because certain documents could be studied at only one place, the Vatican Library in Rome. The Reverend Lowrie J. Daly, a history teacher at the university, conceived the idea of microfilming the most important of these works and making them available in the United States, and the Vatican gave its permission for the undertaking. After four years of intensive work the university had nearly 900,000 feet of film on which were recorded 11 million handwritten pages. The collection includes some 600,000 individual manuscripts dealing with, among other subjects, history, theology, philosophy, music and literature. An Oxford scholar described the project as the "most important single addition ever made to the libraries of America."

St. Louis University is only one of several institutions of higher learning in the St. Louis area with strong off-campus ties. In 1966, for example, the city's professional repertory theater company began productions in the new Loretto-Hilton Center for the Performing Arts on the campus of Webster College. In addition to presenting plays for St. Louis audiences, the company, with financial support from the Federal Arts Endowment and the Missouri Arts Council, makes a three-month tour of the state. Washington University's cultural influence on St. Louis is mainly in the fields of art and music. The university's art gallery, Steinberg Hall, has a first-rate collection and annually brings in three or four traveling exhibits. The institution also maintains an excellent string quartet made up of members of the St. Louis Symphony.

In Minneapolis the town-gown relationship between the University of Minnesota and the city is most notable in drama. The university works in close cooperation with the Tyrone Guthrie Theatre in the training of apprentice actors and operates a drama research center that advises the numerous neighborhood theaters in the metropolitan area.

These are but a few of the colleges and universities playing important roles in the cultural revolution in the Plains States. It is a revolution that involves many kinds of institutions as well as government leaders, philanthropists, and creative men and women in the arts. The major ingredient, however, rests with the people of the Plains States. The interest they are showing in all aspects of culture is the bedrock upon which art depends.

Grant Wood's *Stone City,* painted in 1930, portrayed a real Iowa village that was once a quarrying center, then a ghost town and finally an art colony under Wood's direction.

Painters
of the prairie

The Plains States were long condemned as an American bastion of Philistinism. And yet in the 1930s this region, supposedly so hostile to the arts, produced a group of immensely popular and gifted painters who constituted one of the few truly regional schools of art in American history. The leaders of the Regionalists were Grant Wood of Iowa, John Steuart Curry of Kansas and Thomas Hart Benton of Missouri.

As young men, Wood, Curry and Benton all traveled to Europe and tried to paint in the abstract style that had recently captivated the elite art circles and alienated the general public. But modernist painting did not suit them, and they returned to the U.S., where, celebrating the great body of rural experience, they attracted a large and varied audience by portraying the virtues—and vagaries—of a vital part of American life.

Grant Wood

Born on a farm in Iowa in 1892, Grant Wood had to travel halfway around the world to discover that the wellspring of his art lay not in the flourishing art centers of Europe, but in the rolling fields and rugged farmers he had known as a boy. Although he had at first taken to Parisian life and had even grown a beard and affected a beret, he soon became disenchanted with Continental ways and with the Impressionistic landscapes he was turning out by the score. "It was then," he said, "that I realized that all the really good ideas I'd ever had came to me while I was milking a cow. So I went back to Iowa."

Soon after his return from Europe, Wood's paintings of rural life in Iowa were exhibited in many of the fashionable New York art galleries and were widely reproduced both in advertisements and on magazine covers. Firing the popular imagination by exaggerating and romanticizing familiar realities beyond the commonplace, his paintings portrayed the grim, stalwart Iowa farmers and reminded millions of Americans of their proud pioneer beginnings.

Thought by some to be Wood's greatest achievement and the perfect statement of the American character, *Dinner for Threshers* portrays sturdy Iowa farmers at harvesttime.

Wood's *Arbor Day*, painted in
1932, depicted a group of Iowa
school children planting a sapling
in the yard outside their
schoolhouse. Wood modeled this
work after a real schoolhouse in
northern Iowa and dedicated it
to two of his former teachers,
who taught him, as he put it, "the
wealth of common things."

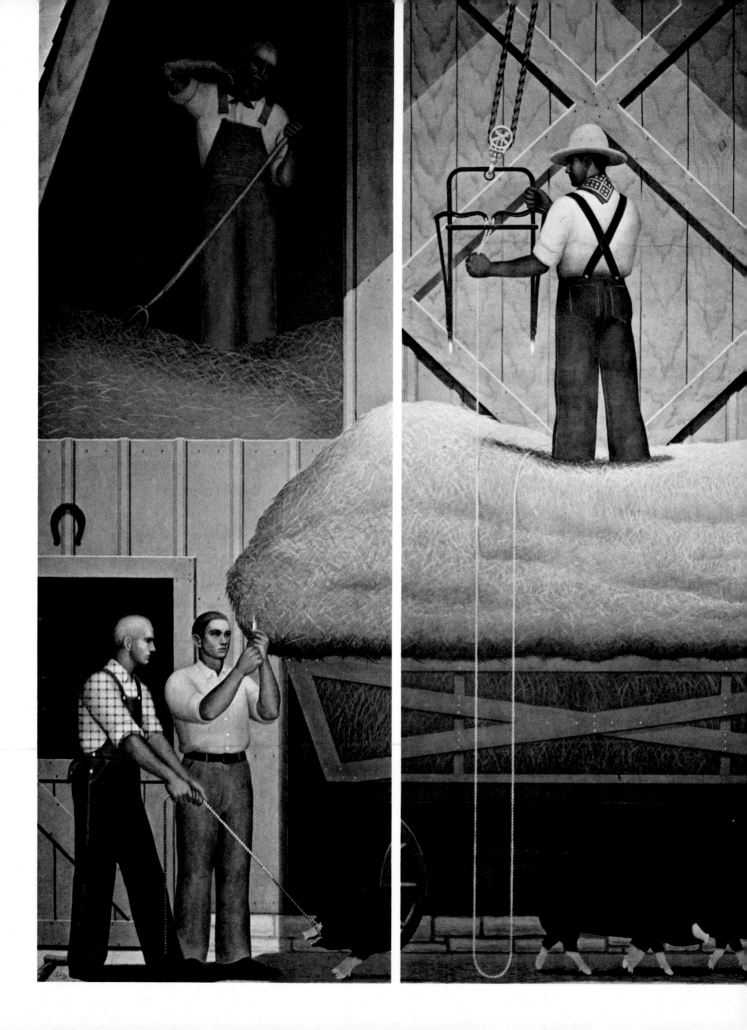

The three mural panels at left, portraying the daily chores of the Iowa farmer, were designed by Grant Wood and painted by artists working for the PWAP, the Public Works of Art Project. When the PWAP was established in 1933, Wood became its director for Iowa, and under his leadership the group produced a large number of fine murals, among them these three, which now decorate the Iowa State University library at Ames.

In 1934 Wood joined the fine-arts staff of the University of Iowa, where he remained until his death in 1942. During this time he continued to portray the Iowa scene with meticulous care. Mulling over mail-order catalogues to observe the minute details of farm equipment, sometimes working as many as 18 hours a day, Wood often took a year to finish a painting. When it was completed, there might be seven or eight layers of paint beneath the surface, any one of which might have been acceptable to a less demanding artist. The painstaking care paid off, for by the end of his life Wood had firmly established himself as one of the most influential and best-loved of American artists.

John Steuart Curry

John Steuart Curry's friend and fellow Regionalist Thomas Hart Benton said after Curry's death in 1946: "Curry never forgot that he came off a Kansas farm, that his folks were plain Kansas folks whose lives were spent with the plain, simple elemental things of the earth and sky. His Art and the meanings of his Art were never cut loose from this background."

Born in 1897 near Dunavant, Kansas, Curry began his artistic career as an illustrator of Western stories for magazines like *Boy's Life* and *The Saturday Evening Post*. But commercial art did not suit him; he was constantly accused of trying to make "museum paintings" out of his illustrations. So, perhaps out of necessity, he turned to serious painting and soon found success. His works, which have hung in the nation's finest galleries, are remarkable for their tense, dramatic style, whether they portray a simple rural ceremony or a stirring scene out of American history.

In *Tornado Over Kansas (above)*, painted in 1929, Curry portrayed the high-pitched emotion and fear of impending disaster felt by a tough, self-reliant farmer and his family as they hurry to the safety of their storm cellar.

Curry's *Baptism in Kansas*, completed in 1928, was one of the artist's first serious works. Evoking the simple religious fervor of the rural Kansas population, Curry brilliantly captured the flavor of this vital part of the plainsman's life.

167

The two murals at right, *Westward Migration (top)* and *Justice Defeating Mob Violence (bottom),* were painted by Curry in 1936 and 1937 for the Department of Justice Building in Washington. In *Westward Migration* Curry summed up one of the most stirring episodes in the American experience, the relentless push of rugged pioneers across the continent. Fascinated by such romantic American figures as Buffalo Bill and Wild Bill Hickok, Curry portrayed the pioneer father in this mural as an oldtime hero, standing on the edge of cultivated land, ready to move onto the frontier where such dangers as outlaws and prairie fires await. A fitting subject to decorate the seat of the federal law-enforcement system, *Justice Defeating Mob Violence* is much like *Westward Migration* in that both murals portray the forces of good and evil at the moment of conflict. Such intense dramatic effects are common in Curry's art and have helped to make him the finest painter Kansas has yet produced.

Thomas Hart Benton

Thomas Hart Benton, shown at right in a photograph taken in 1939, is the most famous and outspoken member of the Regionalists. Born in 1889 in Neosho, Missouri, he began to draw almost as soon as he could hold a pencil. Commenting later on a work he had completed at the age of six, Benton wrote: "Executed first mural with crayons on newly papered staircase wall in Benton home in Neosho. Work unappreciated."

Since that first mural, few of the artist's works have gone unappreciated. For almost 50 years Benton, who called the modernists of the 1920s "an intellectually diseased lot, victims of sickly rationalizations, psychic inversions, and God-awful self-cultivations," has painted scenes brimming over with American vitality. Often evoking the brute force and energy of plains life, his works have captured the American imagination.

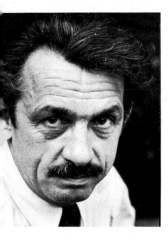

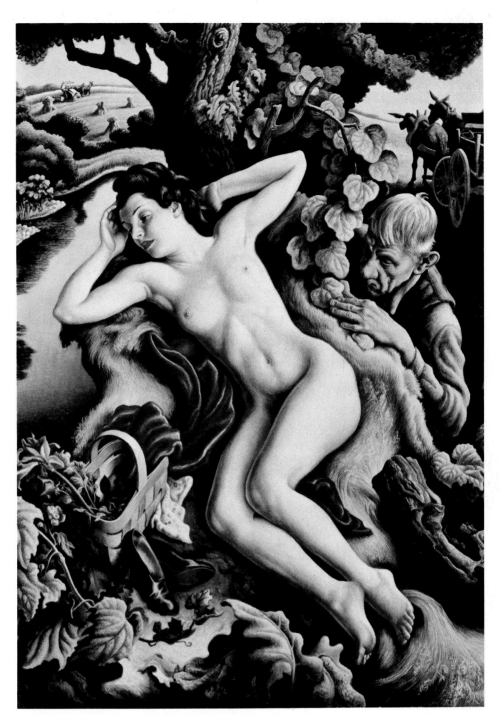

In *Persephone* Benton portrayed Pluto *(right)* and
Persephone as Missouri farm folk. In the Greek myth, Pluto
abducted Persephone, daughter of the goddess of
agriculture, causing winter to come to the land.

Hailstorm (left), painted in 1940, is a striking example of
the Regionalists' frequent use of the turbulent weather of
the Plains States for their subject matter.

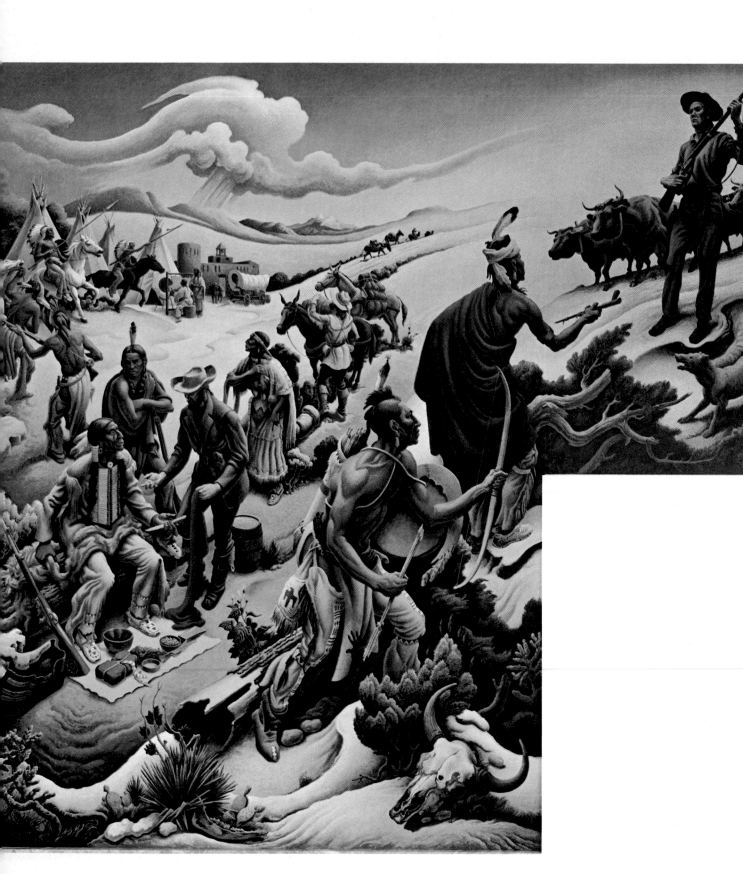

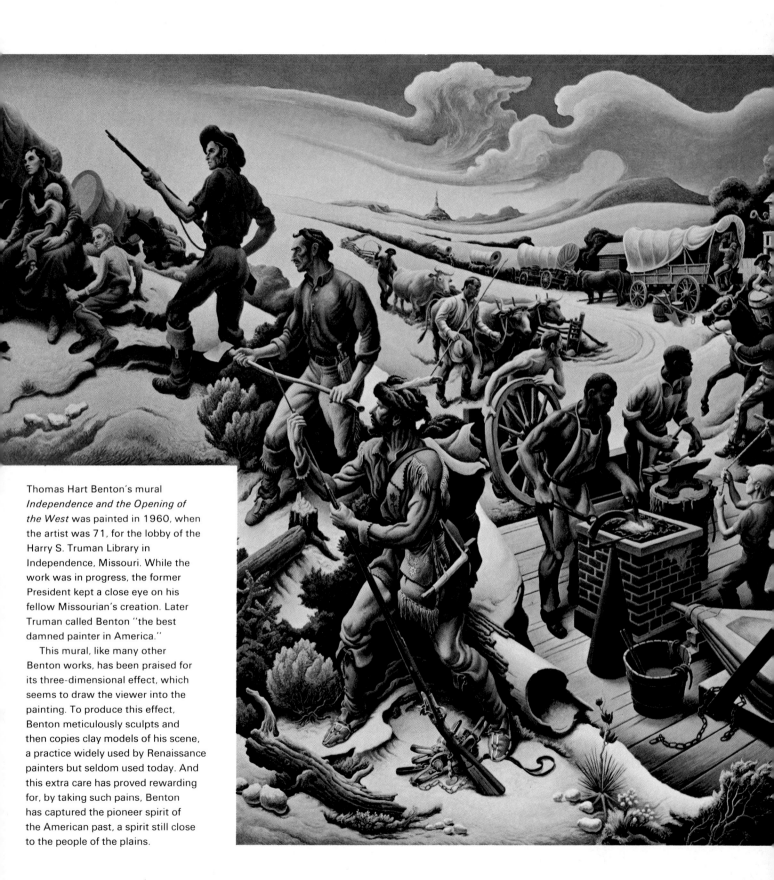

Thomas Hart Benton's mural *Independence and the Opening of the West* was painted in 1960, when the artist was 71, for the lobby of the Harry S. Truman Library in Independence, Missouri. While the work was in progress, the former President kept a close eye on his fellow Missourian's creation. Later Truman called Benton "the best damned painter in America."

This mural, like many other Benton works, has been praised for its three-dimensional effect, which seems to draw the viewer into the painting. To produce this effect, Benton meticulously sculpts and then copies clay models of his scene, a practice widely used by Renaissance painters but seldom used today. And this extra care has proved rewarding for, by taking such pains, Benton has captured the pioneer spirit of the American past, a spirit still close to the people of the plains.

Suggested tours

On the following pages, seven maps show sections of the Plains States that are of interest to the tourist. No attempt has been made to show every road or town. Instead, scenic routes, parks and other special features have been emphasized. The text accompanying each map gives a brief description of the area. Opening dates and hours, especially of the business tours, should be confirmed locally, since these vary during the year. The areas covered are shown in the small map below, along with a key to the symbols used.

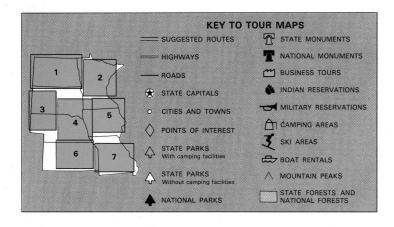

KEY TO TOUR MAPS

- SUGGESTED ROUTES
- HIGHWAYS
- ROADS
- ★ STATE CAPITALS
- ∘ CITIES AND TOWNS
- ◇ POINTS OF INTEREST
- △ STATE PARKS With camping facilities
- △ STATE PARKS Without camping facilities
- ▲ NATIONAL PARKS

- ⛩ STATE MONUMENTS
- ⛩ NATIONAL MONUMENTS
- BUSINESS TOURS
- INDIAN RESERVATIONS
- MILITARY RESERVATIONS
- CAMPING AREAS
- SKI AREAS
- BOAT RENTALS
- MOUNTAIN PEAKS
- STATE FORESTS AND NATIONAL FORESTS

1. North Dakota

With its rugged scenery and abundant fish and game, North Dakota is an excellent vacation state. A logical place to begin a tour is in Fargo, in the southeastern part of the state. Here, in the Cass County Historical Society Museum, there are excellent collections of Indian artifacts, pioneer home equipment and farm machinery. West of Fargo, on Route 10, is Bismarck, the state capital. Visitors will want to see the nearby Menoken Indian Village Historic Site, where an ancient Indian village has been excavated and restored.

Farther west, just off Route 10, is the fascinating village of Medora. The town was built in the 1880s by a French marquis who tried and failed at cattle ranching. His magnificent 28-room château is open to visitors. Buffalo herds and prairie-dog colonies may be seen in the nearby Theodore Roosevelt National Memorial Park.

Northeast of the park, Route 85 leads to Williston, where visitors may tour the Dakota Salt and Chemical Company plant. Almost due north of Williston, via Routes 85 and 50, is the Writing Rock Historic Site. Here there is a 10-ton rock covered with lines, dots, circles and a flying bird. Still undeciphered, the symbols are thought to be of Indian, or even Asian, origin. Continuing east, along Route 2, visitors reach Rugby, near the Geographical Center of North America. North of Rugby, along the Canadian border, a 2,000-acre park and garden has been established to symbolize the peaceful relations between Canada and the United States.

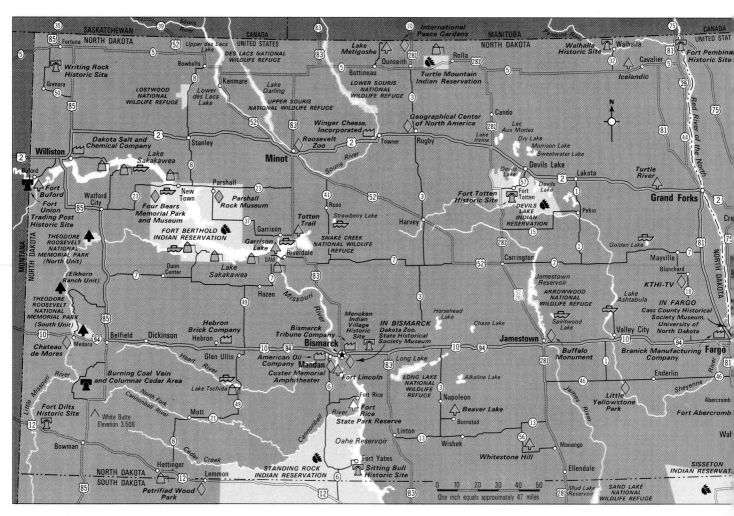

Map labels

Thief Lake · Mud Lake · 59 · Old Mill · AGASSIZ NATIONAL WILDLIFE REFUGE · 219 · BELTRAMI ISLAND STATE FOREST · 89 · 72 · Waskish · PINE ISLAND STATE FOREST · 71 · Big Falls · Rainy River · International Falls · 53 · SMOKEY BEAR STATE FOREST · ONTARIO · MINNESOTA · CANADA · UNITED STATES · QUETICO PROVINCIAL PARK · Crane Lake · ECHO TRAIL

Thief River Falls · 1 · Upper Red Lake · KABETOGAMA STATE FOREST · KOOCHICHING STATE FOREST · NETT LAKE INDIAN RESERVATION · Pelican Lake · Trout Lake · Burntside Lake · Ely

Old Crossing Treaty · 32 · Red Lake River · RED LAKE INDIAN RESERVATION · Lower Red Lake · RED LAKE STATE FOREST · 1 · 6 · BIG FORK ST. FOR. · Bigfork · Scenic · STURGEON RIVER STATE FOREST · McCarthy Beach · Tower-Soudan · 1 · Bear Head Lake

Crookston · 2 · Red Lake Falls · BUENA VISTA STATE FOREST · 89 · CHIPPEWA NATIONAL FOREST · 38 · GEORGE WASHINGTON STATE FOREST · Chisholm · BEAR ISLAND STATE FOREST · Birch Lake · SUPERIOR NATIONAL FOREST · 1

59 · Bagley · Bemidji · Lake Bemidji · Round Lake · Paul Bunyan Statue · Hull-Rust-Mahoning (open-pit mining) · Mountain Iron · Virginia · 169 · Lookout Mountain · U.S. Steel Corporation · Minnesota Museum of Mining · 61

WHITE EARTH INDIAN RESERVATION · MISSISSIPPI HEADWATERS STATE FOREST · Cass Lake · 2 · LEECH LAKE INDIAN RESERVATION · Prairie Lake · Hibbing · 371 · Itasca · PAUL BUNYAN STATE FOREST · Cass Lake · Grand Rapids · WHITEFACE STATE FOREST · CLOQUET VALLEY STATE FOREST · Gooseberry Falls

TAMARAC NATIONAL WILDLIFE REFUGE · Walker · Leech Lake · 169 · SAVANNA STATE FOREST · Independence · Two Harbors · Lake Superior · 61

Buffalo River · Hawley · 10 · Detroit Lakes · 34 · TWO INLETS ST. FOR. · Park Rapids · HILL RIVER STATE FOREST · Savanna Portage · FOND DU LAC INDIAN RESERVATION · 33 · Duluth

Becker County Historical Society · 59 · SMOKY HILLS STATE FOREST · BADOURA STATE FOREST · Woman Lake · LAND O'LAKES STATE FOREST · Cloquet · Superior · IN DULUTH · A.M. Chisholm Museum · Leif Erikson Park · St. Louis County Historical Society · Tweed Gallery

Pelican Lake · 52 · Pelican Rapids · 108 · Big Pine Lake · FOOTHILLS STATE FOREST · 371 · Whitefish Lake · CROW WING STATE FOREST · 210 · FOND DU LAC STATE FOREST · Jay Cooke · 2

Maplewood · Battle Lake · Wadena · PILLSBURY STATE FOREST · Brainerd · Aitkin · RICE LAKE NATIONAL WILDLIFE REFUGE · 61 · Moose Lake · 35 · WISCONSIN · Lake Gordon

Fergus Falls · 210 · 29 · 71 · Crow Wing · Lumbertown U.S.A. · WEALTHWOOD STATE FOREST · SOLANA STATE FOREST · NEMADJI STATE FOREST · 53 · Lake Christina · Lake Miltona · CAMP FORT RIPLEY · Mille Lacs Lake · Sandstone · Banning · SAINT CROIX STATE FOREST · Rice Lake

Elbow Lake · 94 · Elk Lake · Lake Carlos · Lake Osakis · Charles A. Lindbergh · 371 · Mille Lacs-Kathio · Father Hennepin · 27 · 48 · SAINT CROIX · CHENGWATANA STATE FOREST · N · Spooner · 8

Hoffman · Alexandria · Kensington Runestone · Little Falls · Fort Mille Lacs · RUM RIVER STATE FOREST · Mora · 35 · Pine City · 53

59 · Glenwood · Sauk Centre · 52 · Saint John's University · 10 · Milaca · 23

Morris · 29 · Lake Minnewaska · Collegeville · Saint Cloud · Princeton · 61

Ortonville · 12 · Benson · 9 · SHERBURNE NATIONAL WILDLIFE REFUGE · Rum River · SAND DUNES STATE FOREST · 10 · 52 · Saint Croix Falls · Interstate · William O'Brien · 8

Appleton · Monson Lake · Sibley · 372 · Clearwater Lake · Green Lake · 169 · Elk River · Elk River Rural Electric Co-Operative · 95 · IN SAINT PAUL · Indian God of Peace, Minnesota Historical Society Museum, Saint Paul Art Center

Bois de Sioux River · 59 · Willmar · Litchfield · Buffalo · 25 · 10 · Fort Snelling State Historical Park · Bayport · 94 · Eau Claire

Lac qui Parle · Acton · 12 · Lake Lillian · Minneapolis · General Mills, Inc. · Minneapolis Grain Exchange · Saint Paul · Union Stockyards · Dakota County Historical Museum · 64

Montevideo · 212 · Granite Falls · 71 · 7 · IN MINNEAPOLIS · Minneapolis Institute of Arts, University of Minnesota, Walker Art Center · 35W · 53

One inch equals approximately 40 miles · 0 10 20 30 40 50

2. Northern and central Minnesota

Minnesota is called the "land of 10,000 lakes." In fact, it has more than 14,000, and these make the state a vast paradise for swimmers, fishermen, sailors and all others who like the outdoors. A natural place to start a trip is in Minnesota's famous Twin Cities, Minneapolis and Saint Paul. Visitors may find a tour through the Minneapolis Grain Exchange—the largest cash grain market in the nation—an interesting experience. One of Saint Paul's favorite tourist attractions is a 44-foot-high statue of an Indian God of Peace. It is carved in white onyx and slowly rotates 132 degrees every two and a half hours. A short drive north of Saint Paul on Routes 61 and 8 leads to the Interstate State Park, which includes land in Minnesota and Wisconsin along the scenic Saint Croix River.

Farther north is Duluth, a dramatic city built on Lake Superior, the largest fresh-water lake in the world. Since the opening of the St. Lawrence Seaway in 1959,

Duluth has been a major world port, although it is 2,342 miles from the ocean. The town of Ely, which is to the north via Routes 61 and 1, is a good place to go for a lake-country vacation. Here many canoe outfitters set up tours, and it is possible to travel from lake to lake for hundreds of miles through wilderness. To the southwest is the town of Hibbing, which boasts the world's largest open-pit mine. Begun as a small underground iron-mining operation in 1896, it is now a vast pit 3.3 miles long and 535 feet deep.

Due west of Hibbing, via Routes 169 and 2, is Bemidji. Here the Chamber of Commerce will provide Indian guides, who lead tours of the huge Red Lake Reservation. Farther south, via Routes 71 and 29, at Alexandria, is one of Minnesota's most interesting sights, the Kensington Runestone. This 200-pound boulder has carvings that presumably tell of a Viking exploration to the area in 1362, although its authenticity is questionable.

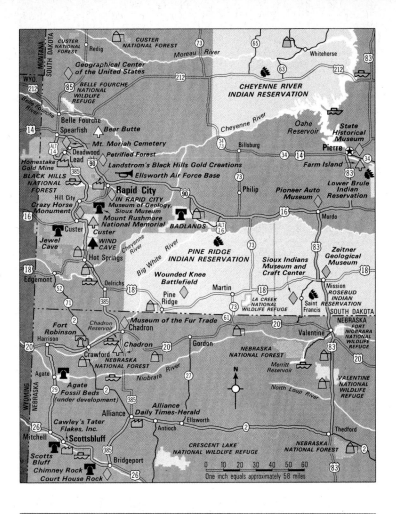

3. Western Nebraska and South Dakota

A circle tour of western Nebraska and South Dakota leads through rugged terrain and past numerous sites of importance in the history of the region's Indians and the white settlers. Starting in Thedford, Nebraska (*bottom right of map*), the tour heads westward to Bridgeport, on the North Platte River. Following the river, the route goes close by the old Oregon Trail, where such natural landmarks as Court House Rock, Chimney Rock and Scotts Bluff stand prominently above the surrounding land. A few miles north of Mitchell are the Agate Fossil Beds, where erosion has exposed the fossils of prehistoric plains mammals. By traveling north to Harrison and then east, visitors reach Fort Robinson State Monument, site of the frontier outpost where a famous Sioux, Chief Crazy Horse, was slain. To the north, above Chadron, the tour enters the Black Hills of South Dakota with their Wind Cave National Park. From Hill City a detour east leads to Mount Rushmore, the impressive monument to four American Presidents. The tour continues northward to the gold-mining center of Lead and to the once notorious town of Deadwood. Turning east at Spearfish, the route leads to Rapid City, site of the Sioux Museum, with exhibits on Indian cultural history, and the Badlands National Monument with its weirdly eroded terrain. Pierre, the state capital, lies to the northeast via Route 83. There the State Historical Museum displays Indian artifacts and relics of the early pioneers. Returning to Thedford, the tour goes through the Rosebud Indian Reservation (*pages 43-57*), where a short detour leads to the excellent Sioux Indians Museum and Craft Center.

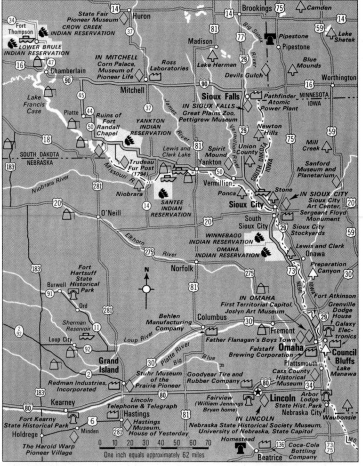

4. Eastern Nebraska and neighboring areas

A tour through eastern Nebraska and nearby portions of neighboring states provides rich rewards for people interested in pioneer and Indian history. A good place to begin is Kearney, Nebraska (*bottom left*) on Route 80, and the nearby Fort Kearny State Historical Park. The fort, which is being restored, was an important stop for travelers on the old Oregon Trail. South of Kearney, at Minden, is The Harold Warp Pioneer Village, which includes one of the nation's most comprehensive collections of American arts and crafts and exhibits on science and technology. Its 22 buildings include an 1869 fort, a land office with old maps and records, a sod house and a train depot with two early locomotives.

About 140 miles to the east, along Route 80, is Lincoln, the state capital. Here one can visit the restored house of the famous orator and statesman William Jennings Bryan. Also in Lincoln the State Historical Society offers many exhibits of Indian and pioneer artifacts. It is only a short drive northeast from Lincoln, on Route 80, to Omaha, Nebraska's largest city. Omaha's citizens are justly proud of their Joslyn Art Museum, which has works by Titian, El Greco, Rembrandt and Goya.

Just east of Omaha, and across the border in Iowa, is the Grenville Dodge House in Council Bluffs, an interesting, antique-filled Victorian residence, now a museum. To the north, in Minnesota, is the Pipestone National Monument, a preserved quarry where Indians extracted red stone for making ceremonial pipes. This place was sacred to many plains tribes. A museum there exhibits Indian pipes and other objects of red stone.

5. Iowa and southern Minnesota

A tour through this area, starting in the southwest corner, offers the visitor many cultural and industrial points of interest. East of the town of Ames, Iowa, on Route 30, is the Mesquakie Indian Settlement, where a powwow with authentic rituals and dances is held each August. To the south of Ames, via Route 35, one comes to Des Moines, capital of Iowa. The Salisbury House in Des Moines is patterned after a 16th Century English manor and has paintings by Van Dyke and Corot.

Northeast of Des Moines, on Route 30, is Cedar Rapids and the nearby Amana Colonies. The Amana folk, who preserve Old World customs much in the manner of Pennsylvania's Amish people, are renowned for their handsome woodwork and woolen goods. About 25 miles south of Cedar Rapids, Iowa City contains not only the State University but Herbert Hoover's birthplace and memorial library; the library contains many of the President's papers and memorabilia. To the north, along

Route 52, the town of Decorah has a strong Norwegian heritage. In town there is a fine historical museum with exhibits of furniture and fishing boats. Near Decorah is The Bily Clock Exhibit at Spillville, a marvelous collection that includes the 10-foot-tall American Pioneer Clock with 57 bas-relief panels depicting frontier life.

Across the border in Minnesota, the town of Rochester is the site of the famous Mayo Clinic, which offers special guided tours and a museum with exhibits relating to human anatomy. Northwest of Rochester, along Route 169, is Le Sueur, where the Green Giant Company presents tours of its immense cannery.

Returning to western Iowa via Routes 169, 60, 71, 18 and 44, visitors reach The Grotto of the Redemption near Algona. Begun in 1912, this structure covers a city block and is made of ornamental stones from every state in the Union. It is considered the largest collection of minerals, fossils, shells and petrifications in the world.

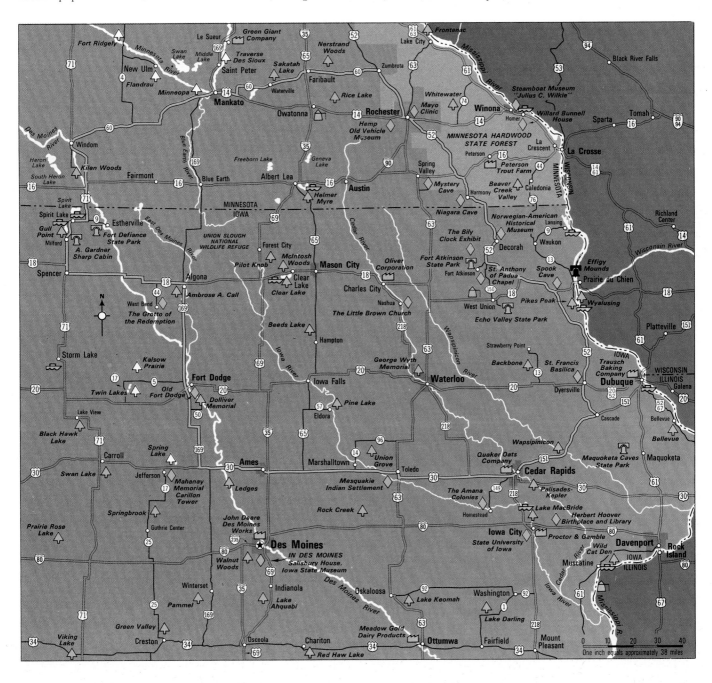

6. Kansas

Though few visitors to Kansas will be startled by the sight of thousands of acres of gently swaying wheat, many may be astonished by the extent to which industry has invaded this state best known for its agriculture.

Lawrence, a food-processing and paper-box manufacturing center near Route 70, is a good starting point for a tour for those entering the state from the east. This town is the site of the University of Kansas and was the stronghold of abolitionist sentiment in pre-Civil War days. There are several fine museums at the university, including the Natural History Museum which has one of the nation's largest collections of fossils and mounted animals. Nearby at the Snow Entomological Museum two million specimens of insects are also on display. Just west of Lawrence, along Route 70, the visitor comes to Topeka, capital of the state. The town was founded in 1854 at the point where the Oregon Trail crossed the Kansas River, thus enabling the inhabitants to profit from the western trade. The Kansas State Historical Society has many interesting displays, including a Concord stage coach and an airplane manufactured in Topeka in 1912. Visitors will find the Hollenberg Pony Express Station northwest of Topeka to be a worthwhile experience. Reached by Routes 70, 77 and 36, it is the last remain-

ing Pony Express Station in the nation to be maintained in its original state and location.

Returning to Route 70 and continuing west, vacationers come to Fort Riley, an outpost for the defense of the Santa Fe and Oregon Trails in the 1850s. Now it is one of the largest inland military reservations in the country and boasts an excellent historical museum. Farther west is Abilene, the end of the old Chisholm Trail from Texas. In the late 1860s and early 1870s more than a million cattle were driven to the shipping pens at Abilene. Today, Old Abilene Town has been reconstructed and looks much as it did in frontier days. The Eisenhower Center, with the former President's boyhood home, a library and museum, may be visited by tourists in town.

Still farther west on Route 70 are two other famous cow towns, Salina and Hays; southwest of Hays, via Routes 183 and 56, is Dodge City, the most renowned cow town of all. Once the world's largest cattle market, Dodge was notorious for vice and violence. On Old Front Street, buffalo hunters, cowboys, soldiers and Indians mingled with famous lawmen like Wyatt Earp and Bat Masterson. Museums in Dodge display mementos of wild West days. A variety show at the Long Branch Saloon recalls the lusty entertainment of frontier days.

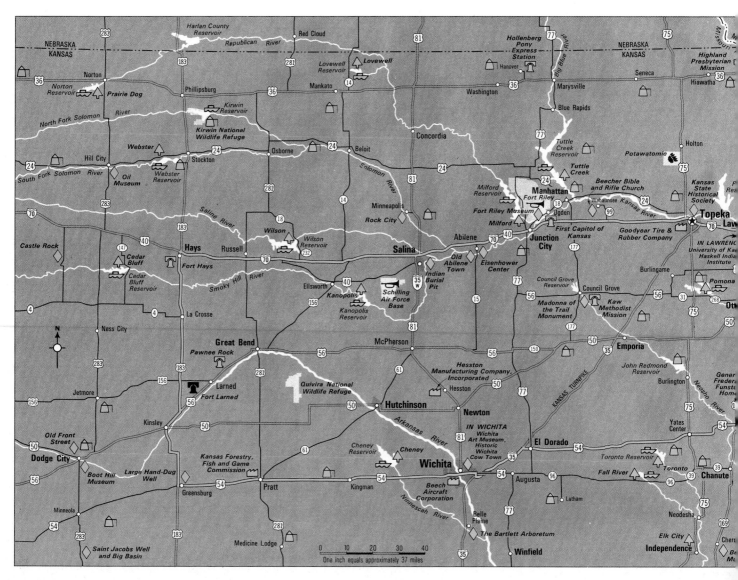

7. Missouri

Offering a blend of Western excitement and Eastern sophistication, Kansas City is an attractive place to begin a tour of Missouri. The American Royal Livestock and Horse Show, held each fall, is an eagerly anticipated event for ranchers and sportsmen. A more sedate pleasure is an afternoon in the William Rockhill Nelson Gallery and Atkins Museum of Fine Arts, which contains a notable collection of European, American and Oriental art. Just east of Kansas City is Independence, hometown of Harry S. Truman and site of the former President's library. Many mementos of Mr. Truman's Administration are on exhibit.

South of Independence, along Route 71, is Lamar, birthplace of Mr. Truman, and farther to the south is Carthage, near the birthplace of the famous Negro scientist George Washington Carver. A national monument near Carthage commemorates Carver's contributions to science and education.

Campers will find the area east of Carthage a delight. Spread out along Route 60 are a number of national forests with facilities for camping, hiking and fishing. Near the junction of Routes 60 and 67 is Lake Wappapello, a good spot for a picnic or an afternoon of boating. Some 70 miles north of Lake Wappapello, off Route 67, is the town of Sainte Genevieve, on the banks of the Mississippi. Its major attraction is the Bolduc House, believed to have been built in 1753 by Louis Bolduc, a prominent merchant. Open to the public, the Bolduc House is luxuriously furnished with 18th Century French Creole pieces.

From Sainte Genevieve it is only a short drive north to St. Louis, the largest and most cosmopolitan city in the Plains States. Among its points of interest is the Missouri Botanical Garden, famous for its orchids and cultivated plants of the Southwest. The garden has the world's first geodesic-dome greenhouse. Also in St. Louis is the Jefferson National Expansion Memorial arch (*page 151*), from whose top can be seen the entire city area.

North of St. Louis, hugging the Mississippi River bluffs, is Hannibal, Mark Twain's hometown, where a museum displays the author's memorabilia, letters, furniture and a collection of first editions.

West of St. Louis, off Route 70, is the town of Fulton. There, at Westminister College, Winston Churchill delivered his famous Iron Curtain speech in 1946. As a tribute to the late Prime Minister, the English church of St. Mary Aldermanbury was moved from its site in Britain and was reconstructed on the Westminster campus.

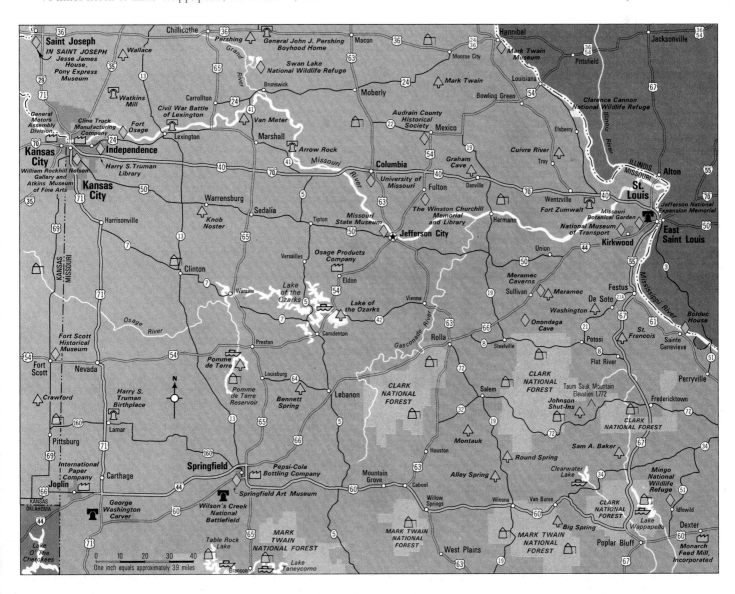

Museums and galleries

Iowa

Decorah
The Norwegian-American Museum, 520 W. Water St. Immigrant pioneer artifacts; Norwegian silver collection; china; glass; Eskimo collection. May, June, Sept, Oct: daily 10-4; July-Aug: daily 9-5:30.

Des Moines
Iowa State Museum, E. 12th and Grand Ave. Geology; Indian artifacts; space exhibits; coins; sporting weapons; Civil War weapons; newspapers; map files; military records. Daily 8-4.

Iowa City
State University of Iowa, Museum of Natural History, McBride Hall. Dioramas show animals in their natural habitats; arrowhead and spearhead displays; Maori and Philippine exhibits. Mon-Sat 8-4:30; Sun 1-4:30.

McGregor
Effigy Mounds National Monument, Visitor Center, three miles north of Marquette. Indian burial grounds; archeological items; audio-visual presentations. Sept-May: daily 8-5; June-Aug: daily 8-7.

Sioux City
Sioux City Art Center, 513 Nebraska St. Contemporary American Midwestern paintings, drawings, prints and sculpture. Tues-Sat 10-5; Sun 1-4.

Spillville
The Bily Clock Exhibit. Hand-carved clocks created by the Bily brothers; 1893 historic house occupied by the Czech composer Anton Dvořák. May-Oct: daily 8:30-5:30.

West Branch
Herbert Hoover Presidential Library. Personal papers and memorabilia of Mr. Hoover and items relating to his life and times. June 1-Sept 15: Mon-Sat 9-4:30; Sun 10-5; Sept 16-May 31: Mon-Fri 9-4:30; Sun 2-5.

Kansas

Abilene
Eisenhower Center, S.E. Fourth St. Boyhood home of the former President; mementos and gifts during Army career and Presidency. Daily 9-4:45.

Dodge City
Old Front Street, 500 W. Wyatt Earp Blvd. Reconstruction of 1870 main street; pioneer and Indian artifacts. Daily 8-6.

Kansas City
Agriculture Hall of Fame, 630 N. 126th St. Large collection of early farm machines. Daily 9-5.

Lawrence
University of Kansas Museum of Art and Natural History Museum, on campus. Contemporary paintings and sculpture; decorative arts; mounted animals in natural settings; fossils. During school session: Mon-Sat 9-4:45; Sun 1:30-4:45.

Topeka
Kansas State Historical Museum, 10th and Jackson Sts. Displays of Kansas, Western and Indian history; military and agricultural galleries. Mon-Fri 8:15-5; Sat 8:15-4; Sun 1-4:30.

The Menninger Foundation Museum and Archives, 5600 W. Sixth St. Exhibits on the history of psychiatry; tape recordings; paintings and prints; letters of Freud. Mon-Fri 9-5.

Wichita
Wichita Cow Town, 1717 Sims Park. Reconstruction of early Wichita period, 1869-1880; school, drugstore, fire station. April-Dec: Tues-Sat 9-5; Sun, hols 10-6.

Minnesota

Chisholm
Minnesota Museum of Mining, Memorial Park. Iron-mining equipment from both the past and the present. June-Sept: daily 8-6.

Duluth
University of Minnesota, Tweed Gallery, 26th Ave. East and 7th St. Sixteenth through 19th Century paintings; early American portraits; 19th Century landscapes. Tues-Fri 8-12, 1-5; Sat, Sun 2-5; eves 8-10.

Minneapolis
Minneapolis Institute of Arts, 201 E. 34th St. European paintings and sculpture; period rooms; pre-Columbian art; Oriental art. Tues 10-10; Wed-Sat 10-5; Sun, hols 1-5.

Walker Art Center, 1710 Lyondale Ave., S. Contemporary art; painting; decorative arts; T. B. Walker collection of jade.

Tues-Sat 10-5; Tues-Thurs eves 5-10; Sun 12-6.

Pipestone
Pipestone National Monument. Indian ceremonial pipes and pipestone objects. Daily 8-5; Memorial Day-Labor Day: eves 5-9.

Rochester
Mayo Medical Museum, Third Ave. and First St., S.W. Exhibits to acquaint layman with biology of man; anatomic models to demonstrate operative procedures. Mon-Fri 10-9; Sat 10-5; Sun 2-4:30.

St. Paul
Saint Paul Art Center, 10th and Cedar Sts. Twentieth Century drawings, paintings and sculpture; African, American Indian and pre-Columbian crafts. Tues-Fri 10-8; Sat 10-5; Sun 1-5.

Missouri

Columbia
University of Missouri, Museum of Art and Archaeology, University Library. Egyptian, Oriental, primitive and modern art; South American and Mediterranean archeological exhibits. Tues, Thurs, Sat, Sun 2-5. Closed Aug 5-Sept 10.

Hannibal
Mark Twain Home Board, Mark Twain Museum, 208 Hill St. Paintings; letters; first editions and other items relating to Mark Twain and his era. Summer: daily 7:30-6; winter: daily 8-5.

Independence
Harry S. Truman Library, Hwy. 24 and Delaware. Paintings; historic documents; collection of political cartoons. Truman memorabilia. Sept 16-May 15: Mon-Sat 9-4:30; Sun 2-5; May 16-Sept 15: daily 10-5.

Jefferson City
Missouri State Museum, State Capitol Bldg. Murals by N. C. Wyeth and T. H. Benton; history and science museums. Daily 8-5.

Kansas City
Kansas City Museum of History and Science, 3218 Gladstone Blvd. Geology, zoology and archeology exhibits; costume collection; Indian artifacts; planetarium. Mon-Sat 9-5.

William Rockhill Nelson Gallery and Atkins Museum of Fine Arts, 4525 Oak St. European and American paintings and

sculpture; Chinese art; decorative arts. Tues-Sat 10-5; Sun 2-6.

Laclede
General John J. Pershing Boyhood Home Memorial Shrine. Restored home of 1858; period furniture; Pershing memorabilia. Tues-Sat, hols 10-4; Sun 12-5.

St. Joseph
Pony Express Museum, Pony Express Stables. History of the Pony Express and St. Joseph. June-Aug: Mon-Fri 9-5; Sun 2-5.

St. Louis
City Art Museum of St. Louis, Forest Park. Egyptian, Chinese, Indian and Western art; Renaissance, classical and medieval paintings and sculpture. Tues 2:30-9:30; Wed-Sun, hols 10-5.

Falstaff Museum of Brewing, 1923 Shenandoah Ave. History of St. Louis brewing industry; bottles; advertising material; tavern furniture. Mon-Fri tours at 2:30, 3:30, 4:30.

Jefferson National Expansion Memorial, 11 N. Fourth St. Old courthouse begun in 1839; Gateway Arch. Daily 8-5.

Missouri Botanical Garden, 2315 Tower Grove Ave. Living plant collection; world's first geodesic-dome display greenhouse. Mon-Thurs 9-5; Fri-Sun 9-9.

Sainte Genevieve
Bolduc House, Main St. One of the few remaining Mississippi Valley houses; French Creole period furnishings. May-Oct: daily.

Springfield
Springfield Art Museum, 1111 E. Brookside Dr. American painting and sculpture; prints; ceramics. Mon-Sat 9-5; Tues-Thurs eves 6:30-9:30; Sun 1-5.

Nebraska

Beatrice
Homestead National Monument, Rte. 1. Items pertaining to the homestead era in America. Summer: daily 8-6; winter: daily 8-5.

Chadron
Museum of the Fur Trade. Indian trade goods; Plains Indian material; furs and trappers' equipment. June-Sept: daily 8-6.

Crawford
Nebraska State Historical Society, Fort Robinson Museum, U.S. Hwy. 20. Indian artifacts;

military items; saddle and harness repair shop; five buildings of historic Fort Robinson. May-Sept: Mon-Sat 8-5; Sun 1-5.

Gering
Oregon Trail Museum, Scotts Bluff National Monument. Art gallery with paintings relating to the Oregon, California and Mormon Trails; works of William Henry Jackson. Memorial Day-Labor Day: daily 8-8; Labor Day-Memorial Day: daily 8-5.

Grand Island
Stuhr Museum of the Prairie Pioneer, junction of U.S. Hwys. 281 and 34. Local history; central Nebraska pioneer history. Mon-Sat 9-5.

Hastings
Hastings Museum, House of Yesterday, 1331 N. Burlington Ave. Rocks; minerals; Plains Indian artifacts; coin collection; planetarium. Mon-Sat 8-5; Sun 1-5; hols 2-5.

Lincoln
Fairview Museum, 4900 Sumner St. Home of William Jennings

Bryan; Bryan memorabilia; furniture and other household items. Mon-Sat 1-4:30; Sun, hols 2-4:30.

University of Nebraska State Museum, 14th and U Sts. Botany, geology, health sciences; herbarium; planetarium. Mon-Sat 8-5; Wed eves 7-9; Sun, hols 1-5.

Minden
The Harold Warp Pioneer Village, Hwys. 6, 34 and 10. More than 20,000 items in 20 buildings; displays show modes of living from 1830 to present. Summer: daily 7-dusk; winter: daily 8-dusk.

Omaha
Joslyn Art Museum, 2218 Dodge St. Ancient and modern art; early Western and frontier art; Renaissance paintings. Tues-Sat 10-5; Sun 1-5.

North Dakota

Bismarck
Dakota Zoo, Sertoma-Riverside Park. Native birds and animals. May-Oct: daily 8-dusk.

State Historical Society Museum, Liberty Memorial Bldg. Items pertaining to North Dakota history; ethnology and archeology of the Plains Indians. Mon-Fri 9-5; Sat 9-4; June-Aug: Sun 1-5.

Fargo
Cass County Historical Society Museum, Minard Hall, North Dakota State University. Costumes; crafts; textiles; farm machinery; Indian artifacts. Tues-Fri 1-5.

Medora
Chateau de Mores, U.S. Hwy. 10. Home of French nobleman built in 1883; French furnishings; personal possessions of the marquis. Daily 8-5.

Theodore Roosevelt National Memorial Park, Visitor Center. Geology; herbarium; partial collection of Roosevelt's ranching effects. Summer: daily 7-7; winter: daily 8-5.

South Dakota

Murdo
Pioneer Auto Museum. Antique

automobiles; sleighs; horse-drawn vehicles; collection of period costumes. June-Aug: daily 6 a.m.-9:30 p.m. April, May, Sept, Oct: daily 8-8.

Pierre
South Dakota State Historical Museum, Memorial Bldg., Capitol Ave. Pioneer and relics of two world wars; natural history; coins; Indian artifacts. Mon-Sat 8-12, 1-5; Sun 1-5.

Rapid City
Sioux Indian Museum, 1002 St. Joseph St. Sioux Indian artifacts. Sept-May: Tues-Sat 9-12, 1-4:30; June-Aug: Mon-Sat 9-4:30; Sun 1-4:30.

South Dakota School of Mines and Technology, Museum of Geology. Mineralogy, geology, paleontology. Winter: Mon-Fri 8-5; Sat 10-12; summer: Mon-Sat 8-6; Sun 2-8.

Sioux Falls
Pettigrew Museum, 131 N. Duluth Ave. Indian and pioneer relics; coins; costumes; natural history exhibitions. Mon-Sat 9-12, 1:30-5; Sun 2-5.

Local festivals and events

Iowa
Steamboat Days—Dixieland and Jazz Festival, Burlington. Display of boats on Mississippi mixed with fine Dixieland jazz. Early June.

Iowa State Fair, Des Moines. A huge fair with outstanding exhibits of agriculture and industry plus races and a mammoth midway. August.

Sidney Championship Rodeo, Sidney. Good prize money and untried bulls make this one of biggest rodeos in the country. Late August.

Kansas
International Pancake Race, Liberal. A pancake flipping race with women of Olney, England, combined with parades, contests and a ball. Every Shrove Tuesday.

National Coursing Meet, Abilene. Test of a dog's working ability in chasing a live Kansas jack rabbit. First weeks in April and October.

Dodge City Days, Dodge City. Parades, rodeo, horse show and dances recall the Old West. Third week in July.

Minnesota
Winter Carnival, St. Paul. Parades and merry-making mixed with numerous traditional winter sports contests. Late January—early February.

Last Chance Bonspiel, Hibbing. Most important curling event in U.S. Early April.

"The Song of Hiawatha" pageant, Pipestone. Outdoor performances presented at sundown. Late July and early August.

Minnesota State Fair, St. Paul. Advertised as the largest state fair in the country, it presents the fine produce of the state. Late August.

Missouri
Maifest, Hermann. Traditional German celebration with dancing, eating and tours of the town and Missouri's only winery. Third week in May.

Veiled Prophet Ball and Parade, St. Louis. The annual visit of the mysterious monarch from Khorassan signals the city's top social event. September.

Ozark Crafts Festival, Marvel

Cave Park. Contests in felling trees, splitting rails and making hand-hewn shingles. Early October.

The American Royal Live Stock and Horse Show, Kansas City. Largest livestock and horse show in the U.S. Third week in October.

Nebraska
Homestead Days, Beatrice. Festival commemorating first application for land under 1862 Homestead Act. Mid-June.

Nebraskaland Days, North Platte. A giant Western festival with rodeo and parade. Late June.

World Champion Steer Roping, Ogallala. Nebraska's largest rodeo attracts professionals and amateurs alike. Late July.

Winnebago Indian Powwow, Winnebago. The Winnebago reservation erupts in lively pageantry of historic past. Late August.

North Dakota
North Dakota Winter Show, Valley City. Huge livestock and agricultural exhibition, including an indoor rodeo. First week in March.

Red River Valley Fair and Machinery Show, West Fargo. A big fair in the heart of the state's richest agricultural area. Mid-August.

South Dakota
Black Hills Roundup, Belle Fourche. One of the country's top rodeos; also parade and carnival. First week of July.

Gold Discovery Days, Custer. Events include outdoor pageant depicting discovery of Black Hills gold as well as a parade, rodeo and carnival. Late July.

Days of '76, Deadwood. Main feature is a parade of pioneer vehicles, horses and famous figures of Gold Rush days. First weekend in August.

Oglala Sioux Sun Dance, Pine Ridge. Indian dance festival highlighted by performance of ancient Sun Dance in which braves torture themselves. First week in August.

Crazy Horse Pageant, Hot Springs. Outdoor staging of conflict between Sioux and white men in 1880s. Monday through Friday at 9 p.m., early June through Labor Day.

Wildlife of the Plains States

A sampling of the wildlife of the Plains States is given on this and the following three pages. In each case both the common name and the name employed by scientists for the plant or animal is used. The information supplied with drawings shown here is not intended to be comprehensive. Those interested in obtaining additional material on the fauna and flora of the Plains States region should refer to the numerous specialized books on flora and fauna. A number of useful reference works that contain such information are listed on page 188.

Mammals

Big brown bat

An uninvited guest in many homes on the plains, *Eptesicus fuscus* is the only species of bat in North America that regularly hibernates in houses.

Raccoon

Easily spotted by its banded tail and black mask, *Procyon lotor* forages along creeks and streams at night. It is widely hunted for its pelt and for sport.

Long-tailed weasel

Mustela frenata longicauda sometimes attacks poultry, but it helps farmers by destroying rodents. Its brown coat *(left)* becomes white *(right)* in winter.

River otter

A shy and retiring mammal, *Lutra canadensis* often lives close to man but is seldom seen. Its thick, lustrous pelt is one of the most durable of native American furs.

Badger

With short legs and long claws, *Taxidea taxus* is a remarkable digger, burrowing after rodents for food and, if pursued, burying itself for safety.

Coyote

Although *Canis latrans* has been tirelessly trapped, hunted and poisoned—because it kills lambs, pigs and poultry—this animal has somehow continued to flourish.

Gray wolf

Canis lupus, once found in great numbers in many parts of the land, has been so avidly hunted that only in a few places, such as the plains, can it still be seen.

Lynx

Often mistaken for a bobcat, *Lynx canadensis* feeds mainly on rabbits. When rabbits are scarce, famine strikes the lynx population and their numbers dwindle.

Black-tailed prairie dog

The plump, squirrel-like prairie dog *(Cynomys ludovicianus)* is an enemy of the farmer, for it destroys crops and its burrow entrances are hazards for horses and cattle.

Plains pocket gopher

Native only to North America, *Geomys bursarius* is an efficient digger, using its sharp teeth and long claws to tunnel as far as 300 feet in a single night.

Beaver

Castor canadensis is noted for the dams—sometimes hundreds of feet long—that it builds out of mud and sticks. It is widely hunted for its warm pelt.

Western harvest mouse

This mouse *(Reithrodontomys megalotis)* is a nimble climber that feeds on seeds and grass tips. It lives inconspicuously in a nest woven from plant fibers.

182

Muskrat

This large rodent *(Ondatra zibethicus)* builds its nest out of water plants and, if particularly hungry, will literally eat itself out of house and home.

Porcupine

Erethizon dorsatum, shielded with about 30,000 barbed quills, is only vulnerable to predators when flipped on its back, thus exposing its unprotected belly.

Black-tailed jack rabbit

Able to ruin acres of valuable crops, these long-legged hares *(Lepus californicus)* are driven into pens by prairie farmers and slaughtered by the thousand.

Wapiti

The wapiti, or American elk *(Cervus canadensis),* is a strong swimmer. It can also run faster than 35 miles an hour and may weigh as much as 800 pounds.

Fish and reptiles

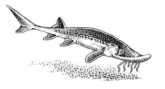

Hackleback sturgeon

Recognizable by its flat, shovel-shaped snout, *Scaphirhynchus platorynchus* spawns in fast-moving water in the spring. Its roe is used for caviar.

Bigmouth buffalofish

A large species of the carp, or sucker, family, *Megastomatobus cyprinella* prefers sluggish waters, for it feeds mainly on mollusks, insect larvae and vegetation.

Brook trout

Basically a cold-water fish, *Salvelinus frontinalis* thrives in clear, cold, spring-water streams and brooks. It is a favorite with anglers and an excellent food fish.

Northern pike

Esox lucius is a voracious fresh-water fish, devouring other fish and sometimes even feeding on its own kind. When hooked, it is a powerful fighter.

Walleyed pike

Stizostedion vitreum prefers clean, cold lakes and rivers. It stays in deep waters during the warm months of the year and surfaces during the winter.

Smallmouth black bass

Generally considered to be—inch for inch and pound for pound— the bravest, most unyielding fish, *Micropterus dolomieu* weighs as much as seven pounds.

Largemouth black bass

Because it is able to thrive in many environments and water temperatures, *Huro salmoides* is in constant demand for stocking ponds and lakes.

Rock bass

Ambloplites rupestris can change its color from silver to black or to silver with black splotches in a few minutes. The female lays as many as 11,000 eggs.

Ornate box turtle

Terrapene ornata ornata is able to withstand extremely arid conditions. It burrows to escape heat, but a rainstorm may bring large numbers to the surface.

Western hognose snake

Sometimes known as the "prairie rooter," *Heterodon nasicus* hisses and looks threatening but never bites. When threatened, it rolls over and plays dead.

Blue racer snake

While not poisonous, *Coluber constrictor foxi* is an aggressive snake that will sometimes strike and draw blood. It is often found in open woodlands.

Bullsnake

Pituophis melanolevous sayi is the most common constrictor in the nation and a destroyer of rodents. It often enters burrows to feed on pocket gophers.

Birds

Western turkey vulture

The only vulture found in most of the West, *Cathartes aura teter* is a regal flier with black and gray wings. It is about eagle-size but has a smaller head.

Greater prairie chicken

Tympanuchus cupido americanus, a brown, hen-like bird, lives in brushy grasslands. Its soft cluck has caused the species to be labeled "the gobbling birds."

Eastern bobwhite

Colinus virginianus virginianus is usually found in small flocks that, when flushed, burst from cover with a loud clatter. The male has black and white head markings.

Ring-necked pheasant

Phasianus colchicus torquatus inhabits grainfields and meadows and is often seen near fence rows. The male is brightly colored with a long, pointed tail.

Western burrowing owl

This long-legged owl *(Speotyto cunicularia hypugoea)* digs nesting burrows and is often seen in the daytime, standing on its burrow or perched on a stone.

Western meadowlark

Sturnella neglecta has a bubbling flute-like voice and sings a variable song consisting of seven to ten notes. Its breast is bright yellow crossed with a black V.

Yellow-headed blackbird

A robin-sized bird with a yellow head, *Xanthocephalus xanthocephalus* has a hoarse, rasping voice that resembles the squeals and grunts of baby pigs.

Indigo bunting

This small indigo-blue bird *(Passerina cyanea)* is often mistaken for a blackbird, as it appears black when viewed from a distance or against the sky.

Flowers and trees

Soapweed

Yucca glauca has stiff, sharp-pointed leaves, and grows in dry soils. Its roots are used as a substitute for soap, and brooms are made from its leaves.

Yellow lady's-slipper

Growing to a height of about two feet, the stalks of *Cypripedium pubescens* (a species of orchid) bear fragrant, shoe-like yellow flowers from May to July.

Pasqueflower

The state flower of South Dakota, the pasqueflower, or wild crocus, *(anemone patens)* is a silky-haired plant that proudly bears a single, bluish-purple flower.

Wild sunflower

Helianthus petiolaris, found only in the U.S., grows in sandy soil and along dry river bottoms. The petals are yellow but the centers may be hues of brown or purple.

Blazing star

Liatris pycnostachya grows to a height of two to four feet and is mainly found on damp prairies. Its purple flowers bloom in clusters during August and September.

Eastern red cedar

Juniperus virginiana is a small, spire-shaped tree. Because moths are repelled by the aroma of this tree, wood from its trunk is used to line clothes closets and chests.

Eastern cottonwood

The most common and one of the largest trees found on the plains —sometimes 100 feet tall— *Populus deltoides* can be grown from a fresh green twig.

Peach-leaved willow

Salix amygdaloides has a straight columnar trunk and a narrow, rounded top. Its leaves resemble those of the peach tree for which it is named.

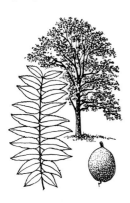

Black walnut

Highly prized for furniture and gunstocks, *Juglans nigra* is one of the nation's finest hardwoods. The nut from this tree is used to flavor ice cream and candy.

Shagbark hickory

The shredded, shaggy bark of *Carya ovata* hangs like warped shingles from its trunk. This arrangement inhibits squirrels from running up the tree.

Ironwood

Ostrya virginiana is appropriately named, for its close-grained wood is so tough that it burns like hard coal. Most ironwood is used to make handles for tools.

Burr oak

Quercus macrocarpa is found in open groves on the prairie. Century-old burr oaks are common since the tree is extremely fire resistant.

Hackberry

Celtis occidentalis produces a sweet, pea-sized berry that is a favorite of many birds. At the tree's top are found dark clumps of twigs called witches' brooms.

Prairie thorn

Found on stony barrens in the plains, *Crataegus pertomentosa* is a small tree with wide-spread branches and a flat crown. It is covered with two-inch thorns.

Silver maple

Blooming earlier than any other tree, *Acer saccharinum* is named for the bright silver underside of its leaves. Excellent sugar is made from its sap.

Box elder

Perhaps the most popular shade tree in the Plains States, *Acer negundo* grows rapidly, bears handsome foliage, and can withstand severe drought.

Statistical information

State nicknames, date of admission, capital

Iowa: Hawkeye State: admitted 1846 (the 29th state); Des Moines.

Kansas: Sunflower State, Jayhawker State; admitted 1861 (the 34th state); Topeka.

Minnesota: Gopher State, North Star State, Land of 10,000 Lakes; admitted 1858 (the 32nd state); St. Paul.

Missouri: Show Me State; admitted 1821 (the 24th state); Jefferson City.

Nebraska: Cornhusker State; admitted 1867 (the 37th state); Lincoln.

North Dakota: Flickertail State, Sioux State; admitted to the Union simultaneously with South Dakota in 1889 (the 39th state); Bismarck.

South Dakota: Coyote State, Sunshine State; admitted 1889 (the 40th state); Pierre.

Population

By state (1968 Editor and Publisher Market Guide, January 1, 1968, estimate):
Missouri: 4,540,124.
Minnesota: 3,646,007.
Iowa: 2,851,293.
Kansas: 2,352,900.
Nebraska: 1,546,818.
South Dakota: 726,789.
North Dakota: 649,522.

By city (region's 10 largest cities are listed below, followed by their population according to the January 1, 1968, estimate of the 1968 Editor and Publisher Market Guide):
St. Louis, Mo.: 655,523.

Kansas City, Mo.: 581,109.
Minneapolis, Minn.: 437,482.
Omaha, Neb.: 364,934.
St. Paul, Minn.: 314,978.
Wichita, Kans.: 314,043.
Des Moines, Iowa: 205,847.
Lincoln, Neb.: 153,840.
Topeka, Kans.: 147,324.
Kansas City, Kans.: 128,971.

Total areas

Minnesota: 84,068 square miles.
Kansas: 82,264 square miles.
Nebraska: 77,227 square miles.
South Dakota: 77,047 square miles.
North Dakota: 70,665 square miles.
Missouri: 69,686 square miles.
Iowa: 56,290 square miles.

Principal rivers (total lengths in miles)

Note: Only the states in the Plains States region that these rivers flow through are named.

Mississippi (Missouri, Iowa, Minnesota): 2,348.

Missouri (Missouri, Kansas, Nebraska, Iowa, South Dakota, North Dakota): 2,315.

Arkansas (Kansas): 1,450.

James (North Dakota, South Dakota): 710.

Cimarron (Kansas): 698.

White (Missouri): 685.

North Platte (Nebraska): 680.

Little Missouri (South Dakota, North Dakota): 560.

Smoky Hill (Kansas): 560.

Red River of the North (North Dakota, Minnesota): 545.

White (South Dakota, Nebraska): 507.

Marais des Cygnes-Osage (Kansas, Missouri): 496.

Neosho (Kansas): 450.

South Platte (Nebraska): 442.

Niobrara (Nebraska): 431.

Republican (Kansas, Nebraska): 422.

Big Sioux (South Dakota, Iowa): 420.

Belle Fourche (South Dakota): 416.

Principal lakes

Superior (Minnesota): 31,800 square miles; maximum depth 1,333 feet; natural.

Lake of the Woods (Minnesota): 1,485 square miles; maximum depth 103 feet; natural.

Red (Minnesota): 451 square miles; maximum depth 31 feet; natural.

Rainy (Minnesota): 345 square miles; maximum depth 156 feet; natural.

Mille Lacs (Minnesota): 207 square miles; maximum depth 35 feet; natural.

Leech (Minnesota): 176 square miles; maximum depth 150 feet; natural.

Bull Shoals (Missouri): 111.31 square miles; maximum depth 243 feet; man-made.

Winnibigoshish (Minnesota): 109 square miles; maximum depth 65 feet; natural.

Lake of the Ozarks (Missouri): 93.75 square miles; maximum depth 125 feet; man-made.

McConaughy (Nebraska): 55 square miles; maximum depth 150 feet; man-made.

Tuttle Creek (Kansas): 24.68 square miles; maximum depth 56 feet; man-made.

Spirit (Iowa): 8.84 square miles; maximum depth 27 feet; natural.

Some U.S. superlatives

Five of the Plains States—Nebraska, Kansas, North Dakota, Iowa and South Dakota—devote more than 90 per cent of their land to farming.

Iowa led the U.S. in number of commercial farms in 1964 with 137,537.

Kansas, North Dakota and Nebraska ranked first, second and third in wheat production in 1966.

South Dakota is the home of the largest gold mine in the U.S.—the Homestake mine in Lawrence County.

Missouri is the nation's largest lead producer.

The world's largest iron-ore mine, the Hull-Rust-Mahoning complex, is located not far from Hibbing, Minnesota.

Agricultural statistics (1964)

	Acreage (in millions)	Number of farms	Principal crops
Kansas	50.3	92,440	Wheat, sorghum, grain, hay.
Nebraska	47.8	80,163	Corn, hay, wheat.
South Dakota	45.6	49,703	Corn, hay, wheat, oats.
North Dakota	42.7	48,836	Wheat, barley, hay, oats.
Iowa	33.8	154,162	Corn, soybeans, hay, oats.
Missouri	32.7	147,315	Corn, soybeans, hay, wheat.
Minnesota	30.8	131,163	Corn, soybeans, hay, oats.

Pronunciation glossary

Abilene (AB uh lean). City in Kansas.
Belle Fourche (BELL FOOSH). River cutting through Wyoming and into South Dakota. Reservoir and dam in South Dakota. City in South Dakota.
Bemidji (beh MIDGE ee). City in Minnesota.
Bois des Sioux (boy deh SUE). River flowing between Minnesota and Nebraska.
Chippewa (CHIP uh wah). River and county in Minnesota. Indian tribe.
Cloquet (kloh KAY). River and

city in Minnesota.
Des Moines (deh MOIN). River, county and the capital of Iowa.
Dubuque (duh BUKE). County, city and university in Iowa.
Duluth (duh LOOTH). Third largest city in Minnesota.
Flandreau (flan DREW). City in South Dakota.
Gros Ventre (GROW Vahnt). Indian tribe, formerly known as the Hidatsa.
Hidatsa (ih DOT sah). See Gros Ventre.
Itasca (eye TAHS ka). Lake, state park and county in Minnesota.

Kearney (CAR nee). City and county in Nebraska.
Kearny (CAR nee). County in Kansas.
Koochiching (COO chuh ching). County in Minnesota.
Maquoketa (ma COH keh ta). River and city in Iowa.
Mille Lacs (Mill LAX). Lake, county and Indian reservation in Minnesota.
Minot (MY not). City in North Dakota.
Omaha (OH ma haw; OH ma hah). Largest city in Nebraska.
Onawa (ON ah wah). City in Iowa.
Osceola (oh see OH la; os ee OH la). County and city in Iowa.

City in Missouri.
Ottumwa (oh TUHM wah; oh TUHM woh). City in Iowa.
Pierre (PEER). Capital city of South Dakota.
Potosi (poh TOE sy). City in Missouri.
Sauk Centre (SAWK SEN ter). River and city in Minnesota. Sinclair Lewis' boyhood home.
Taum Sauk (TOM Sawk). Highest peak in Missouri.
Wapsipinicon (Wop sye PIN ee con). River flowing from Minnesota to Iowa.
Wichita (WITCH ih tah). City in Kansas.
Wishek (WISH ick). City in North Dakota.

Credits and acknowledgments

Maps for front and back end papers by Jeppesen & Company, Denver, Colorado. Maps on pages 174 through 179 © by the H. M. Gousha Company, San Jose, California.

The sources for the illustrations that appear in this book are shown below. Credits for the pictures from left to right are separated by commas, from top to bottom by dashes.
Cover—A. Y. Owen.
Front end papers—Drawings by Richard Boland.
Chapter 1: 8, 9—Michael Rougier. 10—Map adapted from U.S. Department of Interior Geological Survey. 13—U.S. Department of Agriculture (2). 15—No credit. 17—Humble Oil and Refining Company. 18, 19—Larry Nicholson, A. Y. Owen. 20—Theodore David Alles. 21—Dale Nally. 22, 23—Jerry Brimacombe. 24, 25—A. Y. Owen. 26, 27—Fred Schnell. 28—Dale Nally. 29—Anthony C. Reed.
Chapter 2: 30—Smithsonian Institution. 32—Museum of the American Indian Heye Foundation, New York. 35—No credit—adapted from map of Bureau of Indian Affairs. 38—Kansas State Historical Society. 41—Western History Collections, University of Oklahoma Library. 43 through 57 —Gary Renaud.

Chapter 3: 58, 59—Nebraska State Historical Society. 61, 62—Culver Pictures, Inc. 67—Photographs courtesy Fogg Art Museum, Harvard University. 69—Mercaldo Archives. 70—Denver Public Library, Western Collection; Western History Collections, University of Oklahoma Library. 71—Mercaldo Archives. 72—Cliff Young—Western History Collections, University of Oklahoma Library. 73—Mercaldo Archives; Western History Collections, University of Oklahoma Library (7). 74—Sy Seidman—Nebraska State Historical Society. 75—Western History Collections, University of Oklahoma Library; New York Public Library—Union Pacific Railroad, Collection of Wells Fargo Bank. 76—Mercaldo Archives—Kansas State Historical Society. 77—Western History Collections, University of Oklahoma Library—Sy Seidman. 78, 79—Kansas State Historical Society. 80—Kansas State Historical Society—Denver Public Library, Western Collection (3). 81—Western History Collections, University of Oklahoma Library—Mercaldo Archives.
Chapter 4: 82—Sol Studna for *Kansas City Star*. 85—No credit. 86 through 88—Inland Rivers Library, Cincinnati Public Library. 91 through 101—Larry Nicholson.
Chapter 5: 102, 103—A. Y. Owen. 106, 109—Kansas State Historical Society. 110—Nebraska State Historical Society. 113—No credit—

Drawing courtesy Deere and Company, Moline, Illinois. 115 through 129—A. Y. Owen.
Chapter 6: 130, 131—Alfred Eisenstaedt. 132—Culver Pictures, Inc. 134—Denver Public Library, Western Collection. 137, 138—Nebraska State Historical Society. 141—Missouri Historical Society. 142, 143—John Savage for Missouri Historical Society. 144, 145—Missouri Historical Society. 146, 147—Keystone View Company, Meadville, Pennsylvania, The Bettmann Archive. 148, 149—*St. Louis Post-Dispatch*, United Press International (2). 150, 151—Fred Schnell—Sebastian Milito.
Chapter 7: 152, 153—Arthur Shay. 156—Courtesy Grace Hegger Casanova. 157—Walters Studio, Red Cloud, Nebraska. 159—Courtesy Mrs. Katherine Basie. 161—Courtesy Joslyn Art Museum, Omaha, Nebraska. 162, 163—John Barry Jr., Fernand Bourges courtesy King W. Vidor —Fernand Bourges courtesy George Moffett © Associated American Artists. 164, 165—Donald Getsug from Rapho Guillumette courtesy Iowa State University, Ames, Iowa. 166, 167 —Rudolf H. Hoffmann—Whitney Museum of American Art, New York, Donald Getsug from Rapho Guillumette courtesy Hackley Art Gallery, Muskegon, Michigan. 168, 169—Lee Boltin courtesy U.S. Department of Justice, Washington, D.C. 170, 171—Alfred Eisenstaedt, John Savage courtesy Thomas Hart Benton—Joslyn Art Museum, Omaha, Nebraska. 172, 173—John Savage courtesy Harry S. Truman Library, Independence, Missouri.

182 through 185—Drawings by Rudolf Freund.
Back end papers—Drawings by Richard Boland.

The editors of this book wish to acknowledge the help of the following persons and institutions: Clyde N. Bowden, Director, Inland Rivers Library, Cincinnati Public Library, Cincinnati, Ohio; Raymond Brune, Public Relations, Deere and Company, Moline, Illinois; James Casey, Chief of Project Planning Division, Bureau of Reclamation, U.S. Department of Interior, Washington, D.C.; Joseph H. Cash, Associate Professor of History, Eastern Montana College, Billings, Montana; Ralph T. Coe, Assistant Director, Nelson Gallery of Art, Kansas City, Missouri; Frederick J. Dockstader, Director, The Museum of the American Indian Heye Foundation, New York City; Clyde Dollar, Economic and Development Department, Rosebud Sioux Tribe, Rosebud, South Dakota; James T. Dunn, Librarian, Minnesota Historical Society Museum, St. Paul, Minnesota; Ruth K. Field, Missouri Historical Society, St. Louis, Missouri; Jack Haley, Western History Collections, University of Oklahoma, Norman, Oklahoma; Ray Leonard, Public Information Officer, U.S. Army Corps of Engineers, Missouri River Division, Omaha, Nebraska; Vincent Mercaldo, Richmond Hill, New York; Col. William Needham, U.S. Army Corps of Engineers, Washington, D.C.; M. O. Smith, U.S. Army Corps of Engineers, Kansas City, Missouri.

Bibliography

*Available also in paperback
†Available only in paperback

General and historical reading

Adams, Ramon F., *Burs Under the Saddle.* University of Oklahoma Press, 1964.

Billington, Ray, *Westward Expansion: history of the American frontier.* Macmillan, 1967.

Blegen, Theodore C., *Minnesota: A History of the State.* University of Minnesota Press, 1963.

Brogan, D. W., *The American Character.** Alfred A. Knopf, 1944.

Clark, Thomas P., *Frontier America: the story of the westward movement.* Scribner, 1959.

Glaab, Charles N. and A. Theodore Brown, *History of Urban America.** Macmillan, 1967.

Hawgood, John A., *America's Western Frontier.* Alfred A. Knopf, 1966.

Kirschten, Ernest, *Catfish and Crystal.* Doubleday, 1965.

Kraenzel, Carl Frederick, *The Great Plains in Transition.* University of Oklahoma Press, 1955.

McReynolds, Edwin C., *Missouri: A History of the Crossroads State.* University of Oklahoma Press, 1962.

Olson, James C., *History of Nebraska.* University of Nebraska Press, 1955.

Schell, Herbert S., *History of South Dakota.* University of Nebraska Press, 1961.

Smith, Henry Nash, *Virgin Land: The American West as Symbol and Myth.** Harvard University Press, 1950.

Van Every, Dale, *The Final Challenge.** William Morrow, 1964.

Webb, Walter Prescott, *The Great Plains.** Blaisdell, 1959.

Whittemore, Robert C., *Makers of the American Mind.** Apollo, 1964.

Zornow, William Frank, *Kansas: A History of the Jayhawk State.* University of Oklahoma Press, 1957.

Special topics

Baumhoff, Richard G., *The Damned Missouri Valley.* Alfred A. Knopf, 1951.

Benton, Thomas Hart, *An Artist in America.* University of Kansas Press, 1951.

Blacker, Irwin R. and Harry M. Rosen, *The Golden Conquistadores.* Bobbs-Merrill, 1960.

Brophy, William and Sophie Aberle, *The Indian: America's Unfinished Business.* University of Oklahoma Press, 1966.

Castel, Albert, *Quantrill, William Clarke: His Life and Times.* Frederick Fell, Inc., 1962.

Croy, Homer, *Jesse James Was My Neighbor.* Duell, Sloan and Pearce, 1949.

Dale, Edward Everett, *Cow Country.* University of Oklahoma Press, 1965.

Dalton, Emmett, *When the Daltons Rode.* Doubleday, 1931.

The Dalton Brothers and Their Outstanding Career of Crime, by an Eye Witness. Frederick Fell, Inc., 1954.

DeVoto, Bernard, *Journals of Lewis and Clark.** Houghton Mifflin, 1952.

Donovan, Frank, *River Boats of America.* Thomas Y. Crowell, 1966.

Drago, Harry Sinclair:
Great American Cattle Trails. Dodd, Mead, 1965.
Outlaws on Horseback. Dodd, Mead, 1964.

Driver, Harold E., *Indians of North America.** University of Chicago Press, 1961.

Farwood, Darrell, *Artist in Iowa: A Life of Grant Wood.* Norton, 1944.

Gard, Wayne:
The Chisolm Trail. University of Oklahoma Press, 1954.
The Great Buffalo Hunt. Alfred A. Knopf, 1959.
Sam Bass. Houghton Mifflin, 1936.

Garland, Hamlin, *Main Traveled Roads.** Harper, 1909.

Goodrich, Lloyd and John I. H. Baur, *American Art of Our Century.* F. A. Praeger, 1961.

Graham, William A., *The Custer Myth.* Stackpole, 1954.

Grinnell, George B., *When Buffalo Ran.* University of Oklahoma Press, 1964.

Hassrick, Royal B. and others, *Sioux: Life and Customs of a Warrior Society.* University of Oklahoma Press, 1964.

Hollen, W. Eugene:
The Great American Desert. Oxford University Press, 1966.

The Lost Pathfinder, Zebulon Montgomery Pike. University of Oklahoma Press, 1949.

Horan, James D. and Paul Sann, *A Pictorial History of the Wild West.* Crown, 1954.

Hyde, George E.:
Indians of the High Plains: From Prehistoric Times to the Coming of the Europeans. University of Oklahoma Press, 1959.
A Sioux Chronicle. University of Oklahoma Press, 1956.

Johnson, William, *William Allen White's America.* Holt, 1947.

Lavender, David, *Bents Fort.** Doubleday, 1954.

Lowe, Robert H., *Indians of the Plains.†* The Natural History Press, 1963.

McCallum, Henry D. and Frances T., *The Wire that Fenced the West.* University of Oklahoma Press, 1966.

McCracken, Harold, *George Catlin and the Old Frontier.* Dial Press, 1959.

Miller, Nyle H., Edgar Langsdorf and Robert W. Richmond, *Kansas a Pictorial History.* Kansas Centennial Commission and the State Historical Society, 1961.

Miller, Nyle H. and Joseph W. Snell, *Great Gunfighters of the Kansas Cowtowns, 1867-1886.** University of Nebraska Press, 1967.

Nicoll, Bruce H., *Nebraska, a Pictorial History.** University of Nebraska Press, 1967.

Rölvaag, Obe Edvart, *Giants in the Earth.** Harper, 1927.

Russell, Donald B., *The Lives and Legends of Buffalo Bill.* University of Oklahoma Press, 1960.

Sandoz, Mari, *The Buffalo Hunters.* Hastings House, 1954.

Shannon, Fred A., *The Farmer's Last Frontier: Agriculture, 1860-1897.* Holt, 1945.

Sprague, Marshall, *A Gallery of Dudes.* Little, Brown, 1967.

Vestal, Stanley:
Queen of the Cowtowns, Dodge City. Harper, 1952.
Warpath and Council Fire. Random House, 1948.

Wellman, Paul I.:
A Dynasty of Western Outlaws. Doubleday, 1961.
Death on Horseback. Lippincott, 1947.

Wissler, Clark, *Indians of the United States.** Doubleday, 1966.

Natural setting and wildlife

Audubon, John James, *The Birds of America.* Macmillan, 1937.

Burt, William Henry, *A Field Guide to the Mammals.* Houghton Mifflin, 1964.

Collingwood, G. H., *Knowing Your Trees.* The American Forestry Association, 1945.

Conant, Roger, *A Field Guide to the Reptiles and Amphibians.* Houghton Mifflin, 1958.

Fenneman, Nevin:
Physiography of Eastern United States. McGraw-Hill, 1948.
Physiography of Western United States. McGraw-Hill, 1931.

La Monte, Francesca, *North American Game Fishes.* Doubleday, 1945.

Peterson, Roger Tory:
A Field Guide to the Birds. Houghton Mifflin, 1947.
A Field Guide to Western Birds. Houghton Mifflin, 1961.

Peterson, Roger Tory and Margaret McKenny, *A Field Guide to Wild Flowers.* Houghton Mifflin, 1968.

Petrides, George A., *A Field Guide to the Trees and Shrubs.* Houghton Mifflin, 1958.

Sanderson, Ivan T., *Living Mammals of the World.* Hanover House, 1956.

Symonds, George W. D., *The Tree Identification Book.* M. Barrows and Co., 1958.

Terral, Rufus, *The Missouri Valley.* Yale University Press, 1947.

Vestal, Stanley, *The Missouri.** Holt, Rinehart and Winston, 1945.

Zim, Herbert and Alexander C. Martin, *Flowers.* Golden Press, 1950.

Guidebooks

Iowa Writers' Project, *Iowa, A Guide to the Hawkeye State.* Hastings House, 1949.

Kansas Writers' Project, *Kansas, A Guide to the Sunflower State.* Viking Press, 1939.

Minnesota Writers' Project, *Minnesota, A State Guide.* Hastings House, 1938.

Missouri Writers' Project, *Missouri, A Guide to the "Show Me" State.* Hastings House, 1954.

Nebraska Writers' Project, *Nebraska, A Guide to the Cornhusker State.* Viking, 1939.

South Dakota Writers' Project, *A South Dakota Guide.* State Publishing Co., 1952.

Index

Numerals in italics indicate an illustration of the subject mentioned.

189

PRODUCTION STAFF FOR TIME INCORPORATED
John L. Hallenbeck (Vice President and Director of Production),
Robert E. Foy and Caroline Ferri
Text photocomposed under the direction of Albert J. Dunn and Arthur J. Dunn

192

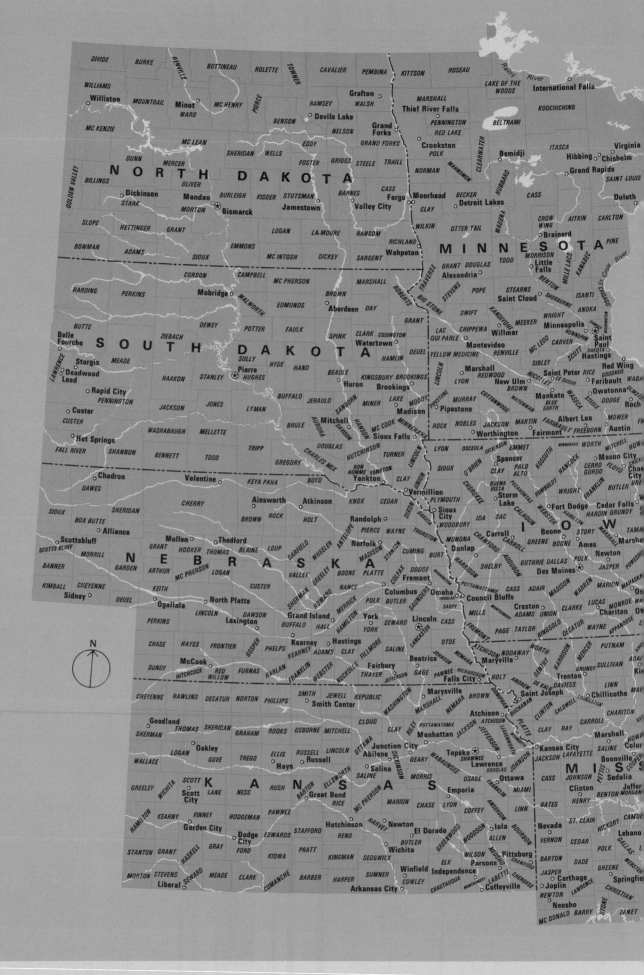